What They *Took* With Them: A Review of *Where's Charlie?* by Tim Soyars

And Jeanie Soyars wrote: *"You know what means even more to me is that look of love and pride on your face when we're in a public place, the praise you bestow when I 've done something wisely or good, the value you put on my ideas, your wonderful tolerance, your appreciation when I strive to please you, your faith in my love and your faithfulness, and most of all the mutual joy we share in knowing our great love for each other."* November 10, 1967

At the same time, Lieutenant Tim Soyars wrote: *"We had an awards ceremony here at Uplift yesterday . . . . I received a Bronze Star for valor and the Air Medal . . . The Air Medal is awarded for flying twenty combat missions. The Sergeant Major told me I flew more than ninety combat missions, but I wasn't counting . . . The Bronze Star is for the raid on the village of Lo Dieu . . . . I long to be near you, to look at you, to touch you, to talk to you . . . . Until then, I'll see you in my dreams."* November 12, 1967

Both exchanges were written during the writhing throes of the Vietnam conflict—what the United States Congress never came to characterize as a "war." The first reflects the deeply committed and loving relationship of a spouse to the war, the second, the metaphors of combat, couched in the security of the first. Both appear appropriately in the appendix as a frame to *Where's Charlie?*, the story of that combat as experienced in the one-year service of an soldier, Second Lieutenant Tim Soyars.

The son of a military-based firefighter and a "housewife" mother of three, Tim Soyars, the youngest of the children, grew up in Norfolk, Virginia. In his family background were generations of forefathers who had stepped up to military service in "answering the call" of their country. In his play, the youngster Tim had been preparing for his own response to serve which came in 1965 when he enlisted in the United States Army at the very moment President Lyndon Johnson had determined to escalate the combat to defeat the Viet Cong and the North Vietnamese and to preserve ce of the democratic South Vietnam.

Where's Charlie? is a story decades in the preparation during which time has clearly filtered the battle experiences of a deeply patriotic and dedicated young American soldier. The narrative itself chronicles Soyars' life leading up to his enlistment in the Army, his courtship and early marriage, his one-year tour of duty in Vietnam from March 1967, and the continuation of his military service stateside until the resignation of his commission in September 1969.

Where's Charlie? is not only the name of the book but also the name of his combat unit, Charlie Company, during Soyars' tour in Vietnam. Refreshingly, the text does not reflect the stains of an apology for another misbegotten American adventure. Readers will find no misgivings at the level of "boots on the ground" regarding the mission of the war or the means of prosecuting it. Rather, *Where's Charlie?* is the unabashed celebration of the thousands of men who dedicated themselves—bodies and souls—to the ideals the United States government projected at the time about the incursion. More pointedly, *Where's Charlie?* is the story of the loyalty and commitment of the members of Charlie Company to their fellow soldiers in the execution of their objectives in the service of those ideals.

At the same time, *Where's Charlie?* is not a polemic on the ongoing Vietnam debate. Soyars' chronicle refrains from attacking the antiwar movement which at times vilified American combatants in the Vietnam conflict. Fortunately for him, Soyars returned to the support and love of his bride and the appreciation of his family which nurtured and sustained him in the sometimes uncomfortable readjustment to service back home and his reintegration into civilian life.

Where's Charlie? is a strikingly and somewhat disarmingly easy read. Soyars' style is clear, and the text glides smoothly from sentence to sentence, unencumbered by syntactical complexities typical, perhaps, of a more reflective narrative. There is little secondary development—explanations of explanation—in the narration, a factor belied by the poignant imagery that peppers the narrative occasionally, suggesting the deep traumas of violence and conflagration and the constant potential for injury and death at every turn in a battle zone. Soyars recounts his argument with a helicopter pilot, to whom he denied permission to unload a palette of American bodies stacked four feet high like cordwood on the floor of the aircraft. At another point, while on night ambush, in close proximity to a squad of reported North Vietnamese regular soldiers, Soyars relates aiming his AR15 at the profile of a moving head in the shadows of brush just off the trail, pulling the trigger, recalling the immediate collapse of the figure, and discovering the body of the slain enemy the next morning. The few combat images that Soyars does share underscore the reality of this conflict and all battle, but Soyars' account is grounded not in the scores of victory, but rather in his sense of duty and efforts to fulfill it, always in the context of the needs of his fellow soldiers.

Tim Soyars survived his Vietnam experiences and learned from them. He notes, "People sometimes asked me if I felt I'd wasted my time by serving in the army and spending a year in Vietnam. I quickly replied, 'Absolutely not.' I'm proud of my service, and it was my duty then as it had been the duty of my forefathers." What readers will take away from this chronicle is a sense of what military service can mean to a person's life. Soyars learned leadership skills that came to serve him in the decades that followed. "My military training provided a great foundation for my future," says Soyars. The wisdom and insight from those experiences Soyars catalogs in his analysis of leadership:

"Leadership is:

- Knowing the team and how to make it work together effectively,
- Inspiring in unpretentious and non-authoritarian ways,
- Planning and leading the mission, but focusing on the strategic horizon,
- Providing clear roles and expectations,
- Mentoring with a focus on the individual and playing to their strengths,
- Doing the right thing and always considering the feelings of others and the consequences of your actions,
- Leading by example, and
- Making yourself dispensable, not indispensable."

What the young Lieutenant Soyars took with him into the military—a sense of commitment, respect for his nation, and the love of his wife and family—sustained him in his service on the field of battle that molded him into the leader he would become afterwards in the business and corporate world, and later in higher education administration.

Geoffrey Grimes, PhD
Professor of English
Mountain View College

Comments about *Where's Charlie?*

In the Introduction to *Where's Charlie?*, Tim Soyars tells us he hopes "this book might inspire some young person to experience the military to its fullest as I did." Tim's sights may have been set too low, for not only is this book truly inspirational to potential military recruits, but also it inspires men and women of all ages. It is a story of honor, courage, and love, and it helps us all increase our understanding and appreciation of those who served during the Vietnam War.

As a United States History Professor, I applaud Tim Soyars for his important addition to the literature on the Vietnam War. In *Where's Charlie?*, Tim provides us with a personal and professional perspective on his service during the war. I always encourage my students to see history through the eyes of the people who participate in it. This book enables us all to gain a greater understanding of that trying period of our history. Tim's inclusion of excerpts from letters exchanged with his bride Jeanie adds a special feature to this memoir, and it reminds us of the sacrifice and love taking place both in Vietnam and at home. Thanks to both for allowing a larger audience to share in their story.

Where's Charlie? is an extraordinary history of one man – and one woman – during one year of the Vietnam War. This book contains a special richness: the organization is superb; the story is engaging and informative; the excerpts from letters between author Tim Soyars and his wife Jeanie are touching; the photos illustrate the people and places; the summary Operational Reports from Charlie Company add texture; the glossary defines unusual terms; and, lastly, don't miss Tim's brief "Reflections on Leadership." I highly recommend this book – it is inspirational and informative on many levels.

Kenneth G. Alfers, Ph.D.
Professor of History
Mountain View College

Comments about *Where's Charlie?*

Captures the essence of OCS life

Jim Stanford
Former third platoon leader
In Charlie Company, Second/Fifth, First Cav

WHERE'S CHARLIE?

Memories from a Time of War, 1965–68

TIM SOYARS

iUniverse, Inc.
Bloomington

Where's Charlie?
Memories from a Time of War, 1965–68

iUniverse books may be ordered through booksellers or by contacting:

iUniverse
1663 Liberty Drive
Bloomington, IN 47403
www.iuniverse.com
1-800-Authors (1-800-288-4677)

Because of the dynamic nature of the Internet, any web addresses or links contained in this book may have changed since publication and may no longer be valid. The views expressed in this work are solely those of the author and do not necessarily reflect the views of the publisher, and the publisher hereby disclaims any responsibility for them.

ISBN: 978-1-4620-1494-1 (sc)
ISBN: 978-1-4620-1495-8 (hc)
ISBN: 978-1-4620-1496-5 (e)

Library of Congress Control Number: 2011907028

Printed in the United States of America

iUniverse rev. date: 07/07/2011

For Jeanie, the girl of my dreams;

our children—Michelle, Chris, and Shannon;

and our grandchildren—Courtney, Justin, Jason, Sean, and Robert

Every day may not be good, but there's something good in every day.

—Author Unknown

I don't think of all the misery but of the beauty that still remains.

—Anne Frank, The Diary of a Young Girl

CONTENTS

ACKNOWLEDGMENTS

Where's Charlie? is dedicated to my wife, Jeanie, who spent many hours proofing and editing, and allowed me to include excerpts from her letters in the appendix; however, she did protest a bit. And to my friend, Donna Millhollon, who assisted with proofing and editing.

I offer a special thank-you to the web master for Tall Comanche, Company C, Second Battalion, Fifth Cavalry Regiment, First Cavalry Division (Airmobile), Vietnam 1965–1972. This site, www.tallcomanche. org/March_1967.htm, provided valuable information to support my memories, and I used selected pieces from the site in the book and appendix.

I mention the names of a number of friends and comrades in my stories and thank them for their service and our association during this eventful time in our lives. I would also like to thank and honor those who serve on active duty, those who are veterans, and especially those who gave their lives for the cause of freedom.

FORWARD

By Jim Stanford
Former third platoon leader
In Charlie Company, Second/Fifth, First Cav

This is a book I almost wrote, and I'm glad that Tim Soyars was the veteran who wrote "his" story. Because this is true history. A personal story of the life of a young soldier in an unpopular war; the story of a young lieutenant charged with the awesome responsibility of leading other young men into the most challenging time of their lives.

The early part of the story seemed like I had written it or that Tim had been spying on my early military career. It was like I was reading the story of my early military career. I enlisted in the fall of 1965, eventually went through OCS, and after a short state-side assignment, moved on to Vietnam and to Charlie Company, Second/Fifth Cav, First Cavalry Division.

I knew Tim only slightly in Vietnam, and forty years later I discovered that we only lived a few miles apart. My time with Charlie Company began just after Tim moved to the S4 office. I was a young lieutenant who took command of the third platoon, shortly after Tim relinquished his command of the second platoon.

I was excited to read the stories of men I knew personally. Some of them are still with us, and some have passed on, but they are all brothers-in-arms who will never be forgotten.

This book is not a compilation of *war stories* although it is a story of war. It's a story of the exciting days, the tragic days, the humorous days, and the downright boring days that soldiers experience in war.

The title, *Where's Charlie?*, could have a double meaning to those of us who were there. It was a question we asked almost daily. *Where's Charlie?* could have meant the elusive enemy we sought to find. But it also was a question we often asked wondering *Where's Charlie?* Company because of the many major moves we would make as a matter of daily routine in our search for the enemy.

I agree with Tim on another point: Vietnam was a war despite what the politicians and think-tankers want to call it. It certainly wasn't a *police action* or a *skirmish*—it was war in its truest sense. Men lived, men died, and men were maimed for life, some physically and some mentally. It was war.

The inclusion of the correspondence between Tim and Jeanie adds a personal view of life in the mid to late sixties while the addition of the monthly summaries of the battalion logs give the story a broader view concerning the activities of the unit and how Charlie Company fit in.

I think this is a good book for those of us who were there and for those who weren't. For those who weren't there, it gives a different perspective of what the war was about and how the soldiers who were there lived their daily lives.

Geoffrey Grimes, PhD
Professor of English
Mountain View College

Where's Charlie? is a compelling testimonial to the experiences of war for an American soldier who not only survived but thrived on his faith in his country, his dedication to the mission and his men, and the love of his wife and family.

At a time in American history when it has long sense been fashionable to question the integrity of our country and the policies that throw many of our best and brightest into harm's way, *Where's Charlie?* is a refreshing reaffirmation of what American novelist William Faulkner once referred to as the "old verities and truths of the heart, lacking which any story is ephemeral and doomed—love and honor and pity and pride and compassion and sacrifice." These are the values that many young men carry into military service; they are not always those with which they retire from the service. Not the case, however, for Vietnam War veteran Tim Soyars who looks back at his hitch in the military and a year of combat in Southeast Asia to reflect on the relationships he formed, the skills he honed, and the benefits he received from his experiences.

Where's Charlie? will leave most readers with a deep sense of pride and respect for our American military service men and women. Winner of a Bronze Star for valor and the Air Medal for combat missions, former Lieutenant Tim Soyars reflects on the positive experiences he received during his tour of duty in Vietnam and what the war experiences earned for him in the years to come.

INTRODUCTION

The late 1960s was a time of war for the United States of America. It was also a time when all eligible young men were required to serve their country, and most of us merely answered the call as our fathers before us had done.

While growing up in the 1950s, stories of World War I, World War II, and Korea were very familiar to me since they were the subjects of storytelling, songs, books, news articles, and movies. They seemed to instill pride and patriotism in all Americans, and all veterans were held in high esteem and honored with great fanfare. As a boy, I often saw myself as Sergeant York, Audie Murphy, or one of John Wayne's many characters. In my daydreams and role-play, I was always a brave leader of men. I knew that someday I would serve my country, and that day came in 1965 when I stepped forward eagerly. Like many soldiers, I returned from Vietnam with pride and honor, a sense of accomplishment, good memories, and the good fortune to have survived without injury.

My wife and children, especially my son, have encouraged me to write my stories for years. I finally started in 2005. As I started, I refreshed my memory by going through copies of my company's operational reports, the daily correspondence between my wife and me, and over six hundred photos I took while in Vietnam. Excerpts of all three sources are included in the book or in the appendix.

I begin with a combat story in Vietnam and then glance backward to my family and my life as a boy. This sets the stage for my desire to be in the army and to give you a glimpse of the boy who would become a man during his time of war. From there I share some of my more significant and often humorous experiences during training, on my way to becoming an infantry second lieutenant in the US Army. The bulk of the book is about the war and my time with the First Air Cavalry. While my stories are about wartime, they entertain and excite with humor, warmth, compassion, honor, sadness, heroics, and romance. My military experience provided the foundation for the rest of my life. I sincerely hope this book might inspire some young person to experience the military to its fullest as I did.

My book title, *Where's Charlie?*, relates to the difficulty we had in finding the enemy (Charlie), especially during 1967, and the fact that I was in Charlie Company. My company made daily combat air assaults all over the Central Highlands and near the DMZ (Demilitarized Zone). My wife tried to monitor my location by keeping a map on the wall and peppering it with pushpins. By the time I got home in 1968, the map looked like a shotgun spray over the Central Highlands with a smattering around the DMZ. She had almost as much trouble finding Charlie Company as I did finding Charlie.

CHAPTER 1

March 1967

It was clear and warm in the late afternoon on March 23, 1967, when my helicopter set down inside the perimeter of Charlie Company. The company was operating in the mountains near the An Lo Valley, northwest of the Bong Son Plains in the Central Highlands of Vietnam. Charlie Company, an infantry unit of the Second/Fifth (Second Battalion, Fifth Cavalry Regiment), First Cav (First Air Cavalry Division), had received causalities during the battle of Phu Ninh on March 11, 1967, and I was one of the officer replacements for the company. The battalion commander escorted me to C Company's mountain camp to introduce me to CPT Don Markham, the CO (commanding officer).

A week earlier, while I was attending new soldier orientation training at Camp Radcliff (headquarters for the First Cav), I was introduced to Captain Markham one evening at the battalion officers' club. The captain was returning from R & R (rest and relaxation) and was scheduled to rejoin his company in the field the next day. He was eager to get officer replacements and welcomed me warmly. As we drank beer and passed the night at the club, he shared stories and the history of the company's activities during his tenure there. One story was about the recent battle at Phu Ninh. Being trained for combat and joining his company in a few days, I was very interested in hearing the details of the battle. He later published the story of this battle in an article for *Assembly*, a magazine for alumni of the US Military Academy at West Point. The article is also posted on the Charlie Company, Second/Fifth website. I have used that article to refresh my memories of the story that Captain Markham told me that night.

Early on March 11, Charlie Company was operating near the village of Phu Ninh supporting a mechanized sweep of the area by the Fortieth ARVN (Army of the Republic of Vietnam) Regiment. Charlie Company surrounded the target area with First and Second Platoons to the north and the Third and Fourth Platoons deployed to the south near the Nui Nieu Mountains. Around 1000 hours, Captain Markham ordered Lieutenant Gerald, Third Platoon, to send a patrol to secure the southern flank. Gerald sent out a squad led by Staff Sergeant Kriedler, who came upon NVA (North Vietnamese Army) soldiers. The squad quickly pursued them, killing one and wounding the other. Hearing the weapons fire, Lieutenant Gerald took another squad to reinforce Kriedler.

Captain Markham was monitoring the radio, listening to the communications between Kriedler and Gerald. Kriedler left two of his men to guard the wounded while he and Specialist Garza searched the area. As they moved into an open area bounded by hedgerows, the enemy opened fire, killing both instantly. Lieutenant Gerald took his patrol cautiously forward. He soon sighted the bodies of Kriedler and Garza, only three meters (ten feet) from the hedgerow. All was quiet. As they cautiously advanced, automatic-weapons fire erupted from the hedgerow. Lieutenant Gerald was mortally wounded, and three of his men were killed outright. The remaining members of the squad took cover and were pinned down within eight meters (twenty-five feet) of the NVA.

Hearing of the situation on the radio, Captain Markham took the remainder of the Third Platoon on a sweep south of their position to try to get to the pinned-down men, leaving the Fourth Platoon in place to block the rear. As they moved, they avoided the trails as much as possible, breaching hedgerows and following the natural drainage ditches. Sergeant First Class Shelly took the lead with Private First Class Watson on point (lead man in the column). As they approached the location where Lieutenant Gerald had fallen, they turned east trying to encircle the area. Moving cautiously along the trail, Watson encountered a lone enemy rifleman, who fired at him and then retreated. They continued their advance when firing erupted again, and this time Watson was hit. The machine gunner, Specialist Beal, sprayed the area, allowing Shelly to rescue Watson. When Beal stopped firing to reload, the enemy fired again, dislodging Beal's helmet but not wounding him.

With every step they encountered NVA fire and more casualties. The barrage of bullets was coming from many locations, which meant the opposition was much larger and stronger than first estimated. With this assessment, Captain Markham decided to keep the Third Platoon in its present position and requested an airlift of the Second Platoon to provide reinforcement.

Staff Sergeant Shoemaker, the Fourth Platoon leader, had been monitoring the radio transmissions and was anxious to get involved. He radioed the CO and offered to lead five soldiers to a position northwest of the pinned-down men. Permission was granted. He carefully moved the squad forward. When they were within fifteen meters (forty-five feet) of the wounded men, the enemy opened fire, and they were also pinned down with little opportunity to advance.

One of Shoemaker's men crawled forward toward the stranded men only to be shot. He was pulled back by his heels. Another attempt was made with the same results. Shoemaker decided to call in Bravo Troop, First/Ninth Cavalry to hit the NVA positions with ARA (aerial rocket artillery). The gunships made several passes, pounding the area with rockets, yet the enemy continued to resist.

The Third Platoon was almost nose-to-nose with NVA, so Captain Markham couldn't call in artillery or rockets to their position and couldn't direct fire to assist Shoemaker either. When the ARA gunships left the area, he ordered Lieutenant Gaffney, the artillery forward observer who was attached to the main element of the Fourth Platoon, to move up to assist Shoemaker. He advanced with his RTO (radio operator), but when he came within sight of the pinned-down squad, he spotted enemy movement and dashed to safety. The NVA immediately fired. Gaffney made it to safety, but his RTO fell to the ground, seriously wounded. The RTO managed to strip off his radio and crawl to cover. Unfortunately, the radio lay on the ground in plain view of the enemy positions with little chance for retrieval.

At 1300 hours, Second Platoon was airlifted to a nearby clearing and was directed to move cautiously along the network of sunken ditches. The going was slow since the ditches were filled with debris. As the point man cleared a patch of heavy vegetation with his machete, the enemy opened up with automatic weapons from within the ditch. They were on the other side of the vegetation, waiting. The point man was killed and two others were wounded. The Second Platoon fired grenades into the area, and the enemy was silenced. Sergeant First Class Salazar, the platoon leader, crawled forward to retrieve the point man's body, and the medic came up to attend to the wounded. The CO ordered the Second Platoon to pull back twenty-five meters to the intersection of two trenches. This proved to be a wise or lucky decision, because, as he found out later, that route of attack was leading the Second Platoon directly into a great trench at the base of the mountain, which was swarming with elements of the NVA.

This mission had placed Charlie Company in the middle of an outpost of the Seventh and Ninth Battalions of the Eighteenth NVA Regiment. The terrain on the Nui Mieu Mountain slopes was an ideal defensive position. The slopes were covered with room-sized boulders with large spaces beneath them that served as natural foxholes and bunkers. Waist-high scrub brush grew among the boulders, providing additional cover. From the ground, the NVA was invisible, so movement up the slopes would have been treacherous, given the enemy's placement there. The base of the mountain contained many natural drainage ditches leading to a major trench approximately six hundred meters (two thousand feet) in length and nearly twenty-five meters at its deepest point. This was the NVA's main defensive position. The army had received a report of enemy activity near the village of Phu Ninh but had known nothing of the NVA's large presence there. In front of the ditches and trench was a patchwork of agricultural plots, mostly enclosed by thick hedgerows. Within the hedgerows, the enemy had made bunkers and created firing positions. The area was a death trap to unsuspecting soldiers moving in the vicinity of the village, and Sergeant Kriedler, Lieutenant Gerald, and their men were the first victims.

The CO left a portion of the Second Platoon in their blocking position in the trench and took the remainder with him to link up with Shelley and the Third Platoon. They moved about fifty meters when two more soldiers were wounded. They tried several more advances but were repulsed each time. The situation was becoming futile. Soldiers were reluctant to move since the enemy seemed to have firing positions all around them. The CO asked for volunteers to search out the immediate enemy positions. Specialist Bennett volunteered to accompany him, and they crawled slowly down a sunken trail. Suddenly, there was a sharp crack close to the CO's face. Only one round was fired, and it struck Bennett. He died en route to the medevac hospital.

Around 1530 hours, the battalion commander, Colonel Stevenson, air assaulted Delta Company to a location about thirteen hundred meters from Captain Markham's position. Delta Company placed one platoon in reserve at the LZ (landing zone), and the company commander, Captain McInerney, led three platoons in a sweep toward the fighting. At the same time, the colonel brought in Alpha Company as backup and airlifted the First Platoon of Charlie Company to a hill on the northern slope of the Nui Mieu Mountains. The First Platoon, led by Lieutenant Dooley, was ordered to sweep down the slope and eventually link up with the Second and Third Platoons.

The First Platoon's landing on the slope was uneventful; however, about halfway down the slope, automatic-weapons fire sent the platoon scrambling for cover. Dooley ordered a squad to return to the top of the hill to protect the platoon's rear, but they encountered fire, with one man mortally wounded. Later, Dooley's RTO was wounded as they moved over a large boulder. With the enemy contact on the slope, the colonel ordered Delta Company to assist them.

Delta Company moved in a column toward the north slope of the mountain. They were, unknowingly, within close proximity of the great trench when NVA firing thundered across the open field, killing or wounding everyone in view. Captain McInerney came forward with the other platoons to assist, and many more soldiers were wounded or died, including McInerney. Staff Sergeant Cuellar assumed command of the company and eventually pulled back to the LZ to evacuate the wounded and to allow room to engage the NVA with artillery. Cuellar ordered Sergeant Dawson, the Third Platoon leader, to go forward and bring back the wounded before he called for an artillery strike, but Dawson got pinned down by deadly fire and could not complete the mission.

Darkness came to the battlefield, and both Delta Company and the NVA retrieved their dead and wounded. It must have been surreal to the American wounded, playing dead, as they watched NVA soldiers walk past their quiet, prone bodies solely to retrieve their NVA comrades. When all of Delta Company's soldiers were accounted for, the entire company pulled back to the LZ. Charlie Company spread its ranks to form a partial perimeter and settled in for the night. They also set up ambushes and trip flares along logical routes but were unable to collect their American dead.

By dawn, the NVA had vanished, apparently fleeing east during the night, leaving many dead soldiers behind. Captain Markham wrote about the morning's discovery as follows: "In the silence of the deserted battlefield we walked the great trench that yesterday had been bloody hell. Only now could we evacuate the bodies of several comrades. There was little talk."[1] In an almost tearful moment, Captain Markham stated that twenty-two American soldiers were killed and twenty-six were wounded at the battle of Phu Ninh on March 11, 1967. They counted eighty-one NVA dead.

As I listened to the story I tried to picture myself there in the battle. I thought of how I might respond to the various situations and the call for volunteers. I thought briefly of the dead and wounded, but I didn't

---

[1] Tall Comanche, Company C, Second Battalion, Fifth Cavalry Regiment, First Cavalry Division (Airmobile), Vietnam 1965-1972, website, http://www.tallcomanche.org/index.html

dwell on the subject. My time to join Charlie Company was close at hand, and I would soon have first-hand experiences of my own. The story of the battle of Phu Ninh presented an accurate picture of the way engagements occurred during the Vietnam War. On March 11, the enemy had fortifications and battle lines; they waited in ambush; they engaged in combat; they disappeared into the night. Finding NVA with large fortifications was not common, but this kind of NVA, hit-and-run contact was a frequent occurrence during the war. However, most combat soldiers, including me, would have preferred the large, decisive battles to the small encounters that were the norm.

I was excited and apprehensive when I joined my company. The battalion commander presented me to Captain Markham, wished me well, returned to his helicopter, and flew back to battalion headquarters. Captain Markham greeted me with enthusiasm and introduced me to the officers and senior NCOs (noncommissioned officers) of the company. After some orientation concerning protocol and mission, the CO turned me over to the platoon sergeant of the Second Platoon, SFC Adolfo Salazar. Sergeant Sal was a seasoned veteran and a fine man, as I'd soon discover. He was in his midthirties, a veteran of the Korean War, and in his second tour of duty in Vietnam. He talked about the history of the company, including the battle of Phu Ninh and the Second Platoon's role, and introduced me to the men of the platoon. With each introduction, we briefly exchanged information about hometowns, family, and service history. Then, Sergeant Sal went over the vacancies on the platoon roster and the orders for the night. Second Platoon was to take a squad of men to a junction along a trail about 150 meters from the company's perimeter and lie in ambush, returning after first light the next day. He volunteered to lead the ambush. I agreed, and I told him that he would be in command but that I wanted to tag along. We departed at dusk to prepare the ambush site. The team consisted of Sergeant Sal, a squad leader, three soldiers, and me. While on patrol earlier that day, the sergeant had identified a well-traveled trail as a good site for an ambush. Upon arriving, the men and sergeants took out entrenching tools and dug a deep trench along the tree line, out of view of the trail. Soon, we settled in for the night. However, no enemy passed our way, and, with little sleep, we returned to camp at first light to begin a new mission.

During the first few weeks with Charlie Company, I spent a lot of time talking to Sergeant Sal, discussing missions, tactics, the men, the CO, the enemy, and the terrain that we patrolled. Like a sponge, I soaked up everything and valued his veteran combat experiences. He was open and easy-going, and it was difficult to think of him solely as my platoon sergeant. We became friends, and I quickly garnered his trust and respect, and soon that permeated the platoon as well.

CHAPTER 2

A Backward Glance

From my position on the heavily wooded ridge, I could see the enemy encamped in the distance. With my binoculars, I could view their activities more clearly. They appeared to be at least battalion strength and well fortified around a small, abrupt mountain. Between the enemy and me lay an open plain. As I continued to reconnoiter the enemy's position, I saw at least one artillery piece at the top of the mountain, aimed in my direction. They hadn't noticed my presence yet, so it was imperative that my unit strikes first. Since the day was young and the sky bright, we couldn't advance across the open plain. The enemy would surely mow us down. I did have one artillery piece, and I planned to put it to good use.

The terrain around the mountain was flat and without natural cover, but the enemy had positioned vehicles of all sizes around the base of the mountain. They hadn't camouflaged themselves, but they looked ready for action and were preparing for an attack. In a way, the camp looked a bit like the German fortifications during World War II that I'd seen in movies. I told my men, "This is going to be tricky, but if we move quickly, quietly, and out of sight of the enemy, we can attack their artillery on the mountain with our artillery and then attack the troops on the ground before they can get a fix on our position." Everyone was eager, so I positioned my men and my artillery along the back of the ridge. I instructed my men to lay low and watch my artillery wreak havoc.

With everyone in place, I took command of the artillery. I knew I needed to make every shot count. After the gun was sighted, I ordered, "Open fire." Boom, boom, boom, and soon the enemy gun toppled over the backside of the mountain. The second shot had hit the target. I said, "Good firing, men." I immediately ordered them to reposition the gun to fire on the enemy ground emplacements. After a few test shots, I ordered them, "Fire at will." Boom, boom, boom continued, and I watched the enemy drop like flies as my artillery rounds pounded them. We were all anxious to attack them on the ground and join in on the enemy's destruction.

Suddenly, I heard footsteps and a familiar voice. "Timothy Ray Soyars, what are you doing shooting those toothpicks all over my bedroom carpet? And your trucks, cars, and toy soldiers are everywhere." "Mom, I'm playing war. I'll pick them up when I'm finished." She continued with a tone of annoyance, "Look at my bedspread; it's balled up on the floor covered with your toys. Pick that up right now." "But, Mom, it's my ridge line." "Is that my vanity case?" she questioned. "Yes, Mom, I'm using it as my mountain. See? This is how I shoot the toothpicks with my cannon. Boom! They go a long ways, and they knock down the men when I hit them." Mom finally gave up, "Okay, but be sure to clean up everything when you're finished and shake out the bedspread to get rid of the dirt left by your toys. And I better not find any toothpicks on my carpet." The battle resumed, and, of course, I was victorious.

History books and novels are filled with stories of young men and women going off to war. In each, the experiences and challenges are as varied as the people themselves. The stories tell of leaders and followers, cowards and heroes. Some of them are wounded in combat, some die, some are awarded medals for heroism, and some perform their duty without receiving awards at all. However, they all make their contributions and share one commonality, the bond of combat. It's well documented how combat can create an everlasting bond akin to brotherhood, linking comrades through fears, tears, companionship, joy, death, patriotism, loneliness, bravery, honor, and memories. All tied to that unique time shared during war.

How do you prepare for war and combat? How do you face the challenges and fears? What makes one person more successful than another during war? Is it luck or lack of luck, depending upon the outcome? My personality, background, and attitude contributed significantly to my approach, my will to succeed, and my contributions during the Vietnam War. Military training contributed to my skills and enthusiasm as a leader in combat. At times during my tour of duty, I believe luck and prayers were with me. I had a few loved ones at home thinking of me and writing often, and I was very thankful for that. The letters made a big difference to my morale and attitude, and I longed for mail call.[2] But before we continue with my story about Vietnam, I'd like to share a few stories to lay the foundation for my participation in combat and my approach to the challenges and fears. I have often heard that a person's past is a good indicator for how they'll handle their future.

As a small boy, I often played war by myself and with friends. As I played, I'd engage the pretend enemy, shooting with my toy weapons and visualizing them falling to their death. I'd run from cover to cover, shooting and sometimes being shot. I'd hit the ground wounded or dead, and then bounce back up, taking on a new character and continuing the battle. When I pretended to be wounded, I rose to greater dramatic heights, leading a charge and showing great heroism. Pretend war took imagination and some scripting, or rather directing, so my playmates didn't always appreciate the role-play. When my friends got tired of this, I'd sometimes continue playing alone. I could always entertain myself using my imagination. I loved watching war movies and could relive the actions in my daydreams, playing out the various parts.

I wasn't born into a military family, but the news and movies in the 1940s and 1950s helped shape my feelings about duty, country, and military service. My wonderful family's many fine examples of military service helped to enhance my attitude and desire to be a soldier. No one in my family was violent or encouraged violence, but all were extremely patriotic. Being a soldier was something I always wanted and planned to

---

2   Excerpts from letters are in Appendix A

do. My dad had a fireworks accident as a boy, losing about one third of his right index finger. This made him ineligible for military service during World War II; he joined the civil service instead. However, his brothers all served in the US Army in both Europe and the Pacific; my mother's two brothers and most of my uncles by marriage served as well. My brother was in the army between the Korean and Vietnam Wars, spending most of the time in Germany, another example that I respected.

I was born in 1945 and grew up in Norfolk, Virginia. My father was a firefighter at the Norfolk Naval Base, and my mother was a housewife (as it was called in those days). I was the youngest of three children, with a brother thirteen years my senior and a sister two years older. Family was the center of existence, with church and country always a big part of our lives.

The middle-class neighborhood where I grew up had many children, and there were at least fifteen boys within a year or so of my age. I probably liked playing war games more than my friends, but sports were important to all of us, and baseball got top billing. After all, it was the 1950s. My neighborhood friends were either Yankee or Dodger fans. The Dodgers were in Brooklyn then, and the rivalry is well-known. We did have one boy who liked the Washington Senators, but he wasn't a very good ballplayer, which could explain his choice of team. Anyway, we played baseball all summer, often having competitions with surrounding neighborhood teams. Besides baseball, we played all of the standard games of the day: kick the can, hide-and-go-seek, and Monopoly. We even created our own Olympic-type events, including somersaults, high jump, endurance racing, tree climbing, fence jumping, marbles, spin the bottle, and, my favorite, raiding neighborhood fruit trees. However, as I matured, I really enjoyed spin-the-bottle.

Fruit trees grew well in our neighborhood. One neighbor's house that backed onto a creek had a five-foot fence and a very large cherry tree that seemed to need care and attention. We boys hated to see the fruit go to waste. After all, mothers in those days frequently chastised their children,

"Eat your food and don't let it go to waste. Don't you know people in China are starving?" or something like that. We certainly didn't want those cherries to go to waste, so we fought off the birds, climbed the tree, and ate and ate until the owner of the house discovered us. This is where our Olympic training would come to good use. We dropped out of the tree, hit the ground running, vaulted over the fence, and dashed across the creek to freedom in some other backyard. The man made good time to the fence, but he had not had our Olympic conditioning, so the fence proved to be a major obstacle. Our adventures were frequent, but we were never destructive and always respectful even when our mouths were full of other people's fruit.

My mom and dad grew up in Danville, Virginia, moving to Norfolk in the early 1940s. My father, Raymond Conrad Soyars, was one of eight children, seven boys and one girl. My mother, Ruth Lee Elizabeth Ashworth Soyars, was the seventh of eleven, nine girls and two boys. Both sets of my grandparents were born in the late 1800s, and their fathers and uncles were Civil War veterans. Being from southern Virginia put the families in Confederate territory. All four of my great-grandfathers were in that war, along with many great-uncles. War stories always fascinated me, especially those that involved my ancestors.

All lines of my family go back many years in America, and my wife has researched my genealogy trying to find the dates of arrival for my first immigrant ancestors. The one ancestor we have a lot of information about is my great-great-great-grandfather, James Soyars—some early records spell the name Sawyers. Since the name Soyars isn't that common in the United States, most, if not all, stem from James. He was sixteen in April 1776 when he enlisted for three years in Captain Torrey's company of the Fourteenth Regiment of the Virginia Line. The regiment fought at Brandywine, Germantown, and Monmouth and was encamped at Valley Forge in the cold winter of 1777–78. He reenlisted in 1779 in CPT Thomas Hord's company and served under COL Abraham Buford in South Carolina. He was in the battle of Waxhaws, also known as Buford's Massacre, on May

29, 1780, where he was severely wounded and taken prisoner by British troops under the command of COL Banastre Tarleton.[3]

At the end of the war, the British released him, and he returned to Danville. There he married and fathered fourteen children, rose to major in the Virginia Militia, served on the Danville School Board and served as sergeant-at-arms for the Virginia Senate from 1823 until his death in 1838. In 1824, he was a member of the escort team to welcome General Gilbert du Motier, marquis de Lafayette, to the Virginia Assembly. The assembly was honoring the French general for his service and dedication to America during its fight for independence. I'd love to expand on this interesting man, but my wife, reading over my shoulder, is telling me to stop and move on to the subject of this book.

During my high school years (1960–63), my brother died unexpectedly in 1961, and my father, who had suffered from heart trouble during those years, died in 1964. These were sad times for our family and impressionable times for me. My mother died many years later at age ninety-two, having lived a full and wonderful life.

After I graduated from high school, I worked and attended a local college for a while, but like many young men of my age, I didn't have a career plan. However, there was never any question in my mind about serving in the military. The Vietnam conflict provided the opportunity, and my family heritage determined what branch. Obviously, I needed to continue the family tradition in the US Army.

---

[3]　Bureau of Pensions, Report No. 66, James Soyars, December 27, 1831.

CHAPTER 3

Basic Decision

Not all decisions are equal. Some are simple, like do I cut the grass or take a nap. Some are major, like do I buy that new sports car or save for retirement. Some are life changing and help to focus or alter the direction of your future. I made a life-changing decision in 1965—a decision that I've never regretted. After high school, I worked full time and attended evening classes at Old Dominion College; today, it's a university. I had a girlfriend away at college and another locally. I had playing around on my mind and didn't apply myself to academics. After a year, I decided I needed to focus on building a future, and to do so I needed to get serious. It was about this time when Uncle Sam started drafting heavily for all branches of the armed forces. Not being a full-time student, I knew I'd soon get the call. I couldn't imagine serving in any branch of the service except the army, so I decided to visit the local recruiter. There, they gave me a few tests and indicated that I could qualify for many jobs in the army. Of course, recruiting was his job, and I knew that, but it did give me encouragement. The sergeant directed me toward the ASA (Army Security Agency), which was looking for people at that time, and I qualified for the ASA based on testing. That sounded like a fun place to learn the spy business. The recruiter also mentioned OCS (Officer Candidate School) and said that it would be more difficult to get an appointment there, but it was another option.

All of this gave me plenty of room to dream about a future. I figured the military would be a great place to get myself together and plan a career. In addition, the military was a requirement for my generation, so I knew I had to serve, and I wanted to serve. After a few years in the army, I'd be ready for college and have a better chance at succeeding, so it sounded like the thing to do. The thought of dying in war crossed my mind, but I was confident and never gave it any serious consideration.

In the fall of 1965 I was inducted into the US Army. From Norfolk, Virginia, I went by bus and train to Fort Jackson, South Carolina, to begin basic training. At the reception center in Fort Jackson, thousands of new recruits from east of the Mississippi were processed, tested, equipped with basic supplies, and given the famous GI (government issue) buzz haircut. Daily routines were hurry up and wait and a lot of yelling by sergeants, but it was fun in its own way. After all, I'd been playing soldier since my early childhood. The GI clothing and haircuts gave all of us a commonality, breaking down ethnic and class barriers, or at least refocusing attention on the common thread, the army. I remember good camaraderie. There was a black recruit from Detroit who was very personable, talkative, assertive, and kept himself at the center of attention. I took a liking to him, and he took a liking to me. We became part of a group that hung out during breaks and after-hours, one of many such groups. Our group included about twenty recruits consisting of Italians, Poles, blacks and those like me who didn't assign any particular ethnic group to themselves. The army had taken a portion of the US melting pot, brought it together, and was mixing it up. It was interesting to interact and converse with people from different parts of America with different accents, backgrounds, cultures, and experiences. This army was going to provide a good educational experience for me.

The Fort Jackson induction center conducted a lot of psychological testing, which was very exhausting. I recall a full day of testing for everyone, and later a few recruits went back for further testing. While there were thousands in the initial testing group, the callback group included only about twenty. I was one of those selected for the second day of testing. It wasn't always clear what we were trying to accomplish with this second series of tests since some dealt with very abstract ideas and appeared to have no one correct answer. After this second round, each of us received counseling about the test results, and the objective of some tests became clearer. In my counseling, they informed me that I showed a high aptitude for electronics and foreign languages, which was odd since I never had any training or interest in either. They also said I qualified for OCS and would learn more about acceptance into that school later in my training. I was feeling good about my enlistment decision.

At last we were ready for basic training and went to join our training companies. Our little reception center group was broken up as we all went separate ways. I ran across a few of them on post from time to time during basic training but not after Fort Jackson. It's incredible how people with little in common come together for a short period, and a bond and camaraderie evolve that could last forever; then, as suddenly as they came together, they part with little likelihood of ever meeting again. We were young, and our army experience would offer many more opportunities for bonding and camaraderie. All are great maturing experiences, although some became sad memories for those we lost in combat.

Military basic training was everything they said and much more; US military training was top-notch. Anything your mom and dad didn't teach you about discipline, the drill sergeants did; they also taught vocabulary my parents probably had never heard.

I had two drill sergeants during basic training, and they couldn't have been more different. One sergeant, Sergeant First Class Sutterfield, was white, about five feet tall and probably weighed one hundred pounds wearing his boots. He was always shouting in a loud, high voice and was very spit-and-polished. The other drill sergeant, Staff Sergeant Horton, was black, tall and large, weighing two hundred plus pounds. He was calm, soft-spoken, and very comfortable and relaxed in his manner of dress. Both were very well suited to their jobs.

I recall the first day of basic. Sergeant Horton called us all together to discuss barrack assignments and to select leaders. He must have had information from the reception center because our barrack had two of the recruits who had taken the second day of testing, and Sergeant Horton selected us to lead the barrack. We wore armbands, one for sergeant and one for corporal. I got the corporal armband. Sergeant Horton assigned me to be in charge of the bottom floor of the barrack, and the acting sergeant took the top floor.

Once all assignments were complete, Sergeant Horton asked if anyone needed anything from the PX (Post Exchange), and a number of hands went up, including mine. He pointed to about twelve of us and asked us to stand away from the others. When we separated, he told us we had just volunteered for KP (kitchen patrol) the next morning beginning at some ungodly hour. It was weeks before anyone would get to go to the PX, but the message about volunteering became very clear to me. That was my only KP experience. It's exactly as portrayed in the movies, continuous yelling and mind-numbing work. In addition, we learned that there is only one way to do things in the kitchen, the army way. Who would have thought there was only one way to wash and dry dishes, hold a pan, or use a mop or a broom? Everything had a prescribed army way. This was part of the army education.

I look back on my childhood experience with KP as a lot more relaxed and fun. My sister and I did chores around the house. My parents were well versed in chores, having grown up in large families. For the benefit of those born after 1960, things were manual in those earlier, black-and-white days. One of our early chores was washing and drying the dishes. My sister, Sheila, took the senior position as dishwasher, and I was relegated to the lesser role of drying. I always tried to make the job more exciting by placing washed dishes back in her stack when she wasn't looking or accidentally splashing water on her as I extracted dishes from the rinse. I never understood why she didn't think that was funny; I enjoyed it, especially her reactions. However, I didn't try any of these tricks when I had KP in the army. If I had, I'd never have gotten off KP.

At Fort Jackson, the American melting pot was evident in my first-floor barrack. We covered all the ethnic groups, all eastern seaboard states, some inland states, and Puerto Rico. Since all of us were new to the army, discipline and duty came in various degrees of competency. Each barrack had daily responsibilities for cleaning everything inside and outside as well as standards for maintaining our bunks and personal items. One of my jobs as corporal was to coordinate all tasks and ensure proper maintenance to standard. Not everyone cared about cleanliness or the army standards, especially as a daily chore. That really wasn't a surprise, and I dealt with it.

I took my duties seriously and worked to motivate everyone to do the same. Tasks went slow at first, and I had to tell a number of soldiers to redo their jobs until they came up to standard. We eventually began to work together as a team, and barrack life became easier. We even got a reward or two for a job well done.

On one occasion, after a long, hard, late day of training, the drill sergeant visited me around bedtime, instructing me to get my floor in order for an early-morning inspection. The captain planned to conduct a white-glove inspection (no dirt or dust anywhere as he wipes his white-gloved finger along surfaces of the barrack). My orders were to get my barrack floor ready that night since we wouldn't have time in the morning. I called the men together to give the order I had just received. I explained our mission and requested that everyone pitch in regardless of the task to get this done as quickly as possible. The moaning and complaining was extensive. Some declared they were going to bed, and I could do the job without them, and then others followed. I tried several tactics to motivate everyone to participate but with little luck. About three quarters of the barrack were in bed and ignoring the order. I walked around the barrack, looking everyone in the eye, saying nothing. After making rounds, I stood by the door and waited for a few minutes. With no response, I yelled that I wanted everyone outside to fight me. "If you win, you can go to sleep; if I win, we clean the barrack as the team we're supposed to be." With this challenge, I exited the barrack. I stood on the lawn making the challenge repeatedly. After a while, the lights came on in the barrack, and I could see men moving about with brooms and mops. Everyone appeared to be up and working, no talking. I went in and joined them, catching a few smiles and an occasional pat on the back. My bluff worked.

In January, our basic training company went on bivouac (a forced march and a week of camping out and playing at war). Unfortunately, it snowed, and many of us came down with the flu. I got very sick, and my company commander sent me to a supply unit in the bivouac area. They put me in a large supply tent with a kerosene heater (what a stinky fuel).

There, I curled up in a sleeping bag, took APCs (aspirin) or some other popular pill of the day, and slept. I continued to have a high fever and chills, and eventually, someone decided to take me to the Fort Jackson hospital. I don't remember being transported to the hospital but woke up there and stayed for about a week, recovering from pneumonia. I missed most of that bivouac experience but got many other opportunities later.

During basic, I applied for OCS. The application included many written documents and a number of interviews with individual officers and a final review board of officers. I never really knew how I was doing in this process, but I received an OCS appointment before graduating from basic training.

After basic, recruits destined for the infantry received assignments to AIT (advanced infantry training). Fort Jackson was creating a special AIT School for those accepted to OCS. For my advanced training, I was scheduled to attend the ASA training program, but my commanding officer asked me to decline the ASA training and join the infantry AIT program, and I did.

It took a little time to fill and organize this OCS AIT session, so I went home and took all available leave. When I returned to Fort Jackson, I joined a conventional AIT training company in progress as a training assistant to the executive officer. He was a recent graduate of infantry OCS, and he became my mentor. He talked about the difficulty of the program and the need to be able to run forever. He took me out to run frequently, and I often became winded. At that time I smoked cigarettes, which didn't help my breathing. He said it would be tough on me if I didn't learn to run long distances. In the movies, the officers drank, ate, smoked, and womanized a lot. I didn't recall them running. I asked, "If I practice the other skills, will I be able to compensate for the lack of long distance running ability?" He either smiled or frowned; I couldn't tell which because of my gasping in a bent-over position.

The OCS AIT company was finally formed, and training there was a lot easier than basic. Since it was the first OCS AIT company, it probably got harder with each new group. After graduating from AIT, I returned home and took more leave until OCS began.

CHAPTER 4

OCS

I flew to Columbus, Georgia, on a Sunday afternoon, taking a cab to the OCS reporting company at Fort Benning. Our reporting time was 3:00 p.m., sorry, 1500 hours. I was excited and apprehensive about what was in store for me but soon lost the excitement and better understood my apprehension. As I off-loaded my duffel bag from the cab, a second lieutenant with an attitude greeted me. I mean a real attitude! "What's your name, scum? Why are you here? Where are you to report? Let me see your orders. Oh boy, you're one of mine. Get that duffel and head up those stairs. Don't ask questions. Follow orders. Move, move, move!" You get the idea. From there on, it got worse.

As I ascended the stairs into the unknown, more second lieutenants were waiting at intervals to ensure no one strayed or regained any of the composure they might have had before arriving at Fort Benning. Several lieutenants were preoccupied with yelling at other newly arrived candidates, so I scurried past, trying to make myself invisible. I entered a large room filled with other victims. Some were in lines, some were being harassed by officers, and some were doing push-ups with officers watching.

Soon, a different second lieutenant inquired if he could help me. I explained who I was and why I was there. Apparently, I said something wrong. He got six inches from my face and explained that I was Candidate Soyars and nothing more, and I wasn't to address him as just sir, but rather "Sir, Candidate Soyars, or yes, sir or no, sir," and I had better say it loud.

He gave me a chance to practice the phrase a few times, but I don't think I pleased him because he had me do twenty push-ups, yelling at me the entire time. When I finished the push-ups, he hustled me toward the line where other candidates were cowering. I assumed this was the running-the-gauntlet-and-waiting-for-the-next-phase-of-humiliation line. I noticed the expressions on the faces of the men around me. Mostly, they displayed shocked timidity. I'm sure I looked the same.

The rest of that evening progressed with more shouting of commands and belittling. I was assigned a platoon and bunk, and then someone yelled something about dinner. Hearing that magic word, I eagerly joined a line, and we all were hustled down halls and stairs, outside along walkways, and to a line heading into another building, which was the line for the mess hall. Harassment was continuous, mixed with the constant sound of "Sir, Candidate Xxxx," "No, sir" or "Yes, sir."

The entrance to the mess hall had about five steps leading to a porch. The porch had a chinning bar, and every candidate had to give ten chin-ups before entering the mess hall. Should he not perform the chin-ups satisfactorily, he had to drop down, do ten push-ups, and go to the end of the line. Many candidates went to the end of the line that first night, but, fortunately, I passed the chin-up test and entered the mess hall. What I saw inside led me to believe that eating wasn't going to be pleasant. Officers were patrolling the tables shouting, instructing, correcting, and sending some candidates outside for more push-ups. I couldn't believe all the contentious, in-your-face harassment.

I finally got to the trays, took one, and proceeded through what was an assembly line; no questions or talking allowed. Each candidate just moved quickly through the line with enlisted men and civilians shoveling stuff on our trays. There was no refusing an item and no seconds. You got what they gave you, and it seemed to be a lot.

As we exited the chow line, a lieutenant greeted us with more shouting and directions as to where to sit. At our table, the lieutenant instructed us to sit on the first six inches of the chair, sit at attention with arms to our sides and look straight ahead with no talking, no eye movement, and no facial expression. I thought, "How fun. We'll have to bury our faces in our trays like pigs and eat until the food is gone." However, the lieutenant instructed us on the proper procedure for eating a *square* meal. (Use your right hand only to pick up the fork; keep your eyes looking straight ahead; capture a small portion of food; lift the fork straight up to the height of your mouth and then move it in a straight line to your mouth. With the food in your mouth, close your mouth and retract the fork in the reverse manner and direction in which it arrived. When the fork reaches the tray, place it upside down with the handle resting on the table and the fork tines on the tray. At that point, your arms are to return to your sides, at attention, while you chew your food.) I thought it was going to take a long time to eat, but the lieutenant, who must have read my mind, said, "You'll be ejected from the mess hall for more exercise if you don't chew quickly." A lesson on drinking followed, which used the same squared pattern as used for the food. Finally finished with the meal, more loud commands followed, hustling us to empty trays, exit the mess hall, and run back to our barrack for further instructions.

By this time, we were all mentally tired and wanted rest. We whispered wishes that all this would soon be over for the night. In the barrack, the lieutenants instructed us, at maximum volume, on how and where to unpack our duffel bags, how to make bunks, how to polish boots and floors, and how to maintain the latrine, etc. We had already learned the army way, now we were learning the OCS way, which was the army way on steroids. The one thing about the army way that was prevalent during basic was cursing, yet OCS had none. No cursing as well as the manner in which we were taught to eat, drink, keep tidy, and clean up were all essential. Upon graduation we received a letter from the president of the United States declaring that by our successful completion of the program, we were now officers and gentlemen.

As we were practicing our new skills, a lieutenant called out the names of four men and hustled them out. Sometime later they returned, telling us of their first experience visiting the platoon tact (tactical) officer. My turn finally came, and I ventured into the hall, where I received several instructions on what my actions should be when I see an officer approaching inside a building. I was to place my back to the wall and stand at attention.

Whichever candidate saw the officer first must hit the wall and turn his head away and yell, "Make way." I got all this information from lieutenants walking the halls while I was trying to get to my destination. The constant yelling was becoming less intimidating to me; it was all I had heard and the only means of communications I had received since I had arrived. The visit with the tact officer, LT James O'Harra, was the best experience of the day. However, when I saw him, I winced. He was the lieutenant with the attitude who greeted my cab upon arrival, but this time he talked calmly and sincerely. He had read my file and wanted me to tell him a few other things about myself, including my reason for being in OCS. He told me a little about the program and himself. I didn't stay there long but left with the impression that he was going to be a good platoon leader.

Sometime around 2300 hours, an order came for lights-out; it was so welcome. I was asleep in seconds but not for long. As we soon found out, it was a custom in OCS to have a more senior OCS company (nearing graduation) visit the most junior company during their first night at Benning, at midnight to be precise. They came to take revenge on us for their first night in OCS. This was their reward for reaching senior candidate status.

While we slept, they quietly positioned themselves throughout our barrack to achieve maximum effect. They came with trash can lids, cans, sticks, hammers, whistles, and anything else they could find to make noise. In unison, they began their serenade, including screamed orders. There was so much noise I couldn't understand the words. Some men got to their feet immediately and were ordered to act like dogs, so they went down on all fours and moved in various directions while barking. Some stayed in their bunks, but the tormentors pulled them out of bed with a thump and offered a bit of extra harassment. Being a very sound sleeper, I was in the latter group. The shouting and harassing continued with no clear purpose. They created chaos and the feelings of uncertainty and helplessness, an experience that we would likely have again one day in combat.

From the chaotic barrack, the senior candidates directed us down the hallway to the latrine. Other men from our platoon were already there, some standing in toilets and one in the sink. They herded us into the shower, where we entered on all fours and continued our barking parade with the water running full blast. It began and ended abruptly. They departed without a word and left us to clean up the mess and find a little time for sleep before reveille at 0400 hours. After the first day's welcome to OCS, a number of candidates lined up to request a release from the program. Other candidates would also leave voluntarily, especially during the first eight weeks of the program.

Not every day was like the first, thank goodness, but some things were consistent. When outside, we were expected to move at double-time (jogging). Our transportation at the fort was largely by foot and always at double-time in platoon formation. At first, I had a problem with the long runs, as the lieutenant had warned me about in AIT. I sometimes dropped out of formation to catch my breath and give my side time to stop hurting, but I always caught up with the platoon and returned to my proper place. Within a few weeks, I had no problem with the running. I wondered if the pneumonia that I'd had during basic had contributed to my difficulties, but I never mentioned having been sick. It probably wouldn't have mattered anyway and probably would have focused negative attention on me. Lieutenant O'Harra would often visit the platoon on Sundays, our day of rest and study, to invite anyone interested to join him in a run. I soon looked forward to the Sunday runs, and by graduation I could run very long distances with ease.

We did have fun from time to time. One evening, a candidate was in the first-floor hall against a wall getting a lecture from his tact officer when a second tact officer approached, shooing a cockroach. The second tact officer told the candidate to kill the cockroach, which he did. At that point, the first tact officer shouted, "What have you done? That was my pet." I think you see where this is going. By the way, I witnessed this out of the corner of my eye. I was also in the hall, braced against the wall, and heard that conversation. It was hard not to laugh or smile.

We scheduled a trial for the murderer and a funeral for the pet cockroach for the next weekend. Everyone in the company had a role in the trial, the funeral, or both. The tact officers assigned roles. One man was appointed judge, others were in the jury, and several were lawyers; also there was a preacher, some family members, pallbearers, mourners, choir, etc. Since I was present at the scene of the crime, I was a witness, and later I was a mourner for the bereaved family. Using initiative, we tried to dress our parts; towels for bandanas and hats, sheets for dresses, a blanket for the judge's robe, etc.

Early Saturday afternoon we started with the trial and ended with the funeral. We invited a junior OCS company to watch, and they really enjoyed the show with laughter and encouragement. Because of the audience, we hammed-it-up more than planned. The tact officers got out of our way during the ceremonies and allowed us to do whatever we wanted. We had fun and milked it for everything we could; fainting, crying, even a fake fight between the murderer and some of the family members. We buried the cockroach, a candidate played taps, and we held the grave site in high regard throughout our program. The grave site was marked with a homemade headstone and a small fence to protect the site; all made from scrounged wood. Occasionally, one of us would serve guard duty at the grave site as punishment for some infraction. It was a special place and event in our OCS lives, and we laughed about it often during our training. It even makes me smile now when I think about it.

OCS was a six-month school, and I have many stories, but I'll only share one more. The last six weeks of training included a lot of academic work and practical use of the higher-level infantry skills previously taught. One critical skill was map reading, and we practiced a lot. An infantry unit's survival in combat might depend on an officer's map-reading skills. After attending many classes, we took a map-reading test to determine our skill level. We went to a distant, hilly, wooded area of Fort Benning, and, after some instructions, they gave us maps, objectives, and staggered start times to begin the course. I really took to map reading and had no difficulty with the course.

As I moved along a trail, I came upon a dejected-looking platoon mate sitting on a large rock. I stopped and asked how he was doing. He explained that he was questioning his choice to be an officer, expressing concern about leading men in combat. He was also having trouble reading the map. He'd been one of the first ones to start the course and still had a ways to go to finish. We talked for a while, and I gave him a lot of encouragement. I also asked him to show me his map and point to his current position. He was lost. I talked through the visible terrain and helped him locate our position on the map. I pointed to our destination and discussed the terrain markings that would lead to the end of the course. Ethically, we couldn't team up; nor could I advise him any more than that, but I told him, "I'm heading to the end of the course, and my focus will be on my map and the terrain ahead. See you back at the barrack," and I took off.

At the end of the course, transports waited to carry small groups of candidates back to the barracks. My platoon mate made it through the course and arrived back at the barrack sometime after me. I neither asked him if he followed me or made it on his own, nor did he mention it. He became a close friend after that day, talking to me frequently about life and other things. On September 14, 1966, my company graduated 118 new second lieutenants. Our OSC class started with 218 candidates. Some men asked to leave, and the army dropped others from the program.

That platoon mate died in action while serving with the Fourth Infantry Division, Kontum Province, Vietnam, in November 1967. He died while trying to rescue several of his men who were wounded during an ambush. That sounds a lot like leadership to me. By the way, the OCS motto is *Follow Me*, and he died living up to that motto. I've thought of him often.

CHAPTER 5

I Dream of Jeanie

As a teenager, I sometimes dreamed about marrying and had an ever-changing image of the girl of my dreams. Marriage was important to everyone in my family, and they always seemed to be in love with their mates. My parents and grandparents were my shining examples. My first image of the ideal girl was from the second grade; she looked like Natalie Wood. Through the years I went through various images based on the current infatuation of the day and definitely more than one movie star. While the girls in my dreams were all cute or pretty, none was the image of Jeanie. After meeting her, she became the permanent girl of my dreams.

My first assignment as a second lieutenant was at Fort Polk, Louisiana, as the executive officer for a basic training company, an appropriate assignment for a new infantry lieutenant. I drove to Fort Polk in my newly acquired, 1966 GTO, arriving about a week before my reporting date in early October 1966. I wanted time to settle into the BOQ (bachelor officers' quarters) and get the lay of the land. I found a few classmates already there, so it was a minireunion. We checked out the officers' club frequently and explored the surrounding countryside.

It was at the O Club (officers' club) that I first saw Jeanie. She was an assistant program director at one of the service clubs for enlisted men. I was having lunch with other officers/former classmates, and she was with a group of her associates. One of the officers at my table, David, mentioned her name and said he had a dinner date with her that evening; I turned to look. There were four young women at the table, but I only saw one, the small blond with the pretty smile and big, expressive, blue eyes. That one turned out to be Jeanie. I recall making a comment to David that she was a little skinny, and he said she was cute, intelligent, and personable. The girls finished lunch and came by our table to visit. After introductions, we socialized for a while. When we were alone, I asked Jeanie to join me for drinks later that evening at the club, and she accepted. That afternoon, I mentioned my date to David, and he seemed upset. That evening, Jeanie informed me that David didn't show up for his dinner date with her. Oh my!

Over drinks Jeanie and I hit it off right away. She was pretty and showed great confidence, intelligence, personality, sense of humor, and maturity. I hadn't experienced that combination in one girl before, and it was captivating. She made me feel very comfortable from the beginning. We had many more evenings at the O Club, movies, restaurants, and just hanging out together over the next few months.

Second lieutenants didn't make a lot of money, so we had to be frugal with the frequency of eating out and entertainment in general. In fact, in 1966, my base pay was $250 per month, but things were cheaper then. In trying to help me save on expenses, Jeanie volunteered to do some of my laundry, and I jumped at the offer. She came with me to my BOQ, and I told her I didn't keep my laundry organized; it was just thrown in my closet. Upon opening the closet door, I heard her laugh and say, "I wish I had a camera." A thigh-high pile of underwear, socks, etc. filled the center of the closet. She inquired if I found it cheaper to buy new underwear than to wash the ones I already had. Actually, the army was always generous with issuing underclothing, and with a full year of training, I had accumulated quite a bit.

Jeanie and I took every moment to learn more about each other. She had graduated from college in 1965 and was two years older than me. I hadn't finished college, so all of that was still ahead of me. I also had a tour of duty in Vietnam somewhere in my near future, and infantry lieutenants had a high incidence of death or wounds in Vietnam. None of this bothered us.

For Thanksgiving, we drove to San Antonio, where she introduced me to her parents and showed me the sights. Things went well there. I liked her parents, and they seemed to like me. While there, Jeanie took me to the famous River Walk and introduced me to Mexican food. In the 1960s, Mexican food was not available throughout the United States; I'd never seen a Mexican restaurant on the East Coast. We ordered drinks as a mariachi band entertained us, and Jeanie explained the various menu options. She recommended enchiladas as an introduction to the cuisine. She also counseled me about the very spicy jalapeno salsa and suggested I sample it lightly. Being a macho man, I didn't see the need to follow her sage advice and scooped up a heaping amount on a large, triangular corn chip. Immediately, my eyes began to water, and my mouth and throat seemed to be on fire. I chugalugged a beer and began looking for water. Jeanie laughed until she cried, and I cried until I laughed. I didn't really cry, but it looked like I was. Actually, I recovered my composure within a few minutes. You acquire a taste and style for eating salsa, and I perfected both in later years. Our San Antonio adventure was wonderful, memorable, and romantic.

Back at Fort Polk, the Christmas holidays were fast approaching, and things at the fort began to wind down. My basic training company had graduated before Thanksgiving, and a new company wouldn't form until January. Since Jeanie worked at a service club for enlisted men, the club had to be open and available to them every day, so she had to work on Christmas. I debated trying to get a flight through the Air Force to Virginia for the holidays. Eventually, I decided that I didn't want to go to Virginia; I'd rather stay at Fort Polk with my girl.

Later that week, I asked Jeanie to marry me; she reacted with all the enthusiasm seen in the old movies. It was a wonderful moment. We discussed plans and agreed not to tell our families until afterward; otherwise, everyone would want to come to Louisiana, and we didn't have much time before we had to return to work. The fort ceased training activities between Christmas and New Year's, so we picked the end of December for our wedding date with a honeymoon in New Orleans.

Several days after we decided to marry, I received orders for Vietnam with a report date of March 6, 1967. I had known orders would come someday, but I didn't expect them this early. I talked to Jeanie about waiting to get married until after I returned from Vietnam, but we decided to proceed. We arranged our wedding with a fort chaplain, collected a few friends, and were married on December 30, 1966.

Tim and Jeanie December 1966

With my new orders, Jeanie decided to resign from the civil service, return to San Antonio to live with her parents, and seek a teaching position while I was in Nam. With the orders, I got a thirty-day leave, so we took a second honeymoon to visit family and friends and sightsee along the way.

We deposited our worldly possessions in San Antonio and drove east toward Virginia to my hometown. Along the way, we had a grand time exploring the Civil War battlefields and just being young and in love. I had read and thought about the battles, the soldiers, and my great-grandfathers who had fought on these battlefields a century before. Three fought with the Army of Northern Virginia. Two rode with J. E. B. Stuart, one with the Second Virginia Cavalry, and the other with the Tenth. One was with the Thirty-eighth Virginia Infantry. All were involved in many major battles of that war, including Gettysburg, with at least two suffering wounds during the war. I knew I'd soon feel a different kind of kinship with my ancestors. Our physical experience would be like night and day, yet our psychological experiences might be very similar. I didn't dwell long on that subject but thought more about my present adventure and future adventures after Nam.

We stayed about a week with my mother in Norfolk then drove to Brooklyn, New York, to visit my sister and her family. We saw many of the tourist sites there, such as the Statue of Liberty, Chinatown, Greenwich Village, and Central Park, and took a few rides on the subway. It was very frigid on top of the Empire State Building in February, and we didn't stay long. I especially remember the lobster Cantonese we had at a restaurant in Greenwich Village. We saw *Sweet Charity* with Gwen Verdon on Broadway, and an off-Broadway play with Richard Benjamin—I don't recall the title. Both were Jeanie's idea, but I enjoyed the shows. At the end of our New York adventure, we were trying to head south, but the weather got worse. We made it to the Verrazano Bridge, but the winds were too much for Jeanie's Sunbeam Alpine sports car (like the *Get Smart* car), and the authorities refused us access. We had to retrace our path and leave NYC by the Holland Tunnel.

After New York, we drove to Gettysburg, Pennsylvania, for another Civil War experience. However, upon arrival at Gettysburg, the weather turned snowy, and the Civil War history adventure turned into a treacherous escape south. I think General Lee experienced that once without the snow. Our vacation time was running low, and we needed to get back to San Antonio. Now the thought of being snowbound at Gettysburg with Jeanie was appealing, but I didn't think the army would appreciate the excuse.

The drive through the Shenandoah Valley was slow and treacherous but beautiful. The snow was heavy and continuous, and Jeanie's sports car, with the top up and heater on full blast, stayed cold the entire trip. That was a really drafty car. We stopped at every town along the way looking for a place to stay, but we found no vacancies until Harrisburg, Virginia. It was dark when we arrived and finally settled in for the night.

The next morning the sun was bright, and we decided to end the sightseeing and head west toward Texas. The drive was a lot easier on that day, since the snow plows had done their job during the night. Jeanie took over the driving in southern Virginia and unconsciously started pacing another car that, unfortunately, was going eighty-five miles per hour. As we approached the Virginia/North Carolina/Tennessee borders, a state trooper took notice, pulled both cars over, and instructed us to follow him to the local JP's office, which was in a small town a bit like Mayberry. Come to think of it, the trooper looked a bit like Barney Fife. The JP's office was in the town's general store. Several hours later and several dollars lighter, we were back on the interstate heading for Texas, driving considerably slower.

In San Antonio, we continued our playful adventures, visiting the hill country, trips to the River Walk, and even the opera. Once was enough for me; actually, I'd prefer a trip to the dentist over the opera. We also traveled about two hundred miles to San Angelo, Texas, where Jeanie's grandparents and other relatives lived. Texas was delightful in the late winter that year, and we enjoyed the drive and stops along the way. In San Angelo, we had a grand time visiting High Hopes (her parent's retirement property), eating home cooking, playing games, and having general old-fashioned family fun. Jeanie's grandfather took us to his favorite fishing spot. We didn't catch a thing, but we have the memories.

My in-laws were rock hounds who searched for treasures all over the state of Texas. This was a serious hobby, and they really got into it. My mother-in-law bought me a pocket-sized rock book and gave me a crash course in geology. I followed along with interest but never took to the demonstrations my in-laws constantly gave for licking or spitting on newly found rocks—they didn't actually lick them, but I teased them about that possibility. It seems that when you first find a rock, you need to wet it to bring out the color. It must be an acquired taste. My mother-in-law had marked a few pages in my new rock book, which showed rocks common to Vietnam; one of them was a crusty-looking thing that often contained a ruby. I hadn't heard of Indiana Jones at that time, but I think I heard the music as I daydreamed about finding precious stones with one hand and shooting NVA with the other. We shall see!

March 6 was drawing near and preparation began for the l-o-o-ong journey and l-o-o-ong stay in Nam. It's tough going off to war. The unknown and the threat of battle and death loomed in my mind. I prayed for safe passage and a safe return home, but the future suddenly became less clear or certain. I had so much to live for, especially now that I had found the girl of my dreams. I enjoyed being with her so much, sharing everything. A year suddenly seemed like an eternity.

CHAPTER 6

The Rainbow

The day of departure for Vietnam arrived too soon. Jeanie and I had a quiet morning preparing to drive to the San Antonio airport. We'd had a wonderful two months to prepare ourselves for this day, so the good-bye was short but filled with many promises. Our future was full of hopes and plans, and I wanted to come home safe and sound. I'd always had confidence that I'd be successful in Vietnam and that I'd return home safely.

The first leg of my flight from San Antonio took me to Oakland, California. It was a long, boring, lonely, and thoughtful journey. While I waited at the Oakland airport, it rained. As I watched the rain and planes from the observation deck, a very large, beautiful rainbow appeared at one end of the runway and extended over the airplane that was preparing to take me overseas. It went out over the bay and toward the ocean so far that I couldn't see its end. It seemed to spread over the mighty Pacific to a distant land. While I couldn't see its ending, I could see its beginning, America, my home. I felt a satisfying peace, a sense that it was a message from above to comfort me as I departed the United States. I was ready to do my duty. I thought of that rainbow often during my tour in Vietnam, and when I did, I felt that same peace. I looked forward to returning to its beginning, as its message seemed to imply.

The rainbow, Oakland Airport 1967

The flight from Oakland was jammed full of military troops of all ranks and branches, but we all had the same destination. It was a quiet flight. I guess we all had a lot of thinking to do. I remember the airline giving everyone an International Date Line certificate—I wonder whatever happened to mine. I also remember being wakened by the guy next to me, who didn't appreciate my using his shoulder as a pillow—still seeking my Jeanie, I guess.

We arrived at the Saigon Airport early in the morning. Most soldiers arriving in-country without specific unit assignments, me included, went from the airport to the Ninetieth Replacement Battalion at Long Binh, the army holding location. As casualties occurred in field units, replacement requests came to Long Binh. The drive from the Saigon Airport to Long Binh was very congested with all types of traffic. Military traffic was heavy, but the local traffic dominated the roads. The Vietnamese population was mostly on foot or bicycles, but some drove three-wheeled, motorized vehicles and some drove automobiles. I saw several people pushing wheelbarrows with passengers; go figure. Traffic laws didn't seem to exist; the traffic moved randomly everywhere. The sites, sounds, and smells were so different and intriguing.

I vaguely remember the camp at Long Binh, although my photographs quickly bring back some memories. Speaking of photographs, Jeanie had a small 35 mm camera that she let me carry while in Nam. I regularly took slides and mailed them off for processing and then on to Jeanie in San Antonio. Jeanie and her family really enjoyed the slides but often had many questions that would have to wait for my return home. One early complaint from her was that none of the slides were of me. I was able to remedy this when my RTO volunteered to take pictures of me from time to time.[4]

At the officers' quarters in Long Binh, we passed the time talking about the war and possible assignments, and drinking beer, and playing cards. The army took our US currency and replaced it with military script, which looked like monopoly money. It bought things at the PX and clubs and from Vietnamese merchants throughout the country. I still have a few pieces of script stashed away; however, I hope I'll not need that form of currency again. One of my poker friends at Long Binh was a Special Forces first lieutenant who had previously served as a platoon leader in an infantry unit in Vietnam more than a year earlier. After his first tour of duty, he returned to the States to attend Army Special Forces School and returned as a Green Beret officer for his second tour. Within two days his orders came in, and he was off to join his unit attached to the First Cavalry in the Central Highlands. I don't remember his name, but I later found out that his back was broken in a helicopter crash during a mission in 1967.

My orders came through on March 13. It's hard to express the emotions that I felt, but it was somewhere between excitement and apprehension. I did experience fear during my tour but never the paralyzing fear that causes panic, nausea, loss of bladder control, etc. I was probably too young

---

[4] Some photos are included in the book, and others can be found on my website at: www.timsoyars.com

and cocky for that kind of fear, even as I came up against life-threatening situations.

Thinking back to my childhood, my parents talked about how I seldom showed fear and often sought out risky situations. When my sister and I were little and got into trouble that deserved punishment, my mother dealt out spankings. My sister was terrified, crying and promising not to do it again. I'd ask to be first, so I could go back out and play, seldom crying from a spanking. This exasperated my mother. She eventually tried different tactics for my punishment, like confinement to my room, but with all my toys and vivid imagination, that didn't work either. I could entertain myself for hours in my room.

My sister frequently talks about me as her fearless protector during our early childhood. She always laughs as she tells of the time she and her second-grade friends were playing dolls in a neighbor's yard, and several boys their age came by and started picking on them. I was playing in our front yard when I heard my sister's cry for help and saw the boys and their mischief. I was five years old, but I ran to her rescue shouting, "Don't worry, Sissy, I'll save you." She said I growled as I ran toward them. Just before I arrived on the scene, the boys scattered and ran from the neighborhood. I was small for my age, but I had no fear. I'm lucky to have reached adulthood considering my size and sometimes fearless nature.

I was relieved to receive my orders and pleased with my assignment to the First Air Cavalry Division. I'd read and heard only good things about the division. My assignment was with Charlie Company, Second/Fifth Cav (Second Battalion, Fifth Cavalry Regiment). The Fifth Regiment is nicknamed the Black Knights, and, as I later discovered, it was formed in 1855, first under the command of COL Albert Sidney Johnston and then under LTC Robert E. Lee. It had a long and respected regimental tradition, and I hoped to add to its proud heritage. On March 11, Company C had run into the Eighteenth Regiment of the North Vietnamese Army. A battle ensued, and a number of soldiers had died or suffered wounds. Company C needed a new platoon leader, and I was it. Once my orders arrived, Long Binh wasted no time in arranging transportation to the headquarters of the division.

The home of the First Cav was at Camp Radcliff, An Khe, in the western Central Highlands. The division insignia was visible from the window of the C130 as we approached the camp. A large mountain, Hon Cong Mountain, bordered the camp, and near the top of the mountain was a very large, flat boulder with the insignia painted on it. If you're not familiar with the First Cav, the insignia is large and unique. The yellow, triangular shield has rounded corners; a black, diagonal stripe extends over the shield from upper left to lower right; in the upper right section is a black horse's head cut diagonally at the neck. I remember hearing soldiers of other divisions describing the patch, in jest, as, "The horse they couldn't ride, the line they couldn't cross, and the yellow speaks for itself." I think someone was jealous. In combat our insignia was camouflaged OD (olive drab) green and black to match the OD jungle fatigues.

After being assigned quarters in their new units, new arrivals to Camp Radcliff went through a week of in-country training and orientation. The training was called remount (an appropriate name for a cavalry unit). Three things stand out in my memory about remount training. One, we went on patrol outside the perimeter of the camp. As I recall, every new person went through the training regardless of MOS (military occupational specialty). We had cooks, clerks, chaplains, infantry soldiers, etc. in this training. We even spent one night outside the perimeter (many more of those to come in my future). Two, we went to the rifle and grenade ranges. While at the grenade range, a soldier died when his grenade prematurely exploded. At that point, I wondered about the safety and quality of the munitions, but this was a freak malfunction. I was next in line behind him. The soldier was an enlisted man about my age who had been with me throughout the training. He wasn't an infantryman; his job was in finance. No one is safe anywhere in a war zone. Three, all the infantry types went through a rappelling course. We climbed along an easy path to the top of a small cliff next to the training course. We learned the proper technique and then jumped over the side of the cliff and bounced our way down. We did this several times until the instructors were satisfied with our performances. Since the First Cav used helicopters for most missions, the training was valuable for situations that might require soldiers to leave a helicopter that couldn't land due to the terrain. Although we didn't rappel frequently, it did occur during my tour. The experience would be useful to me.

Before leaving for the field, I stored my personal belongings in my duffel bag until time to go home. The battalion had a secure area for the safekeeping of personal items, or, rather, safekeeping was the plan. The only thing of value I had in my duffle was a hunting knife that my brother had made. It had a six-inch blade set in a fiberglass handle reinforced with sinew; the scabbard was hand tooled. I'd wanted to carry it in the field, but the sergeant major advised me to leave it behind and use the army-issued knife, which he thought would be more versatile, so I did. I later discovered that someone had broken into my duffle and stolen the knife. I should've taken it with me or left my inherited treasure at home.

After remount training, I caught a flight on a C130 to LZ English, the forward base camp for the brigade, and then a chopper ride to join Charlie Company. LZ English was located north of the village of Bong Son in Binh Dinh Province, and Charlie Company was west of there. My journey as platoon leader had begun.

CHAPTER 7

Coconut Cocktails and Odds 'n' Ends

The first several weeks with Charlie Company went by really fast. Every day I encountered something new (jargon, patrols, and camp and radio protocol), and I was absorbing everything like a sponge. When conditions permitted, we had a daily routine. We rose at daybreak, washed, shaved, and prepared for breakfast. After that the men broke camp, and the CO met with the platoon leaders to issue marching orders for the day. We sometimes moved as a company unit, and other times we had platoon missions. Most days involved making one or more combat air assaults to pursue reports of enemy activity. Being in the field and on a combat mission was never boring, and time flew, but it wasn't all work and no play. Boys will be boys even when they're trying to be men.

Water

After a long, hot mission, a cool drink was always welcome but seldom available. Canteen water was a valuable commodity, and most of us carried at least two canteens of water on every mission, so we adjusted to warm drinks.

Being a member of the First Air Cav had advantages. We had helicopters assigned to our battalion, which gave us the ability for resupply in the mornings and evenings or anytime we needed it as long as a landing site was available. Every day, each platoon received its ration of water to fill canteens. We shared the remaining water for washing ourselves. To accomplish this task, we filled our steel pots with a bit of water. The steel pot is the outer steel of the infantryman's helmet. Inside the steel pot is the lightweight helmet liner, which is removable and adjustable to fit various-sized heads. The outer steel of the helmet is to protect the head, but it's also a good sink. Soldiers have found many uses for the steel pot, including a washbasin, a container for cooking, or a seat when nothing else was available. A little hand soap and water from a local river, a well, or the ocean in a steel pot constituted an infantryman's bath. It was awkward and inconvenient but better than no bathing at all.

There were times when water ran low during a mission, and we had to fill canteens from streams. When we used stream water, we always looked for water from sources above the surrounding countryside, like mountain streams. The rice paddy water was contaminated with human and animal waste and could be deadly. When we did use stream water, we added iodine tablets to the canteen to kill bacteria. Iodine-treated water tasted like chemicals, so I always emptied my canteens when water resupply came. However, water is water when you're humping hills in hundred-degree-plus weather.

Uniforms

We changed uniforms if they were torn or when the complaining from platoon mates became too much. I tried to wash myself daily, especially certain vulnerable areas, using scrounged water. A little washing always made me feel better. I usually ordered a new uniform at least weekly. Being dirty with soiled clothing was a difficult adjustment for me. Most soldiers didn't wear underwear, but we changed our socks daily to avoid fungal infections. We often waded through water, so our feet were usually wet and had to dry while patrolling or in the evening when we removed our boots. In one letter, my wife asked about the socks. She seemed to be concerned about the waste. I told her not to worry. The GIs made good use of the stinky, soiled socks by making a stew with them. You can imagine the flavor. Actually, our socks were recycled. The company sent them to the laundry at Camp Radcliff, where they went back through the system after washing.

Luggage

Collectively, everything a soldier carried into combat weighed between twenty and thirty pounds. At times, it felt like a lot more. Soldiers were assigned weapons based on their training specialty, such as a machine gun, grenade launcher, or M16 automatic rifle. All officers and some NCOs carried a .45-caliber pistol as well as an M-16; however, soon after my arrival, Charlie Company received a few AR15 automatic rifles for testing, and I chose to carry that rather than the M16. The AR15 operated very similar to the M16, but it had a collapsible stock that made it less bulky to carry. It was my rifle of choice.

Everyone carried a bayonet, survival knife, hand grenades, smoke grenades, and a supply of ammo magazines and extra boxes of ammo. We also carried an entrenching tool, canteens of water, canteen cup, mess kit, air mattress, rucksack, C rations, P38 (can opener), dog tags, water-resistant poncho and liner, insect repellent, iodine tablets, malaria pills, and various personal items, such as snacks and razors. Some soldiers were assigned to carry a flashlight, machete, flares and claymore mines. In addition, I also carried a compass, maps, and a number of personal items, including watch, wallet, camera, pictures, pen, writing paper, wedding ring, towel, a book, and letters from Jeanie. I always made room for more letters from home.

Coconuts

When we took a break, we often looked for palm trees to provide shade from the sun. On one occasion, my platoon and Third Platoon were camped for the night under a grove of palm trees beside a large network of rice paddies. The company had divided into several search groups during that morning, so the company was camping in several different locations that night. The CO was with the First and Fourth Platoons. After we were bedded down for the night, except for those drawing perimeter guard duty, a grenade went off near the Third Platoon perimeter; fire opened up, and a claymore mine was detonated. Sergeant Sal, SFC Francisco Kumangai and I rushed to our perimeter closest to the action. No, we weren't in our pajamas. A soldier in the field slept in his pants, socks, and a T-shirt or no shirt. We always had our weapons and boots within reach. We were up, in unlaced boots, with our rifles and on the perimeter very quickly.

I wrote Jeanie on March 30, "Last night was hectic. Around 2200 hrs, a VC tossed a grenade into the Third Platoon perimeter. They opened fire and continued to do so for at least an hour. Finally, I issued an order to my men that if anyone fired, they'd better have a dead VC at the end of their bullet." My men stopped firing and watched the perimeter for signs of activity. The Third Platoon leader and I were in communications with each other and with the CO. After a while, the CO ordered the Third Platoon to cease firing, watch, and listen. While we doubted the enemy was still out there, we instructed everyone to be alert. I slept soundly for the remainder of the night since there were no further encounters. At the time, I thought that the grenade probably came from a Third Platoon soldier rather than from Charlie. The Third Platoon was sometimes a bit lax in discipline, or it seemed that way to me.

When morning came, my platoon stayed in place while the other platoons continued to patrol. As the morning progressed, we noticed several Vietnamese working in the rice paddies about 150 meters from our position. I sent a squad to investigate, and they returned with several suspects. We held the prisoners for later transportation to battalion for interrogation, but, in the meantime, someone suggested that a coconut would make a very good midmorning drink. One of the prisoners volunteered, with prodding, to climb a tree to drop a few for us. He went up the tree with remarkable speed but with a very strained expression on his face. I don't think he did this for a living, but he managed to knock a number of large coconuts to the ground. Sergeant Kumangai, who was from Samoa, demonstrated the proper technique for disrobing a coconut with a machete, and then we put our machetes to work. In no time we were drinking cold, refreshing coconut milk. One of the prisoners had been carrying baskets of food and supplies on a pole across his shoulder. Several of my men practiced carrying the load and found the task more difficult than it looked, but they had fun trying, and it was good entertainment.

We found a volunteer to fetch coconuts—Central Highlands

Not as easy as the natives make it look—Central Highlands

We didn't encounter any additional enemy activity that day but did form a habit of taking breaks near coconut palm trees. Sergeant Kumangai and my first RTO, Thomas Jarrett, and a few others also learned to shinny up trees and drop refreshments to the ground. At first, they all had a tough time with the climb, but they improved with practice. On one occasion, one of my men had some Kool-Aid, and we experimented by adding it to the coconut milk. It was surprisingly good. At my request, Jeanie sent a variety of Kool-Aid flavors from time to time. I shared them with my platoon, and we continued to enjoy our coconut cocktails.

Beer

Before leaving the subject of cocktails, at least monthly the battalion sent trash cans filled with Budweiser and a variety of soda. The beer always outnumbered the soda; I wonder why. It was always a welcome relief, breaking the tension and allowing more relaxed conversation to evolve. The quantities were enough for two cans per man, and those who didn't drink beer found new popularity on beer day. For some, the ice was a more welcome choice. I'd take a few chunks of ice myself from time to time.

Beer time at Charlie Company—Central Highlands

Naps

We always welcomed a break, and a cool, refreshing coconut drink was helpful. I found a short nap to be very refreshing and energizing for me. I never seemed to get enough sleep while in the field. Sometimes during breaks from patrol, I'd catch a quick, Eisenhower nap. I learned to fall asleep quickly and wake up refreshed with ten to fifteen minutes of napping. In fact, I'm still good at napping today, although I now prefer longer naps in a Lay-Z-Boy.

Communications

We had frequent radio communications with the CO and other platoons, and the CO maintained dialogue with the battalion concerning missions and needs. The radio was vital for successful operations, and every unit in combat had a call sign to use when talking on the radio. Obviously, the call signs were a unique identification for the individual and the unit. The call signs changed frequently in order to confuse anyone who might be trying to figure out who was who, and I think to confuse us as well, which happened from time to time.

Having decided to write my memoir almost forty years after leaving Vietnam, I naturally don't recall all of my call signs. Operational orders prohibited me from putting them in my letters, so memory will have to serve. When I first arrived, our company had a series of Indian tribe names, such as Comanche and Apache, and theme names, such as Mad Merlin. In addition, within a company, key positions used a numerical and alphabetical reference. The company commander was six, so his call sign would be Comanche six or Mad Merlin six. The platoon number designated the platoon ID. The First Platoon leader was Comanche one-six. Since I was the Second Platoon leader, my call sign was Comanche two-six. Mike was the identifier for sergeants, so their call signs would be Comanche six-mike for the company first sergeant or Comanche two-six-mike for the Second Platoon sergeant. Radio operators were the key to successful communications, and their identifier was alpha. Thus, my radio operator was Comanche two-six-alpha. With every change of call signs, we'd have fun with the name and the mistakes— "Mad Merlin Comanche two-six-alpha, this is mad two-six-mike, over."

A legitimate radio conversation between the CO and me might go something like this:

> Mad Merlin two-six, this is Mad Merlin six, over.
> This is Mad Merlin two-six, over.
> This is Mad Merlin six. What is your current position, over?
> This is Mad Merlin two-six. I'm located at L7254 and D6020, over.
> This is Mad Merlin six. Is there an LZ near your location, over?
> This is Mad Merlin two-six. Yes, at approximately L7254 and D6020, over.
> This is Mad Merlin six. I'm sending choppers to pick you up; get ready to pop smoke, over.
> This is Mad Merlin two-six, roger, over.
> This is Mad Merlin six, stand by for further orders, over and out.

Sometimes our communications weren't strictly by the book, but the above gives a good idea of the dialogue.

Slang

Learning the radio language and military terms unique to the First Cav and to the war was part of daily life, and after a few weeks in the field, they became a natural part of my vocabulary. I also learned a few Vietnamese words or phrases. When in a foreign land, you should learn to speak the language, but learning the language from other soldiers isn't the recommended method. However, when it's your primary source, you do what humans have always done; you copy the language you hear. I didn't receive any language instruction during any of my training, so on-the-job instruction would have to do.

One of the first local words I heard from other GIs was *di di mau*. When we patrolled along Highway One or in the more populace areas, children and sometime adults would show interest in the soldiers, or, rather, in what the soldiers might give them. With our objective to accomplish, their closeness could become dangerous. The GIs told me that *di di mau* meant *go, go quickly* and when I said the phrase to annoying beggars, they would sometimes go away. When that didn't work, I'd say it again in a rougher tone of voice. I never really knew if it was the phrase, the tone of voice, or the weapons I carried, but the combination always worked.

The other word I learned early on from my men was *boom-boom*. I first heard the phrase in the village of An Khe, especially as I passed certain merchants' storefronts. Occasionally, the phrase would come up while on duty at the Bong Son Bridge along Highway One. Often the phrase came in conjunction with a body motion, which explained the meaning clearly. Something was for sale from the oldest profession in the world. I'd respond quickly, "*Di di mau!*" I learned other words and phrases for communicating with the ARVN, but I don't recall them. The above two phrases were generally enough for the infantry soldier, so I was indoctrinated.

The Enemy

The US military used many terms to describe the enemy. The NVA referred to the North Vietnamese Army. The Viet Cong was the communist army based in South Vietnam, also called VC or Charlie. The first letters of **V**iet **C**ong, VC, were transposed to military call signs **V**ictor **C**harlie; thus, the Viet Cong became known as Charlie. We often used the word *Charlie* to refer to both the NVA and the VC.

CHAPTER 8

A Full Day's Work

During my stay with Charlie Company, we spent most of our time in and around the Central Highlands. Our missions were either on the plains or in the mountains and valleys east and west of the plains. In 1967, military intelligence reported VC and NVA activity all over our operating area, and the Second/Fifth chased these leads daily. As we later found out, the enemy's strategy was to build up forces all over the south, avoid battles now but prepare for battles in 1968 during *Tet*, the New Year's celebration. Our goal was to find and engage the enemy then capture or kill him. I feel sure the enemy knew our mission, but we didn't have a clear understanding of theirs. We did find them from time to time and disrupted their strategy. With our supporting helicopters, we moved at a moment's notice and ventured into both familiar and unfamiliar territory often.[5]

One morning, I received orders to take my platoon on an air assault to a valley at the base of a large mountain range. Intelligence reported enemy activity in the mountains, and our company was to investigate. Our assigned area didn't have trails, so we needed to make our own way up the mountain. Since the climb would be too slow and noisy for a full company, my platoon was sent to clear an LZ at a prescribed coordinate on one of the smaller mountains. The rest of the company would fly in by

---

[5] Appendix B includes Charlie Company, Second Battalion, Fifth Cavalry Regiment, First Cavalry Division operational reports March 1967 to March 1968. Taken from the following website: www.tallcomanche.org

helicopter and join us for the next leg of the mission. While Second Platoon was gone, the rest of the company conducted patrols on the plains.

My platoon was airlifted to the base of the mountain to begin our climb. The weather was hot, and the climb was difficult. Without a trail or path, we had to clear brush with machetes and make our own way. Most of my men were young and full of energy, but I rotated the point man frequently to keep a fast pace. We reached our objective faster than Captain Markham expected. We established a perimeter and began the task of clearing the LZ. My men worked fast and had fun talking, joking, kidding, and singing as they worked. One area was used as a resting place and was designated our HQ (headquarters) since it had a small tree to provide a little welcome shade. The men worked in shifts, allowing plenty of time for rest before taking another turn. We finished clearing the LZ before noon and prepared to take a break before the rest of the company joined us. About that time, the CO radioed to inform me of a new mission for the Second Platoon. Battalion planned to pick us up by helicopter at our mountaintop location and take us to LZ English, our brigade HQ. My mission was to secure two 750-pound bombs that had dropped harmlessly to the ground from an Air Force cargo plane in the vicinity of LZ English. The remainder of the company continued their patrols and was to move to the new LZ in early afternoon.

At LZ English, I got the rest of my orders. I was to take two squads (about fifteen men) to search for the bombs and leave the remainder to rest and help with guarding the perimeter; I left Sergeant Sal in charge at English. It didn't take long to find the first bomb, which lay at the edge of a rice paddy along a tree line near a village. I reported this, and they ordered me to secure the site.

A Chinook helicopter with an engineering crew came to our location to lift out the bomb. It took a while for the engineers to secure the bomb for lifting, so I sent one squad to search for the second bomb. They returned, reporting no luck. The engineers finished securing the bomb to its harness, and the Chinook slowly lifted it off the ground. As we watched, we started receiving sniper fire from the far side of the village. We returned fire and moved closer to the village but saw no enemy activity. With the first sound of gunfire, the Chinook detached its load and left the site until I gave them an all-clear. I called in an artillery strike, which was precise and heavily damaged the village and the surrounding area. I thought, "See, Mom, letting me practice soldiering with cannon and toothpicks just saved the day." I should have written her about that, but I don't believe I did. She would have laughed. When the artillery finished, I took a squad to search the area but found no signs of inhabitants. The village showed many signs that it was an active village, yet no one was there. I reported my findings by radio to battalion HQ, and then the Chinook returned, retrieved the bomb, and carried it to safety.

I was preparing to resume the search for the second bomb when battalion HQ radioed me with orders to rejoin my company in the mountains. Helicopters were in-bound to my location, and I should stand by to pop smoke on the helicopter commander's instructions. While I was on the bomb mission, the rest of my platoon with Sergeant Sal had airlifted to join Captain Markham. In the early afternoon, the CO moved the company into the mountains using the LZ that we had previously cleared. From this LZ the company began blazing a trail along a densely covered ridgeline in pursuit of reported NVA. Other companies of the battalion had made contact with the NVA and were in pursuit of them in the An Lo Valley. Charlie Company was to serve as a blocking force along the mountain range above the valley.

The mountain terrain was heavy with brush and trees, and there was absolutely no landing zone for a chopper anywhere in the company's vicinity. They made camp on a heavily wooded hilltop and cleared enough room to lower replenishing supplies by rope. I only had fifteen men with me, and the battalion apparently hadn't considered allowing me to camp away from the company, so off we flew to join our company by any means possible.

As we flew to the mountain campsite, the CO informed me by radio of the situation and lack of an LZ. The sun was setting fast, and it would be dark by the time we arrived. I briefed my men and joked about the amusement park ride ahead for us. The chopper pilots were advised of the situation and had the necessary equipment to get us to the ground. When you have time to wait, you have time to think. What was the mission this night? Pursue NVA activity reported in the area. Well, if NVA was there, dangling men from a helicopter would certainly flush out anyone wanting easy targets.

Hovering over the darkening landscape, I could see apprehension and fear on the faces of some men as we prepared ourselves to rappel from the helicopters. I tried to stay calm and offered last-minute instructions and encouragement. My chopper came in first and hovered three to five stories above the night camp for Charlie Company. The chopper used its spotlights to light the ground, where I could see only a small opening between trees. The chopper swayed, with its lights bouncing all around, as I jumped backward out the door of the chopper, taking the correct posture as I had been instructed. I think some of my boyhood, Olympic-style training and adventures helped prepare me for this type of challenge, but I was most thankful to have had the rappelling class at Camp Radcliff. Dropping from a cherry tree in my neighborhood is a bit different from dropping from a helicopter at night in a war zone. I don't remember any rappelling training while stateside, but in the First Air Cav, many new opportunities in warfare were being developed, and I'm sure new training was continually added to the stateside programs. I descended to the ground just as they had taught me during remount training. On the ground, the rest of my platoon greeted me with cheers. I knew I'd better do it right with the entire company watching as well as the men in the choppers above, waiting to follow my example. It was slow going, but we finally got everyone on the ground. Most did fine, but there were some less than perfect drops when some men became tentative, stopped, jerked, and swung a bit. With coaching and encouragement from the ground, everyone landed safely.

It was completely dark by the time the last man descended. I congratulated everyone on their accomplishments, and we all joked and laughed a bit at the sight of soldiers dropping from the night sky from perfectly good helicopters. We had chow and prepared for the night, going to bed tired and welcoming sleep at the end of a full day's work for an infantry soldier.

CHAPTER 3

Frenchy to Montezuma to the Sea

In early April 1967, our battalion went north to relieve the Marines at Duc Pho near the DMZ. Enemy encounters had been frequent for the Marines there, and after a long stay, they were moving to another operational area. Near the village of Duc Pho was an old, French, dirt airfield left over from the Indochina War. It was designated LZ Frenchy, and Charlie Company airlifted in first to secure it. Soon, the entire battalion arrived and brought artillery and engineering equipment. There we established a new, forward base camp for the battalion. Our infantry mission was to guard the perimeter at Frenchy, conduct search-and-destroy missions in the surrounding area and provide support for engineering units working to reconstruct the airfield and build roads in support of the mission.

The people in the village were friendly and interested in the new GIs. They entertained us, and we reciprocated. The children really loved to hang around the soldiers, and we welcomed them. The atmosphere at Frenchy was casual and friendly during the daytime. The villagers were definitely used to a foreign military presence, since the French had been there for many decades before the US military arrived.

SFC William McCarson with village children—LZ Frenchy near DMZ

We'll have to work on that salute—LZ Frenchy near DMZ

The boy is crippled. He couldn't walk on his legs, but he had mastered walking on his hands—LZ Frenchy near DMZ

After dusk, the environment and attitude around Duc Pho changed dramatically. Every evening the enemy mortared the LZ, and snipers attempted to disrupt our activities. This caused our artillery and 90 mm machine guns to unleash their wrath in the direction of the enemy fire. They put on quite a show since they had their guns loaded with tracer rounds to mark their aim. It was like horizontal fireworks. One morning at dawn, I photographed a house burning in the village. It wasn't clear if the enemy or the army had caused the fire, but the villagers were very busy hauling water to keep the fire contained. We pitched in to help, and, as a team, we put out the fires by midmorning.

House on fire—LZ Frenchy near DMZ

While at Frenchy, the village chief invited some of my men to visit his home. We were new to the area so this could promote goodwill, and it would be interesting to see how a village chief lived. I advised the CO, then Sergeant Sal and I, along with several of our men, paid our respects. Because the chief spoke no English, an interpreter accompanied us, since our Vietnamese wasn't appropriate. The chief showed us around his home and property, and through our interpreter we had a conversation. He was tired of the VC and NVA destroying his country and was glad we came to help him and his people. Our conversation was short, but he did give us a good tour of his village. The chief and some of the villagers looked of military age, but the army had checked them out and said they were friendly. They sure looked like some of the VC we had seen on earlier missions, and someone was mortaring us every evening.

We only had a short stay at LZ Frenchy. When other units came in to take our place, Charlie Company went farther north. Our company split in many directions to various sites near Duc Pho. The Second Platoon went to a spot perched atop a hill in the middle of a large valley. My helicopter landed at what the Marines had called LZ Montezuma. As the last Marine helicopter lifted off, I could see that they looked dirty, scruffy, and tired. They probably said the same about us since that's the way of field combat units. The LZ overlooked a vast landscape in all directions and was well fortified and strategically located. It did need cleaning and maintenance, so I put my men to the task. My platoon was the only one at this location, but the camp layout was for a full company. Sergeant Sal, Sergeant Kumangai, and I took the two-room HQ bunker, and Sergeant Sal assigned each squad to defensive positions around the camp. The camp was comfortable, and the valley looked very peaceful; however, our predecessors would've disagreed with peaceful since the Marines had lost a number of men during their stay there. I sent out daily patrols without any contact or incident.

LZ Montezuma with SPC Felton Cooper on duty—near DMZ

Again, my platoon didn't stay very long—so much for the nice, large accommodations. I received orders to accompany Captain Markham to the coast to protect the navy as they built a seaport. The purpose of the port was to off-load heavy equipment, build roads, and establish a major defensive position in the area. At first, it was relaxing duty. As time permitted, we took turns skinny-dipping in the South China Sea, which was very refreshing. However, my platoon also went on frequent patrols along the beach and in the surrounding countryside.

The building of the seaport provided a very different atmosphere for us. The navy dredged the coast just off the shoreline, and in no time a large navy transport ship docked and off-loaded a lot of heavy equipment. The first to disembark was a tank company, followed by heavy, artillery, and engineering equipment. We went from our usual silence to a buzz of excitement and noise, which increased by the hour. Captain Markham and the first sergeant went aboard the ship at the naval captain's invitation. They returned, obviously well nourished, with a load of goodies for us. The navy supplied themselves well, and we appreciated their sharing.

On our second day, I led a patrol of about six men south along the beach. My mission was to accompany a team of navy divers and three tanks. The divers were looking for alternative sites suitable for building another seaport. The tanks were there to provide firepower should we encounter difficulties. The navy knew how to go on patrol as well as eat.

Every mission was likely to encounter enemy fire, and most missions did. Normally, a sergeant would lead a patrol with as few as six men. In this case, the navy had two officers, and the tank commander was a captain. Since the mission required infantry tactics and strategies, an infantry officer had to lead the patrol, and I was designated mission commander. I was the lowest ranking officer on the mission, but I was in charge; I liked that idea. We started the mission with everyone riding on the tanks. When we reached the marked coordinates to begin the search, we disembarked and provided security while the navy divers explored the coastal floor.

I positioned my men along the inland, grassy area on the beach, while the tanks spread out, pointing their turrets inland. The navy worked quickly and moved southward at a rapid pace. All three units were in radio contact, so we could coordinate and change our positions southward as the navy continued its search. Most of the inland coast to this point had no villages or buildings of any sort, but on the southern horizon I could see several houses sitting in a clump of palm trees about 150 meters from the shore. We kept our sights on the west flank, occasionally looking forward and to the rear, watching for signs of activity, but we saw nothing.

When we reached the area of the houses/village, bullets suddenly started whizzing past and popping in the sand around my feet. We were in an open, flat area of the beach without sand dunes and totally exposed. We dropped to the sand and returned fire toward the village, but we saw no signs of the enemy. I ordered two men to run to the small dunes closer to the village, where they would have some protection from further enemy firing. We provided cover, firing into the village as they ran. When they were in position, I ordered them to open fire on the village to cover the rest of us as we advanced to the dunes. As I approached the sand dune, bullets again whizzed by and popped in the sand around me. My RTO and I hit the ground uninjured behind a small dune. The enemy seemed to be going for the guy with the pistol on his hip near the radio operator. Who would have thought? You can see why the life expectancy of infantry lieutenants in Vietnam was short. Bullets continued to pop near my position, yet we couldn't see the source. I thought about playing war as a kid; I often pretended that I was being shot at, wounded, or even killed. I'd jump up and take on a new persona and continue the battle, but this was not pretend. I knew this enemy meant to kill for real, and I directed myself and my men with that thought always on my mind. I radioed the tank commander to open fire on the village. He enthusiastically complied, and soon the village was on fire and in shambles. "That'll teach them to mess with me," I thought, "especially while I'm walking my tanks." I ordered the tank commander to cease firing, and we observed the area for signs of life. Seeing nothing, I led my men toward the village to conduct a search. We found nothing living or dead and returned to our mission. The navy found the coastal depth they were looking for, and we all returned, riding our tanks back to our base camp.

As we rumbled down the beach, we encountered a group of Buddhist monks marching southward. They wore colorful maroon and yellow robes and the typical Ho Chi Minh sandals. You might ask, "How do you tell if the monks are real or VC in disguise?" We really couldn't tell, but since each carried an umbrella and both hands were visible, we felt safe to approach them. We frisked them, but they carried no weapons or communications equipment and spoke only a little English. We reported our findings to the battalion S2 (army intelligence). In this instance, they already had information concerning those monks and advised me to let them continue on their journey, and we continued ours. We never knew how the VC might dress. The civilian population and the VC were indistinguishable. However, the NVA wore uniforms, a sure giveaway.

Buddhist monks traveling the beach—near DMZ

Eventually, I bought a pair of the Ho Chi Minh sandals while visiting the village of An Khe. They're really uncomfortable but cheap. The Vietnamese make these sandals from used tires and inner tubes, so, naturally, they left black marks on the feet, especially when wet. I wore the sandals around occasionally and can attest to the dirty, hard-to-clean feet.

After we returned to our base camp, the navy officers invited me to join them on board the ship for food, drink, and a shower. All three words were magic to my ears but especially the shower. I had sand in every crevice of my body from the continuous helicopter activity, and a hot shower sounded wonderful. It had been a least a month since I'd had a real shower. We had an enjoyable visit, drinking cold beer and eating tasty deli sandwiches. It was late afternoon, so it was too early for the evening meal. The sandwiches were fresh and excellent. I took a thirty-minute shower, savoring every second. I returned to the beach refreshed and the envy of my platoon. I wished they could've joined me, but I was the only one permitted to go. By the next morning, I was all gritty again. Thus is the life of an infantryman.

My platoon received a number of missions to search for enemy in the villages west of the new seaport. We encountered resistance with every mission in this area; one mission in particular comes to mind. I have an even temper and usually control my emotions well, especially when I was a young lieutenant, but on this day, I had to play the outraged tough-guy role.

Our mission was to follow a major road leading inland from the new seaport, escorting an engineering company as they repaired and built roads through the countryside. The road was notorious for sniper fire on passing vehicles and booby traps on the road. We had a crew of men minesweeping the roads, and my job was to protect the engineers from the snipers. While near a village, an army truck convoy passed by, and bullets began to pop around us. The gunfire was coming from a village about fifty meters on the other side of a rice paddy, west of the road we were patrolling. The road was slightly below a natural embankment, so I quickly directed my platoon to spread out along the embankment and return fire toward the village. I ordered the grenadier to fire his grenade launcher in the direction of the enemy fire. The machine gunners laid down fire at each end of the village, moving from the outer perimeters to the village center. I heard the grenade launcher fire once and then a commotion from some men nearby. I turned to witness the grenadier holding his launcher above the embankment, keeping his head and body below the rim, and firing a second round somewhere into the rice paddy. I yelled the soldier's name and said, "Get your head above the embankment and aim your weapon."

At the same time, I reached his position, but he continued to cower, so I placed my boot hard on his rear. He came to his feet quickly with fear in his eyes, probably more from what I might do next than from the enemy. After all, I had an AR15, a 45 pistol, a bunch of hand grenades, and a knife and was now practically on top of him. I yelled into his face (as close as I could since he was over six feet tall, and I'm five feet eight), lecturing how stupid his actions were, given the trees between the embankment and the rice paddy, and the potential danger he was causing my platoon. I took the launcher away from him and fired several rounds into the targeted area. By that time, the launcher had lost its impact since the enemy had had plenty of time to escape. I called for one of my sergeants to put the private under close supervision, and if he did anything like that again, to take away all of his weapons. The private was relatively new in-country and was only eighteen years old. I was twenty-one and also rather new in-country, but a few years in age and good training can mature a boy.

I took a squad to search the village, finding nothing. The rest of the platoon continued to escort the engineers, and I soon rejoined them on the highway. We covered more than six thousand meters that day and received sniper fire from three different locations along the route. Since our mission was to provide cover for the engineers, I decided to call in artillery on the sources of the enemy firing. I also received orders to burn the villages associated with the sniper fire. During my first three months with Charlie Company, our orders were to search and destroy (destroy only when resistance was encountered). Battalion issued orders to search but not destroy in June 1967.

Later, I discussed the situation concerning the private with Sergeant Sal, and we decided to reassign the grenade launcher to a more experienced soldier and continue to give the private close supervision until he proved himself ready for more independence. I briefed the captain on my experience with this man, and, as I can best recall, he was reassigned to the mortar platoon, where he wouldn't be in close combat on a daily basis. In the business world, a second chance may be appropriate when you make mistakes, but in front-line combat, you only get one chance. Too many men's lives were at stake to take a risk with a soldier like that. We did the best thing for the platoon and for the private.

We only stayed in the north for a few weeks before returning to the Bong Son plains. On the day we left the north, we conducted searches near the DMZ and captured a few prisoners. Our mission ended when I received orders to find a landing zone as fast as possible and prepare to make an assault south. We weren't operating as a company but were conducting platoon missions spread out across the area. Upon receiving orders, I moved my platoon to a nearby rice paddy, and soon, another platoon joined us. They had several prisoners; one was an old man, probably in his 60s—that doesn't sound so old now. The platoon leader was absent, away on R & R. The Third Platoon sergeant (acting platoon leader) was harassing the prisoners and telling them about the chopper ride that they were about to experience. He'd convinced them that accidents often happen to prisoners who ride in helicopters. I overheard the sergeant asking the old man if he knew how to fly and saying that he'd better learn fast because in a few minutes the chopper would be in the air, and he'd soon follow. I saw fear on the faces of the prisoners, and upon hearing the sergeant's last statement, I ordered him to release the prisoners into my custody. He complained that he was only kidding, and I answered, "I'm not."

My platoon took charge of the prisoners, and during the flight the old man sat at my feet looking at me then out the chopper's open door. When I made eye contact with him, his expression showed concern but not fear. He continued this routine of looking at me and out the chopper until we landed. We delivered the prisoners safely to our CO upon landing at our rendezvous in Bong Son. I explained my actions and reasons for taking charge of the prisoners; the CO commended my decision. I didn't see that sergeant again after that incident, but I felt good about helping the old man.

CHAPTER 10

Bong Son Plain

After spending several weeks in the north, we returned to the Bong Son Plains to resume operations there. The plains and valleys of the Central Highlands were the least physically challenging terrain for a patrol, but the topography of the land made patrolling a constant risk for enemy attack. We airlifted by helicopter into an area based on intelligence reports of enemy activity, but our arrival seldom surprised anyone. Every helicopter mission to an unsecured area was termed an air assault, and helicopter gunships preceded all air assaults. The gunships pounded the LZ with rockets and machine-gun fire in an attempt to provide a secure landing and off-loading of soldiers. Because of the landscape and agriculture of the plains, many landings were in rice paddies and totally exposed. These landings would've made great sites for an attack if the enemy wanted to do so.

Our missions varied, but usually upon landing on the plains, our first objective was to search surrounding villages. Many were the homes of VC as well as sources of supplies, hiding places, and ambush sites for NVA. We would occasionally encountered sniper fire as we approached villages. When this occurred, we employed one of two options. We'd move closer to the source of the sniping, seeking to flush him out and to determine the strength of the enemy, or we would hold our position and call in artillery or ARA on the contact area. Often sniping occurred from VC with the objective to disrupt our mission. The latter option was expedient and allowed us to resume our mission quickly, and if the sniping was from VC, we foiled their objective. If NVA was present and prepared for a fight, they would not snipe. They would wait in ambush for us to move close to their positions and then open fire. Most villages were surrounded by hedgerows, with palm trees planted throughout the area to provide shade. The hedgerows shielded runoff ditches and other structures and were often planted near trails, providing good opportunities for concealment.

After searching one village, we moved along the trails or rice paddies to other villages. For some missions, the ARVN or South Vietnamese police would accompany us. We would air assault in the early morning or fly to an area near the targeted village late in the evening and establish a camp for the night. Just before dawn, we would move to the village and surround it. With first light, the ARVN or police would arrive by helicopter to conduct a physical search and interrogate the villagers, paying particular attention to military-age males. Sometimes the missions with the ARVN and police provided good information for military intelligence.

View of village, trees, and hedgerow—Bong Son Plains

We conducted many such missions throughout the Central Highlands during the spring and summer of that year. In mid-June 1967, we were patrolling toward the Dam Tra O Lake west of a village, slowly following a trail, and looking for signs of VC or NVA. The Second Platoon was on point when we came upon several pungi pits camouflaged with leaves, dirt, and other debris. Since the pits were so close to the village, we knew we weren't going to have a friendly visit. The pits were lined with bamboo spears coated with feces and who knows what else. Fortunately, we found the pits before any of us stepped into them.

Pungi pit along a trail, vicinity of Dam Tra O Lake—Central Highlands

Just ahead was a thick, parallel line of hedges several meters from the trail and about seventy five meters long. I set up a machine gun facing the village and proceeded to check out the hedgerow. While we reconnoitered, the machine gun suddenly opened fire on a man in black pajamas running just beyond the village. I turned in time to see the runner drop to the ground. The CO ordered me to pursue, so I took two squads and instructed the first sergeant to cover us. We found the pajama-clad runner lying dead. I had one squad continue to search the immediate area, and I accompanied the other squad with the body to a designated assembly point near the village. The CO searched for papers and used our interpreter to find out from the villagers what they knew of this man. The CO was in communication with the battalion, reporting that the dead man was much taller than the average Vietnamese, around six feet, which suggested to Captain Markham that he might be Chinese. The dead man didn't show the signs of having worked with his hands as you would expect from local villagers. We didn't find any papers on him, and the villagers provided no information of value. Soon several crying women came, begging to take him away. They indicated that he was a son and husband and not VC or NVA, but they couldn't explain why he was running and couldn't explain the pungi pit either. After conferring with battalion for a while, the CO allowed the women to take care of the body. Our orders were to perform a thorough search of the village and surrounding area, which kept us occupied for most of the afternoon.

The company split into platoons, and each searched in different areas near the lake; my platoon was searching south and east. After several hours, we stopped to rest at a shrine overlooking the lake not far from the village. While there, a young girl (approximately fifteen years old) approached us; we checked her for weapons and found nothing. She proceeded to tell us how unhappy she was in Vietnam. She looked out over the lake and told us of her strong desire for life in a better place. She said her father was dead, and she lived with her mother but saw no opportunities for herself there. She asked if she could come with us and maybe go to America. She'd heard wonderful things about America. It was sad hearing her beg to go with us, but, of course, we couldn't help her. After a rest, I got the men ready to resume patrol and told the girl to return to her village. We didn't want her to get in the way or to be injured. She left in the direction of the village with her head bowed. From time to time I've thought of her, wondering if she found a way to come to America. I'll never know.

Girl at the shrine with Robert Parker, vicinity of
Dam Tra O Lake—Central Highlands

Before we completed our patrols around Dam Tra O Lake, the CO
called to advise me to get to an LZ and stand by to pop smoke. He told
me that the helicopters were bringing flak jackets, and every man was to
wear one for our next mission. We moved south to assist Bravo Company
of the First/Fifth, which had run into a large NVA contingent from the
Eighteenth Regiment of the Third NVA in the village of Va Thien, south
of the lake near a major highway. A tank company would join us to assist
in the operation. Alpha Company of the Second/Fifth was airlifted into the
mountains south of the point of contact to act as a blocking force. Charlie
Company landed near the First/Fifth to assist with their attack and siege
of the village. We landed without any bombardment to the LZ since we
were in close proximity to other US units. Upon landing, we moved into
position next to Bravo Company. Our company's placement was on the
west side of the village, extending to the mountain south of the village.
During landing and while moving into position, we didn't encounter any
fire.

When we reached our positions, it was dusk, and I could hear the tanks approaching from the north. Medevac arrived to carry out the wounded from Bravo Company; at the same time, the battalion commander arrived in his helicopter to direct the battle. As the commander's helicopter circled the area, automatic-weapons fire erupted from the village. I heard a radio report that enemy fire hit the commander's chopper. No one was hurt, but this caused the helicopter pilot to move away and land behind our lines. The colonel joined our CO to review the situation from the ground. About that time, the tanks arrived. They positioned themselves in front of companies B and C. It was now dark, and as soon as the tanks were in position, they opened up. They pounded the village for thirty minutes or more, doing a lot of damage and putting on a noisy but dazzling show. Our orders were not to fire unless the enemy was in clear sight. When the tanks finished their work, it became very quiet. After several more hours of lying on our bellies, watching and waiting, we received orders to assign guard posts and sleep at our present positions. We drank from our canteens and ate cold C rations since no resupply would occur that night. We put out claymore mines; soldiers were positioned and assignments given, and we settled in for the night. Most men slept in full gear if they slept at all. I unbridled myself from my backpack and web gear, but I slept fully clothed, wearing my flak jacket. All was very quiet for the rest of the night, but it was a tense night for most. In the morning, we swept the village and the surrounding countryside. The official report shows 101 NVA killed and one wounded. Bravo Company reported eleven men killed and eighteen wounded. Alpha and Charlie Companies incurred no casualties.

Several weeks after we left the lake area, a company from the First/ Ninth Battalion visited the area north of the lake near the village where we patrolled. They were greeted by an NVA unit entrenched along the hedgerows. The battle of Dam Tra O ensued, and the operational report for June 1967 recorded eighty-six NVA killed and three captured. The report doesn't mention the US casualties, but with that many NVA killed, there had to be some.

Patrolling the valley—Central Highlands

In the month of June, Charlie Company continued to make combat air assaults all over the Central Highlands. We would be in rice paddies, in the mountains, on the beach, and back and forth. A lot of enemy traffic was reported during this time. Also, Army Intelligence reported a large number of NVA sightings on the beaches, especially at night. The NVA was using small boats to move along the coastline to strategic villages to collect supplies and then return with their goods to their unit encampments in the mountains or other hideouts along the coast. The beaches were a favorite destination for many of my men as well. While patrolling the beach areas, we would sometimes arrange a long break or make camp for the night there. This gave us time to play in the surf and sand. We had many missions along the coast and also some success in finding the enemy.

Air assault near South China Sea—Central Highlands

One evening around dusk, the company was airlifted to a beach on the South China Sea and set up camp. In late evening, the navy arrived in transports and carried us to another beach location to prepare a night ambush. Upon landing, we quickly and quietly moved onto the beach and into the nearby sand dunes, where we established a company ambush position. Our purpose was to wait for NVA moving from the sea to the inland villages. Normally, an ambush consists of a small contingent of soldiers; this was the entire company, around 150 men. We were in close proximity to one another and positioned to view the landscape in all directions.

Soon NVA came. It wasn't clear how many there were, but some were very close to my platoon's position and walking from the sea inland. Firing broke out along our front, and one NVA crossed my line of sight, running parallel to my position. The moon was bright and silhouetted the target. I took aim and shot once toward his head, and he disappeared immediately. Sporadic firing continued, but soon army helicopters arrived to spotlight the area around our position and saturated the surrounding area with machine-gun fire and rockets. During the commotion, the fire from one chopper accidentally hit a soldier in our company, but his wound wasn't serious enough to medevac him that night. The platoon medic treated him, and the next morning medevac took him to a local medical unit. With all the gunfire, we killed, wounded, or scared off any other NVA that might have been in the area. After all, intelligence reported that they were there for resupply and not battle. We took turns sleeping and watching throughout the remainder of the night with no further enemy sightings. At dawn, we found a number of dead NVA scattered along the beach. We did find an NVA with a bullet in the side of his head, lying dead in the general area where I had fired. I had a strange feeling of pride when I saw him. I've never quite reconciled that feeling, but killing was my job in 1967.

Later that day, many soldiers in the company, including me, displayed flu-like symptoms. How do you call in sick when you're an infantry soldier in a combat zone? You don't; you just take APCs and keep on going. However, with so many soldiers sick, it was difficult to conduct additional search missions. Battalion ordered our company to move to a nearby village for stand-down (a period of rest and refitting—no combat operations except for security needs) for a two-day period to allow the sick soldiers time to recover. Those well enough to work were mustered to patrol the surrounding area.

Since so many were feeling puny, the battalion doctor flew out and gave us shots of penicillin, and that did the trick. The next morning all of us were up and ready to go; however, the company stayed put for another day, allowing more time to recuperate. It was a good thing we stayed there since several of us continued to have fever for a few more days. During the doctor's visits, he also went to nearby villages to administer vaccines to the local children. The parents liked the idea; however, I think some of the children objected.

Most trails in the lower elevations in the Central Highlands led to water. As we conducted our daily missions, we encountered water often. It was a visual anomaly to see a well-traveled trail end at a river's edge and, far across on the other side, rise up to the bank as if it had tunneled under the river. The trails crossed the rivers at natural fords, so the rivers were usually navigable by wading at various depths no more than waist high; otherwise, we needed a bridge or boat. We employed many methods for crossing water, but wading was the most common.

It took a little personal preparation before and after we crossed a river. We needed to secure papers, maps, letters, etc. to higher altitudes on our bodies to keep them dry, usually in our helmets. Because of these wading adventures, one of the most valuable items in the company was a piece of trash. That trash came from the discarded plastic wrapper of newly installed radio batteries. The plastic was very heavy, about eight by twelve inches, and was perfect for protecting letters and maps. I seemed to have two bags partially filled at all times. Jeanie wrote to me daily, and I kept every letter. Periodically, I'd send a bag of letters to An Khe with the first sergeant. He'd secure them for me at company headquarters, and then I'd box them and mail them home at the first opportunity.

Notice the map and letters secured in my helmet
to stay dry during water crossing

Whenever my platoon had the point, I always positioned an M-60 machine gun along the bank of the river to provide cover in case we encountered enemy fire during the crossing. Then I'd lead a squad of men across, leaving the rest of the platoon/company to wait until I secured the other side. I always carried one machine-gun crew with me to protect the crossing from the opposite bank. We never encountered any enemy fire while crossing the rivers, but we were prepared, and everyone appreciated the security of the machine guns on both banks of the river. I was told that before I arrived, the company had not employed this tactic. However, it soon became a standard operating procedure.

Machine gun in place on bank to secure crossing—Bong Son Plains

Whenever we wadded a river, we always checked ourselves and each other for leeches. A lit cigarette was the best method of removal. My first experience with this was very much like the scene in the old movie *The African Queen.* You may recall Humphrey Bogart pulling the boat through swamp water and periodically stopping while Katharine Hepburn squealed as she knocked off the leeches. Well, we didn't have a Katharine Hepburn, but I think we did have a bit of squealing, probably more of a yelp, when someone was accidentally burned by a cigarette. On one occasion, we crossed a deep, slow-moving river that was full of leeches. Upon reaching the other side, we inspected our bodies and found we were covered with the little buggers. Every man in my platoon had leeches thickly coating his body from armpits to ankles. It took nearly thirty minutes to remove the leeches and shake out our clothing. That would have been a great ambush site; Charlie would have caught us with our pants down, literally.

On another occasion, I led about ten men on a search mission late one afternoon. I believe this was my first solo mission without my full platoon or cadre of sergeants. We encountered some sniping, so I led the men in chase after the culprits. Our pursuit took us off the beaten path, which caused me to pay particular attention to the terrain and my map. Without trails, you could easily lose your way if you didn't read the maps carefully. I didn't want to get lost, and dusk was fast approaching. We never found the enemy, but we did encounter a deep, narrow river. One of my men wanted to swim across, but that wouldn't have been prudent. Instead, I sent several men to look upriver and downriver for a viable crossing. The men who went upriver returned with several rowboats in tow. They had found them adrift; we may have been right on Charlie's trail after all. We made several trips ferrying everyone across. Once on the other side, we headed for base camp as the sun was getting low in the sky. I stayed in frequent radio communication with the CO, and, according to my map, we were about fifteen minutes away from our company. We made it safely back just as the sun was setting. At that moment, I was thankful for the extensive amount of time spent on map reading during OCS. This mission introduced me to the nature of the enemy and his tactics. I don't know if the sniping was from VC or NVA, but they weren't interested in a fight. They sniped and fled, this time causing no damage to my men. They were most likely there to visit the local villages after dusk for resupply.

With all the water we encountered during patrols, our boots and socks stayed wet most days. Drying was only possible at night when we made camp for the evening. I developed a fungus on my feet. I don't recall problems with the fungus while in Nam, but when I returned to the United

States, the condition became more visible and itchy. Both military and private practice doctors applied various treatments but to no avail. The condition recurred regularly through the 1970s then gradually disappeared in the 1980s. I guess it had finally succumbed to treatment or died in the healthier environment. I still get an itch in those places from time to time, which triggers memories from long ago.

In recent years, I read that the United States treated the Central Highlands and the DMZ with Agent Orange and other defoliants. I was in the midst of the heavily treated areas my entire tour. The army didn't publicize that fact to the soldiers. However, that might account for some of the ailments that I've encountered since the late 1960s.

CHAPTER 11

Mountain Missions

We often flew into mountain clearings in search of the enemy. Sometimes our missions were in open terrain, but most patrols were in the more densely wooded areas where NVA often hid their camps. The mountains provided a good physical workout, great scenery, and occasional treacherous climbs. They also provided other excellent opportunities for an enemy ambush.

Patrol up the hill, like ants in a column—Central Highlands

Most of the mountain ranges had foot trails, some of which had been in use for many generations. For the VC and NVA, the mountain trails were the favorite means of transporting supplies, delivering new recruits, moving wounded, and traveling to and from their base camps. While most enemy movement on the trails was at night, they would sometimes travel during the day, especially on trails more heavily covered with foliage and shielded from aerial observation.

The enemy also used the mountains to build fortifications for storage, sleeping, hospitals, etc. Many were in caves or dug into the ground and camouflaged. We frequently found signs of activity, and on occasion we had physical contact with them. At times, we made our own paths through the mountainous foliage, looking for an enemy camp or newly created footpaths.

One afternoon in the spring of 1967, I took a small patrol up a mountain range looking for signs of NVA activity; our company was camping in the valley below. This was a typical day's work for the First Cav: one or more platoons would spend three-plus hours searching an area in the morning and another three hours in another area in the afternoon and then return to camp for dinner and a night's rest. The remainder of the company would hang around camp, relax, and be prepared to support a patrol should it encounter the enemy. The CO attempted to allocate the patrolling and resting equally among the platoons.

Captain Markham and Lieutenant Soyars
reviewing a mission—Central Highlands

This particular day my platoon got the mountain duty—great exercise! The mission didn't require the entire platoon, so I assembled two squads (about twelve men), and we followed a small path up the mountain until it began to move away from our assigned scouting area. Captain Markham instructed me to move into the higher wooded area of the mountains to look for fresh signs of the enemy or newly created trails. The terrain was steep and heavily wooded, but we moved quietly in a well-spaced column upward through the rugged terrain. After several hours of climbing, we came upon a beautiful pool of mountain water with a small waterfall. The area appeared untouched, and this was the first recollection I have of hearing a bird during my stay in Nam. Until I heard the bird, I hadn't really thought about the lack of wildlife. War can have a significant impact on the environment as well as the people.

Heavily forested with thick underbrush—Central Highlands

My men were excited about the pool of water. "Can we please swim, can we, can we?" They really didn't sound like children, but they were excited. Well, it was almost time to begin our descent back to camp before dusk anyway. Without much hesitation, I said, "It's time for a break." I thought a little swim would be a nice reward. When would we find such an idyllic place again? I sent one squad to search the surrounding area and assigned several men to guard the perimeter. The other men undressed and jumped into the water. The squad returned from patrol and reported that the area was seemingly untouched with no signs of any kind of human traffic. I gave them thirty minutes or more to play in the water. While they played, I took the guard duty and made sure everyone had a turn in the water. I wish I had a picture of them, but they were skinny-dipping. They laughed and played like little kids, although they were careful not to make too much noise. I also wish I could've let them have more time there, but the mountains could be treacherous at dusk, especially if the enemy was about. Before we left, I took a short turn in the water, and it was cool and refreshing.

While the men played in the water, I noticed a fist-sized rock that looked like one of those Indiana Jones rocks my mother-in-law asked me to be on the lookout for. I picked it up and examined it. I didn't lick it, but rather spit on it and rubbed it to see the color. What did I know! It just looked like a rock, but I put it in my backpack to send home. I looked around and found one more for her collection. Later in the year, Jeanie wrote to tell me how thrilled her mother was to receive the rocks. She had examined them with great care and reported that I had probably found petrified dinosaur dung. Now I was really glad I hadn't licked them.

We eventually made it back to camp without incident. We found no sign of other human activity during that patrol. The other squads that patrolled the flatland around the camp had similar reports. Early the next morning, helicopters picked us up for the next assignment.

We visited the mountains near the coast many times in search of the enemy. Usually we flew to a mountain clearing, where we off-loaded one chopper at a time. However, for one mission we landed in a valley and climbed almost straight up to a well-manicured plateau. It was a long and exhausting climb. The entire company moved slowly up the jagged stone face of a cliff. I remember thinking that if the enemy were anywhere near us, they could've picked us off one at a time from the top of the cliff or from the valley below. If one man fell, he'd take one or more soldiers with him on the way down. We reached the top of the plateau thirsty, exhausted, and without incident, and, again, there was no sign of the NVA. The plateau was like a mountain oasis. The grass was green and manicured. It was a site used by Buddhist monks, and I could see why. It provided a beautiful, remote, cool place with perfect scenery for contemplation. It provided us with a great place to rest, eat, and take a few pictures after the long trek.

On a mountain plateau, near the coast—Bong Son Plains

One of my more unforgettable ventures into the mountains occurred when the company air assaulted to the southwest end of a mountain range near the coast to investigate NVA sightings. Whenever we conducted an air assault, it would involve a large number of choppers, so the entire company could arrive in quick succession. Since it was impossible to know if an LZ would be hot (taking fire from the enemy), the choppers moved fast, keeping a close formation. Gunships, loaded with ARA and machine guns, led all air assaults into potentially hostile areas. The ARA and machine-gun fire would disrupt any threats by an enemy, but it also warned them that we were coming.

On April 22, 1967, the Third Platoon was assigned point, and they loaded up about six choppers and lifted off; Second Platoon came next, and then the rest of the company followed close behind. The Third Platoon landed on the mountaintop and received sniper fire, with one soldier reported shot as he entered an existing foxhole on the LZ. Normally, soldiers in the first choppers to land moved off the LZ immediately to provide protection and to make room for the next wave of choppers with their cargo of soldiers. When the Third Platoon landed, everyone stayed in the foxholes or lay prone on the LZ. The LZ was only about twenty feet by twenty feet, with one narrow trail leading into the adjacent mountain range. All other sides of the LZ were sheer drops. Unfortunately, the Third Platoon didn't report the situation accurately to the CO. The platoon leader reported the sniper fire and the wounded soldier but nothing else.

I was always in the lead chopper for my platoon, and when we arrived I could see the mass of soldiers lying all over the hilltop, with only the knoll of the mountain left for a helicopter to land on and no place for my men. I radioed the CO and reported what I saw. He ordered me to land anyway. Once on the knoll, we would have no place to go except to crouch beside the helicopter. The Third Platoon leader was busy spying for the sniper; thus, he failed to call in the landing situation accurately and wasn't taking any action to move off the LZ. I radioed the CO again, advising him of our predicament. The entire company monitored the same radio frequency, and during air assaults the choppers were on our radio frequency as well. The chopper pilots took orders from the infantry commander in charge of the operation, in this case, Captain Markham. I explained the situation again and requested that he give orders to abort the landing for the Second Platoon or order the Third Platoon to get off the LZ immediately. The Third Platoon leader indicated that we had room to land, and the CO said to proceed. However, he also ordered the Third Platoon to move off the LZ, but they didn't move. The time from my first radio report to my landing was only a matter of minutes, so quick and decisive actions were imperative.

My chopper slowly descended to the hilltop. The pilot had little choice but to go slow; too many soldiers were in the way to put down safely. If the snipers were still around, we would be sitting ducks, or rather, hovering ducks. The pilot eased the chopper down, and we off-loaded, stepping between horizontal soldiers as they hugged the ground. I couldn't believe the landing was still on! The Third Platoon leader wouldn't give an order to move, and he had the only avenue off the hilltop blocked. I really dislike disorganized and indecisive leadership. I was preparing to take my men through the Third Platoon and onto the mountain that lay ahead. Before

I could react, another chopper was moving in to land. My radio operator and I hugged the ground as the chopper hovered above us. I shouted for the other soldiers to move closer together and away from the center of the LZ to give my men room, but they lay scared, frozen to the ground. All of this was happening as the chopper descended, and many others were hovering and circling, waiting their turn.

I was on my back between two rocks, each about fifteen inches high, talking on the radio, advising the chopper pilot, "Your tail blade is a foot, no, inches away from my chest; no, if you don't stop rocking, it will be in my chest!" My RTO was shouting and waving his arms for the chopper to take off, but it continued to bounce, causing the tail blade to seesaw up and down within an inch of my chest. It contained six of my men, who were slow getting off since very little space was available for them on the knoll. After off-loading several men, the chopper lifted off, to my relief; however, he only lifted briefly and returned to force me once again to the ground. Somehow, while all of this was happening, I was able to convince Captain Markham to cease landing any more choppers until the Third Platoon moved off the hill. However, I wasn't able to convince the chopper pilot to lift off without getting rid of his remaining soldiers. It seemed like this process took hours, but it really was only minutes—too many minutes. The chopper finally rose, and I prayed a big thank-you and briefly thought about my rainbow! For years, I relived this experience, seeing the tail blade a hairsbreadth away from my chest. If I were to die in war, I wouldn't want it to occur due to the indecisiveness or mistakes of others! Later that evening when I wrote to Jeanie, I didn't tell her about the incident, but I did write an emotional, poetic letter.

By the time the Third Platoon left the hilltop, the NVA was long gone. We only found indications of a small camp. We searched the mountains for some time with no further contact with the enemy. In the afternoon, we left the mountains and went to a new location and another assignment.

By the way, before the chopper and I played seesaw, I saw the soldier who was shot, propped up in his foxhole, eyes open and staring blankly in my direction. He'd died almost instantly. The soldier had been in-country for about seven days and was in his midtwenties, married with a young child. I'm not sure why, but often the new troops in the field were the ones that were wounded or killed in action. If you made it for two months, you felt good about making it all the way. Sometimes soldiers were victims of their inexperience. In this instance, the sniper had about forty soldiers to shoot at, but the one he shot and killed was a rookie.

CHAPTER 12

Patrols in the An Lao Valley

We frequently patrolled the An Lao Valley, or VC Valley as the soldiers called it. The valley was remote, dense, and surrounded by mountains of all sizes. There were frequent aerial sightings of the enemy but few battles occurred there during my tour. It was difficult to surprise anyone due to the preemptive ARA strikes. We searched there and in the surrounding mountains many times while I was with Charlie Company.

Patrol in the An Loa Valley—Central Highlands

Patrol near the An Loa Valley—Central Highlands

The enemy peppered the entire country with tunnels. Some were new and some were dug during their years of war with the French, and the An Lao Valley and surrounding mountains had its share. The NVA and Viet Cong used them for cover during travel but mostly for encampment. Often, when the enemy was encamped, US units would unknowingly come upon a campsite while conducting a mission, and if the situation was right for the NVA, they would spring an ambush. This occurred many times during the war and was the situation described in the first chapter of this book.

One of my sergeants, Francisco Kumangai, loved the tunnels. He was from the Solomon Islands. The islands had natural caves/tunnels, and he often played there as a boy. Whenever he saw a tunnel, it seemed natural for him to go inside and explore. I let him poke around in a few, but they were all empty. When we found one tunnel entrance, we'd fan out and look for others, since they were sometimes connected. I'd have one man drop a grenade in the main opening and instruct the others to watch for disturbances in the surrounding area. Sudden dust or smoke could indicate another entrance. With each entrance found, we continued to drop in grenades and to look for signs of disturbance. Our CO preferred that we not venture into the tunnels due to bobby traps, so we used this next best approach.

On one morning assault, our mission was to search the valley and move up a mountain path looking for signs of the enemy or their recent presence. We found little in the valley, but a short way up the mountain trail, we came upon a maze of foxholes and tunnels, and saw clear signs of recent activity. With every grenade dropped into a hole, we saw dirt fly all around the trail and from a number of locations in the woods. We had found a large, complex network of tunnels. After dropping a number of grenades and searching the area, battalion ordered us to continue up the trail and advise them when we reached a certain grid on the map. At that point, they dropped bombs on the trail and in the surrounding woods to demolish the tunnel complex as well as kill anything that might be hiding there. It was hard to find NVA or Charlie unless he wanted you to, and, in this case, he'd likely moved on before our visit.

The climate in Vietnam varies by region; the Central Highlands are pleasant to very hot from April to September. The monsoon season starts in October and continues through March. The monsoon season made all duties miserable.

Rain, rain, and more rain—Central Highlands

On one mission in the VC Valley around May or June, it was extremely hot with little wind as I took my platoon on a morning patrol. The valley had some well-worn trails with dense foliage on both sides. The trails were heavily used, and I don't believe the GIs were the only ones using them. We patrolled slowly and with heightened vigilance. As we moved along the trail, we came upon a cleared site containing dead and decaying bodies of VC/NVA, at least a week old. The area had bomb craters as well as foxholes and a few tunnels. We passed other decaying body parts and clothing. All appeared to be casualties from a bombing. When I reported my findings via radio, the CO ordered me to ignore the debris and continue the patrol. It was eerily quiet, especially with no wind, no wildlife, and dead bodies lying about.

The next day I took a small patrol to search in another direction toward a small mountain ridge in the western part of the valley. The main body of the company stayed camped and was prepared to support us should we encounter Charlie. Two other patrols from our company went in other directions. While my patrol covered different territory than the day before, it went very much like the previous day. We saw signs of recent activity but had no contact in the valley. We reached the base of our targeted mountain ridge, but there was no visible trail going up. I radioed the CO to report the situation, indicating that we'd need to cut our way up the ridge, making our location known to anyone in the area. I suggested continuing farther west looking for a place more easily ascended, but I received orders to continue cutting our way to the top of the ridge, cutting and climbing slowly up the mountain.

The brush was extremely thick, making the climb very slow, so I rotated point men frequently. The point man led the way using his machete to clear the trail. It was tiring work, extremely hot, and there was no hint of a breeze. I later found out that the temperature was 125 degrees that day. We drank water and swallowed salt tablets, but the heat was too much. Heat exhaustion overcame all of us. My radio operator was the first to succumb. I ordered everyone to stop, drink more water, and take more salt tablets. Fortunately, I had the platoon medic along, who told everyone to remove their shirts, sit still, and put water on their heads to cool down. We were a sight to see, and not one of us was combat ready. With a little rest and a lot of water, most of us recovered quickly. However, my radio operator, Thomas Jarrett, didn't, so I called in medevac to lift him out. The CO told me to stop my patrol and return to camp as soon as we recovered enough to travel. We made good time back to camp, and later I found out that Jarrett had malaria as well as heat exhaustion. He hadn't mentioned any symptoms before the mission. The heat must have aggravated his condition, and the combination of the two caused him to become very ill. He was sent to Japan and didn't return to duty until the fall of 1967. My medic told me that Jarrett would sometimes joke about taking the malaria pills, and he suspected that Jarrett tossed them into the bushes. The medic lectured everyone about the consequences of not taking the pills. Some people just dislike pills, and perhaps Jarrett was one of those people. I asked my platoon sergeant to get me another radio operator, and Jim Henby became my new two-six alpha. I was very fortunate to have had two highly competent, loyal, and all-around nice guys as RTOs. Some officers weren't as lucky.

During another mission in the An Lao Valley, Charlie Company landed late one afternoon. We were to set up a night listening post and conduct early morning searches of the area. We arrived too late to be resupplied that evening due to the distance from battalion HQ. Our resupply order would come in the morning, but that night we had to eat C rations. While we set up camp and prepared for the evening, the CO asked me to send a squad to reconnoiter the area around the base camp and look for a site to place a listening post. I selected SGT William Clanton to lead his squad on the patrol. Clanton had been a specialist when I joined the Second Platoon, and I had recently promoted him to sergeant. This was his first solo patrol. I instructed him where to search, and the platoon sergeant offered words of wisdom as he and his men left.

Setting up camp for the night—An Loa Valley, Central Highlands

The patrol had been gone about twenty minutes when a loud explosion occurred to the southeast of our perimeter. Sergeant Clanton radioed me immediately, advising that his patrol had walked into a booby trap, and everyone was down. I asked if they were under fire or in contact with the enemy. He reported no. I told him I was on the way and so was the medevac helicopter. The CO had called for medevac on his radio while monitoring my conversation on the company radio. I quickly assembled a few men, the CO joined us, and we rushed to Clanton's aid. The trap appeared to have been a US Air Force cluster bomb, and everyone was on the ground with torn clothing and blood everywhere. The medic attended to the men, and the CO and I tried to comfort them the best we could. Clanton watched me the whole time as if waiting for me to tell him everything was okay. I assured him that he'd have the finest medical attention available, and I'd pray for his quick recovery. Clanton appeared to be the most seriously injured. He'd been walking point and got the full impact and the most shrapnel. The medevac choppers arrived, and the wounded were loaded aboard. I took Sergeant Clanton's hand, and he smiled at me and said, "I'll see you soon." The enemy acquired all kinds of US munitions to use against us. Cluster bombs were dropped from US aircraft and exploded in midair, sending many small bomblets to the ground. On impact, they were supposed to explode and kill enemy troops or destroy vehicles. Unfortunately, some didn't detonate upon contact with the ground, and the enemy turned these unexploded bomblets into weapons against US and ARVN ground forces.

That was a solemn night. We had lost some good men and friends. We prayed, each in our own way, for their safety and quick recovery. All of them were sent to the army medical facilities in Japan for treatment. I lost track of them for a while, but I know that all but Sergeant Clanton returned to Vietnam. I've thought of him often over the years, hoping some day to see him again.

The next morning, before breaking camp, we performed a weapons check, called a *mad moment* by the army. We did a weapons check periodically to ensure readiness when confronted by the enemy. For this exercise, everyone finds a place on the perimeter of the camp, and on command fires his weapon(s), emptying one clip per weapon. The machine gunners were free to fire until other firing subsided or until they were satisfied with the test. Since I carried a rifle and a .45 pistol, I emptied both weapons. This was always a good activity, helping to relieve tension or frustrations as well as to test our weapons. During this particular *mad moment*, we talked about hoping the NVA was lying in ambush, waiting for a chance to pounce. Our test would fix them, and this one was for

Sergeant Clanton and his squad. The Second Platoon shot a few more rounds than normal that morning.

On another mission in the valley we encountered snipers, but we couldn't find the source. In searching the direction of firing, we found a small, empty Buddhist temple. The temple wasn't active, but someone had recently used it. We found a few pieces of trash scattered about, a mandolin with a small bullet hole, and a Buddhist prayer shawl. We took the abandoned items back with us to the CO.

Sniper fire—Central Highlands

Back in camp, Captain Markham thought our captured items would make good souvenirs and offered them to me. Generally they forwarded items on to the S2, but he thought these would be of little value to them. No one else had an interest, so I claimed them. I sent them with our first sergeant back to An Khe for safekeeping. Later, during one of my visits to Camp Radcliff, I packaged and mailed them to Jeanie. As a music teacher, she was pleased to receive the mandolin, and I now keep them in my study along with other memorabilia.

CHAPTER 13

Stand-down

I don't know if the phrase *stand-down* was common to all military units in Vietnam, but it was in the First Cav. A stand-down was a term used when we got a break from normal patrol or air assault duties. We stayed busy patrolling most days, but occasionally we had stand-downs. Several were at field base camps, where the company took turns with perimeter guard duty. At least once we had several days off at our home base, Camp Radcliff in Ah Khe, but most stand-downs occurred wherever we happened to be camped the previous night. They were always welcome since they gave us time to catch up on letter writing, reading, relaxing, and visiting with soldiers. They also provided an opportunity to get our hair cut. One of my men had clippers and willingly performed that task. I think he might have been a barber in civilian life. Our hair didn't give him many challenges since we all maintained the standard, short GI haircut. Most frequently, stand-downs weren't for the entire company; usually one platoon or several squads would have to patrol the areas near our encampment.

Our company had a medic who loved to read, and he had a constant supply of paperbacks from the States. He shared his treasures with everyone, and I often took advantage of his generosity. His supply consisted of new fiction and nonfiction as well as some classics. I read a few Steinbeck novels and a few nonfiction authors, and I started *The Source*, by James Michener, several times, finally finishing it in 2005—that's a long book. Actually, I reread the book from the beginning in 2005. Reading was pleasurable and took me away to other places and times.

Stand-downs also gave the medic time to perform his duties more thoroughly. The medic passed out malaria pills to everyone in the platoon on a daily basis and administered aspirin and first aid as needed. He also conducted weekly inspections of each soldier, NCO, and officer under his jurisdiction. As a precaution, he'd examine feet and genitals for infections from dirt, moisture, etc. Soldiers recently returned from R & R were of the most concern since many of them participated in activities prone to venereal diseases. It was common to see the medic administering shots to a few men during his inspections. I remember one soldier who was so far gone with VD that he was sent to the States for medical attention. I couldn't imagine how an in-the-field infantry soldier could get that badly infected from one R & R and a few visits to the An Khe brothels. I'd have thought his pre-Vietnam physical would have caught preexisting infections.

Once, my company drew guard duty protecting the Bong Son Bridge along Highway One. The bridge was a major military and civilian crossing and had continuous daytime traffic. While this was a mission, it was like a stand-down since at least half of the company was relaxing at any one time. It was a refreshing change of pace. The men took turns in the guard bunkers watching the perimeter. While it was relaxing duty, the time went slowly, and most of us got bored quickly. I got restless after one day and was ready to return to the field.

Bong Son Bridge on Highway One—Central Highlands

We didn't purchase things from the local economy while in the field. Even in the larger towns on the major highways, there was very little worth buying. However, having guard duty in a populated area did provide the opportunity to make a few acquisitions. At the Bong Son Bridge, local merchants would set up portable stores outside our perimeter during the day, closing before dusk and opening again the next morning. Some vendors would sell food, but most sold Tiger beer, a strong local favorite. I wouldn't eat the local food, and I advised my men to use caution. Now the beer was different. I figured all that strong alcohol would kill any bacteria. I allowed my men to drink in moderation when not on duty, and the sergeants would take turns monitoring the purchases so no one would overindulge. That system worked well. I managed to taste a few Tigers myself during those days at the bridge. It was stronger than American beer, but it was a good change of pace from canteen water and coconut cocktails.

One of the strange things that one of the bridge vendors sold was betel nut. Many of the Vietnamese thought this nut was a delicacy and chewed it often. The nuts were in large seedpods about the length of a man's forearm. The locals would crack the pod and chew the black nut inside. We saw villagers all over the country with black mouths and teeth, and occasionally we'd see them in the act of chewing. The nut did disgusting things inside a mouth—a dentist's delight. None for me, thanks!

While on duty at the Bong Son Bridge, we conducted patrols in the surrounding countryside, on the lookout for suspicious activity. We never came across anything worth mentioning except for a funeral in the town of Bong Son. As we entered the town the funeral procession was assembling, so we paused, as a sign of respect, and watched the procession assemble and move down the street. The people moved with graceful dignity to music played on drums and flutes, with elaborate decorations all around. Most were dressed in everyday Vietnamese clothing; however, a number of women were dressed in long, white dresses and white veils that dropped below their waists in the front and back. Some children wore white headgear of various designs. Some of the members of the funeral looked at bit suspicious, so I reported this to the CO. After discussions with battalion, he responded that some South Vietnamese government people were present in Bong Son, and we should leave the funeral alone. It was impossible to tell the friendly from the enemy from the government people. What a war!

Funeral procession in the town of Bong Son—Central Highlands

One unexpected distraction/entertainment came when Jeanie sent a set of darts in one care package. I thought, "That's all I need, another weapon to carry," but the darts became a real treat for my men and me. For targets, we often created disposable dartboards from empty C ration cartons, which were burned with the other trash before leaving a campsite. The darts were very popular with my men, and from time to time men from other platoons would ask to borrow them. Someone had *Playboy* magazines, and they put up a few centerfolds as targets. You can imagine the areas of the photos that scored the most points. When the *Playboy* photos were used, a crowd would often assemble, with cheering, laughter, and general enthusiasm dominating the atmosphere of the camp.

Often on Sunday mornings and on religious holidays, we slept a little longer. Monthly, the battalion chaplain would visit the company in the field to hold services. When the chaplain visited, the services had a large attendance. On other Sundays, one of the company soldiers conducted services for those interested. It was great to be able to hold services with some regularity.

Sunday worship held by my men—Central Highlands

For one stand-down, our battalion spent a week at Camp Radcliff, An Khe. This one was special. The company had been humping the hills and sloshing through the rice paddies for many months, eating C rations or mess hall chow flown in by chopper. The battalion had earned its seven- to ten-day stay in An Khe to rest, relax, and retrain—very little of the last one occurred, as I recall. During my time with Charlie Company, we only had one such visit to Camp Radcliff. Later, when I was in Battalion S4 (army supply and logistics), the entire battalion had another stand-down there. These short assignments at An Khe provided a good break from the war since the camp had a stateside flavor to it, with clubs and post exchanges, and we didn't need to carry weapons or field gear, not even in the town of An Khe. Army military police patrolled and guarded the town, so it was a safe zone for soldiers.

I did do a few work-related activities during the day while at Camp Radcliff, but nothing significant stands out. We sometimes took jeeps into the town to get a local Tiger beer, shop for souvenirs, get a massage, or, if you were so inclined, get a *boom boom* at one of the local brothels.

I was newlywed and fearful of getting a disease, so I declined the latter. While in the town, I purchased some locally made pottery for Jeanie and crossbows for my brother-in-law and myself. I bought the crossbows from some local Montagnards (hill tribesmen). They set up along a road between the town of An Khe and Camp Radcliff and offered their goods for sale or trade. The Montagnard people were different from other Vietnamese in looks, customs, and clothing. The Vietnamese considered them primitive, second-class citizens and shunned them.

Montagnard people near An Khe—Central Highlands

While at Camp Radcliff, I was able to pack my purchases, along with the letters I had received from Jeanie, and mail them all home through the US Army mail service. Uncle Sam provided free mail delivery from Nam, and Jeanie received everything I sent quickly. Mail coming the other way was less reliable and a lot slower. I'd sometimes go for weeks without mail, and then, suddenly, five or more letters arrived in one day.

I also occupied my time playing cards and visiting the officers' club, where I played my first slot machine. I didn't play them much, and I've tried a few slot machines in other locations since 1967, but I came away with the same feeling—not for me!

A few nights before we were to return to the field, we had a platoon cookout coordinated by my sergeants. They borrowed several grills made from old barrels and procured enough T-bone steaks for two or three per man and more Budweiser than we could drink in a week. We partied, ate, sang, joked, and enjoyed each other's company into the early morning hours. I sometimes think about the fun that everyone had that night and how much that event meant to me and, I hope, to my men. I had only been in-country for about a month at that time, and this gave me an opportunity to interact in an informal setting. We learned much about each other and became a closer group of men. Sometimes, the simple things or events can have the greatest impact on our lives. We created new bonds that night—bonds that would help us through the days ahead.

CHAPTER 14

Village of Lo Dieu

On May 9, 1967, Charlie Company's mission was to make a night landing in order to perform a dawn cordon and sweep of Lo Dieu, a small village on the South China Sea. Located at the base of a rugged mountain range southeast of Bong Son, it was cut off from the plains by mountains and a strip of boulders and rocks along the north and south boundaries of the shoreline. With limited accessibility, it was ideal for NVA infiltration, since the mountains were a favorite hiding and traveling site for the NVA, allowing them easy access to the village. US troops had limited opportunities to surprise the enemy at that location.

In late afternoon of May 9, my company was airlifted to a distant beach, far south of the village of Lo Dieu, so that our landing would have no impact on our target. At our new beach location, we set up camp and were given time to swim, write letters, read, or just relax. The plan was to make an amphibious assault on the village of Lo Dieu in the early morning. Around 2300 hours, we broke camp and boarded two navy amphibious landing craft that had arrived in the breakwater along the beach. We waded into the surf to board and were transported out to sea to wait until the appointed time to land. It was very dark, so we couldn't see how far out we were, but land wasn't in sight from my position. The sea was rough, at least to me, so we pitched and yawed, causing some soldiers to get a bit seasick. The movement of the boat made it easy for me to sleep, rocked by Mother Nature. However, many men stayed awake, too anxious about what lay ahead.

We stayed at sea for several hours until navy swift boats came to accompany the landing craft as we moved up the coast toward the village. As soon as the swift boats arrived, we started preparing for the landing. We really didn't know what to expect. Were we surprising the enemy, was he waiting to surprise us, or was he in the area at all? As we traveled to the village, some men quickly ate cold C rations, but most of us just waited. Around 0300 hours, the landing craft came slowly onto the beach. The CO had told us earlier that we would have a quiet landing; however, the navy began bombarding the base of the mountains to the west of the village as we were coming ashore, reminiscent of the Marine landings in World War II. The noise was deafening—so much for surprise! When the landing craft hit the beach, we exited by the front ramp into water about waist high. On shore, Captain Markham called the officers together to give a final briefing. As we stood there, I heard a *very* loud noise close to my left ear. The noise was so loud that I didn't hear what the captain had said. I told him about the noise and asked the others huddled around me if they had heard anything. Apparently I was the only one, so I asked the captain to repeat his last sentence. I think it was shrapnel from the bombardment. I'm still amazed that no one else heard that loud sound.

My platoon and First Platoon were to cordon south of the village, and Third and Fourth Platoons would cordon the north. I started the Second Platoon about 150 meters south of the village by posting Sergeant Sal in charge of the beach. We put one machine gun there, and I took the other one with me. Moving west, we came upon a well-worn trail, where I put the second M60 machine gun and the ammo bearer. I placed men every fifty meters, which took us to the southwest side of the village. Beyond the machine gun, the terrain became thick with bushes, hedges, and trees, all of which made it more difficult to keep straight-line contact between men. With the exceptions of the two machine guns and the RTOs, soldiers were alone and fifty meters apart. My RTO, Jim Henby, and I took up positions along a small path southwest of the village, and I placed my last two men west of me. The CO established his HQ just west of the Second Platoon, with the First Platoon spread out toward the mountain.

After I placed my last man and returned to my post, Captain Markham ordered the navy to cease firing, so as not to endanger the platoons moving toward the mountain range. Before I could settle into my position, automatic-weapons fire broke out in the middle of my line. I radioed Sergeant Sal, but he had no news about the firing. I called out to the soldier east of me and asked him to relay information to and from the man next to him. I was preparing to head east to investigate when the firing slowed. As I was talking on the radio with the CO and Sergeant Sal, I saw a figure appear about twenty meters in front of me moving along the path directly toward Henby and me. In the dark, the figure first appeared as a blur but came into focus as he approached. I still couldn't tell if the figure was one of my men, so I called for him to halt and identify himself. Instantly, the figure turned and ran. I opened fire, and the figure disappeared into the bush, and once again firing started all along the Second Platoon's line. I couldn't see any other movement from my location, so I took Henby and began moving toward the soldier east of me. I softly called to him that I was coming, and he acknowledged. I moved from cover to cover and position to position just as I had done in my imaginary play as a boy, but this time I had the threat of a real enemy with real bullets.

As I traveled, I called the CO, explaining what I was doing. I moved from location to location; no one had seen any movement until I reached the M60 machine gun, where SPC Robert Parker and SPC Robert King were operating the gun that covered the trail. The shooting had begun from this site when a column of men approached them from the village. Parker and King told me their stories, and with dead NVA lying about, I listened intently.

Parker was on the gun, and King was handling the ammo. The approaching column was very quiet and surprised them. The enemy column, which hadn't seen my men either, was several feet in front of the machine gun when Parker saw them, recognized them as Vietnamese, and opened fire with the M60. The NVA fell to the ground or ran in various directions along the trail. Somehow, two NVA soldiers ended up in the machine-gun pit with Parker and King. They were behind Parker but in front of King, who was loaded down with ammo, doing his primary job of feeding the M60. Since the activity began quickly and moved with great speed, King didn't have time to retrieve his M16 rifle. Parker continued his focus on the NVA in front of him, not fully aware of what was going on behind him. Cassius—a nickname given to him because of this action— King started pounding the two NVA with his fists and ammo belts. He had been a scrapper in his youth in Houston and wasn't afraid of a good fistfight. He pounded; the two NVA flailed and clawed their way out of the pit and fled back toward the village. Parker continued firing down the trail, taking both of them to the ground.

Shortly after I arrived at the machine-gun position, the sun was rising, and everything started to settle down. On the trail, we found five dead NVA. On the beach, Sergeant Sal and his men had rounded up twelve who were trying to escape the barrage. They were heading to several boats secured on the beach. We searched the dead and handed our findings and prisoners over to battalion S2 who had arrived to escort the prisoners back to battalion. The Second Platoon was the only unit of the company to have made enemy contact, and while we handled the prisoners, the other platoons searched the village for more NVA but found nothing.

Later, battalion confirmed that our captives were NVA. They were in the village to collect food, ammunition, medical supplies, etc. S2 also gathered some good intelligence concerning NVA activity from the prisoners. For that day's action, a number of my men received medals for valor, calmness, and composure while in contact with the enemy and for bravery and success in accomplishing the mission. Parker and King were awarded Silver Stars, and Sergeant Sal and I were awarded Bronze Stars. After all that, we were ready for breakfast. Battalion S4 delivered scrambled eggs and bacon for a picnic breakfast on a South China Sea beach near a village called Lo Dieu.

KIAs at the village of Lo Dieu—Central Highlands

Prisoners from the village of Lo Dieu—Central Highlands

We operated around this area at least one more time during my tour with Charlie Company, but that time it was during daylight. We made an air assault on the beach in the early morning, and the company established a perimeter and sent out platoons to search in different directions. My platoon searched south of the village, working our way from the company perimeter toward the southern tip of the mountain range and the sea. When we reached the south end of the beach, we followed the base of the mountain back toward the company perimeter.

Near the base of the mountain, we found a well-worn trail moving in a northerly direction. It was probably the southern end of the trail from our previous action on May 10. I reported our location and findings to the CO, who ordered us to follow the trail. I told the platoon to move slowly, cautiously, and with plenty of distance between men. The trail quickly opened onto a field, so I halted the platoon to view the terrain ahead carefully. The trail led to a hedgerow and a ditch. The ditch was at a thirty-three degree angle across the trail, leading southwest to the mountain and northeast toward Lo Dieu. Before proceeding, I set up a machine gun on the edge of the field, and then took a squad down the trail. We were about fifteen meters from where the trail entered the hedgerow and ditch, when a metal-on-metal sound echoed loudly from the hedgerow ahead of us. By instinct, we all hit the ground, pointing our rifles toward the hedgerow. No one opened fire. We watched, listened, and waited. We neither saw nor heard anything else. Later, Sergeant Sal and the men around him in the rear of the column reported hearing the metallic sound as well and expected the sound of an AK47 to follow, but it didn't. I ordered my point man to toss a grenade into the ditch and another man to fire a clip into the ditch left of where the grenade exploded. I also radioed the situation to Sergeant Sal and ordered him to move west toward the other end of the hedgerow. West would've been the most logical escape route since it was dense with brush; the other direction was more open. As Sergeant Sal went to investigate, I took the squad cautiously toward the ditch only to find it empty. We searched in both directions, looking out for booby traps. Sergeant Sal reached the western end of the hedgerow and reported no signs of the enemy; however, we both noted that the ditch had had recent foot traffic. We couldn't confirm the metal-on-metal sound, but the entire squad recognized the sound of a gun's firing action. Surely some of us would've been casualties if the enemy had fired on us. We were thankful for the apparent equipment malfunction that day. I reported to the CO, requested further orders, and informed him of the potential enemy presence to the west toward the mountains. He advised me to return to the company perimeter since he'd just received orders to prepare for another air assault.

Those were the typical operations for Charlie Company in 1967. We killed and caught some NVA and may have been on the trail of others, but intelligence reports from other areas of battalion operations took us elsewhere. So off we went on another adventure.

CHAPTER 15

Cs, Sundries, and Doughnuts

Those wonderful C rations! They aren't so wonderful when you have better options, but if you're hungry and that's all you have to eat, they're wonderful. I always seemed to be hungry at that age, and especially while in the field in Vietnam, so I didn't intentionally miss meals, C rations or otherwise.

Most soldiers carried a sock stuffed with C ration cans tied to their backpack. The infantry in the field always had C rations for lunch, and sometimes that was all we had for breakfast and dinner as well. After being in-country for a few weeks, most soldiers had gotten around to tasting everything Uncle Sam had to offer in those meals and had formed their likes and dislikes. We received resupply of C rations several times a week, and the grabbing and bartering began.

Notice the sock filled with C rations and three
canteens of water—Central Highlands

Everyone seemed to like the cheese and crackers, and every ration pack included them, but some soldiers would seek to collect as many cheese and crackers as they could and use them exclusively for a meal. Somehow, I liked the one ration that no one else in my platoon liked, the ham and lima beans, so more of that was available to me than I wanted or could carry. When warmed, I thought that meal tasted more like real food than the others did. I also liked the scrambled eggs if I could get them, but they were very popular.

Sergeant Sal always carried a bottle of hot sauce, which really helped the flavor of C rations. Jeanie eventually sent me a bottle or two, so we had plenty to share. The name of my sauce was Texas Pete. I remember having that sauce in our pantry through the '70s, but I haven't seen it in stores since then. Actually, I really developed a habit of adding hot sauce to food and continued to do so for some time after I returned to the States.

Occasionally we received LRP (long range patrol) food packs. They were the modern (1960s) version of C rations but dehydrated in a foil pack and much lighter in weight. You merely added water and a little heat, and, presto, a complete and tasty meal. However, we got so few that I don't have a good recollection of them, but they tasted good and were sought after by most everyone in my platoon. We continually ordered them, but seldom received them. The LRPs were for use by the Army Rangers and Special Forces units and were relatively new to the United States Army food chain in 1967. Later during my tour, I discovered that the LRPs were sought by other branches of the US military and were sometimes used by army supply people to trade. This added to the supply shortage.

Since the First Cav used helicopters for resupply, finding a good landing zone was a priority each evening because it meant a hot meal along with our supplies and mail. Most evenings, the company would set up camp late but before dusk. This gave the supply choppers time to land and off-load in the daylight. The battalion cooks did a fine job of making some good meals. The food would arrive in army marmite cans to kept food hot. Once a week we'd have beef, potatoes, gravy, a vegetable, rolls, butter, iced tea, and a cobbler. That is a very fine meal for an infantry soldier in the boonies. We had other hot food items, but I remember this one as being tasty, satisfying, and served frequently. The choppers would return at dawn to collect the mess utensils and cans from the previous evening. They often brought grab-and-go-type breakfast items along with them—coffee in plastic containers (similar to present-day milk containers but more flexible), doughnuts (glazed and cake), and occasionally some hard-boiled eggs. The doughnuts were plentiful, and at first I looked forward to them, but soon I couldn't stand to look at another one. It was many, many, many years after I left Vietnam before I ate doughnuts again.

The most important time of the day for our company was the arrival of the resupply helicopter with the evening supplies. You might think food would be what was most anticipated. Well, it was important, but more important to many soldiers was the mail. When mail call came to the Second Platoon, several soldiers suddenly gained popularity and attention. One soldier got many packages of cookies and other sweets from home, which he gladly shared. Another got the hometown newspapers almost daily and shared with anyone showing an interest. I got attention because of the powder Jeanie sprinkled in her letters. The squad leader started asking me to smell the platoon's bundle of letters before distribution to determine if

I had a letter there. I could always identify the smell of Jeanie's letters. My identification of letters did three things: first, other men wanted to smell the letters before I disappeared with them; second, if I didn't get a letter, they knew my mood wouldn't be very good; and third, it was fun, and everyone seemed to enjoy the ritual. With my constant encouragement, Jeanie began including a picture of herself in many letters. Of course, I loved to get them and had them close at all times, looking at them during breaks and before bedtime. Occasionally, my RTO or another soldier would ask to see them. Before long, many men were asking to see my pictures. Not all of my men received pictures, so I let them look but only briefly.

*My pinup Jeanie in her ao dai—traditional Vietnamese
dress—that I purchased in An Khe*

After being in Vietnam for about three months, I got a bad case of homesickness for my wife. I thought about her continuously and felt melancholy from time to time. I looked forward to her letters and pictures, and I'm sure they contributed to my attitude. Like a kid before Christmas, I could barely wait until R & R—one week of rest and relaxation after being in-country for six months, and Jeanie and I thought and wrote about our reunion in paradise often.

In addition to the daily mail call, each platoon received a sundry box once a week. These boxes contained cartons of various brands of cigarettes, cigars, pipe tobacco (not used in Charlie Company), pipe cleaners, matches, candy of all sorts, stationary tablets, pens, razors and blades, shaving cream, soap, toothpaste, etc. We always had leftovers, which went back with the choppers for distribution at battalion. With all the goodies, we created a lot of trash. Our resupply helicopters carried away most of our discards, but we burned the boxes and paper at a central company fire pit. When the mission or conditions didn't permit burning, we dug a hole and buried the trash.

I rarely ate candy in those days, but we had so much in the sundry packs that it often went back on the helicopters. Most everyone took a few pieces to snack on and some to share with the villagers. One morning I took several bags of M&Ms and stuffed them in my pockets. As we patrolled, I munched. After munching for most of a morning, I was sick to my stomach. I don't know what made me eat so many, but that was the last I ate during my tour. To this day, I seldom touch M&Ms.

My wife and sister sent a number of goodie packages to me, and each was a great and welcome surprise. Both were generous with the amount of stuff sent, so I was able to share. My sister, Sheila, made baked goods most of the time, but once I received a rather large, crushed package from her. Upon opening this mashed, moist box, I found several broken jars of her wonderful, homemade spaghetti sauce and other appropriate food items meant to create an Italian dinner. The contents of the box were a mess. The package took several weeks to get to me, and the jars must have broken early during its journey. Mold covered much of the sauce and the other items, but I was thankful for her thoughtfulness. I left the package for Charlie. He might think the mold was betel nut and eat it, and then my sister could be proud to know that she took out a few VC with her moldy sauce.

CHAPTER 16

Pop Smoke

Being shot at by the enemy is a soldier's expectation during combat, but friendly fire is a needless and abysmal event during war. Since arriving in Vietnam, I had heard a number of stories about friendly fire causing injuries to American soldiers. In some instances, the friendly fire occurred because of someone's bad judgment, such as calling in artillery, mortars, napalm, bombs, or rockets too close to friendly troops. In the case of artillery and mortars, generally the infantry commander in charge of the mission or a forward artillery officer provides a map coordinate to direct the fire. The ground commander directs the firing for napalm or rockets, usually by popping a colored smoke grenade to identify the location of the ground unit and by providing instructions where to drop the munitions. Each soldier in a company carried various colored smoke canisters, and, to avoid confusion, they wouldn't pop smoke without permission to do so.

A smoke grenade directs helicopters to our location—Central Highlands

May of 1967 was a very busy month for Charlie Company. On May 7, our company made three combat air assaults before noon. All three were to follow up on reports of NVA activity in the valleys and mountains in the Bong Son area. In the early afternoon, we made our fourth air assault to a valley on the western side of the mountains with instructions to move up the heavily wooded slope toward the mountaintop to check out reports of enemy troop movement. Our landing site was a friendly LZ, and upon landing, Captain Markham called his officers together to issue orders for the mission. He put Second Platoon on point, leading the column.

As I mentioned before, the point platoon was the trailblazer and sometimes was an easy target should we make contract with the enemy, either in person or by booby trap. Platoons generally followed a prescribed formation, and in my platoon I always traveled near the front of the column and the platoon sergeant always traveled near the rear. The first man in the column is the point man and is most often a more seasoned soldier. Most of my men considered it an honor to be on point, and I'd have multiple volunteers if I asked for them. However, I usually called out a squad leader's name and told him, "I want you on point today." The squad leader assigned the point man and the marching order of his squad. Sergeant Sal and I frequently talked about the squad leaders and platoon members and their readiness for leadership roles, so I generally made informed decisions concerning the point position. My platoon usually proceeded in the following order: the point man, a rifleman, a grenadier, a rifleman, the lieutenant, the radio operator, a rifleman, the two-man M60 machine-gun crew, a squad leader, and so on to the end of the platoon column. Because we patrolled most days, often without any contact with the enemy, it was easy to become complacent. Knowing this, I led with caution and alertness, and my men followed my example.

On this day there was no trail, so we had to blaze our own way. I generally tried to keep the point man walking about ten to twenty-five meters ahead of the column, depending on the terrain, looking for danger signs. My instructions to the second man in the column were not to lose sight of the point man. I kept a close watch as well, since we had to be ready to assist if needed. The ridge was steep and heavily wooded on both sides. Fortunately, the brush wasn't too heavy so we only needed to use machetes occasionally. To the west was a valley, and to the east was a deep, dry riverbed that rose abruptly to a much larger mountain. As we approached the upper quarter of the ridge, automatic-weapons fire erupted from my point position. Of course, we all hit the ground, taking aim at the distant trees for signs of the enemy. The point man of my column was within twenty meters of a column of NVA who apparently were blazing a trail down the ridge and heading our way. He saw the NVA before they saw him, and with the firing they scattered. I took up a position on the right side of the ridge and surveyed north and east down to the riverbed below. As I was surveying, my point man opened fire again, yelling that he'd spotted more enemy movement ahead of his position. At the same time, I noticed a small group of NVA moving in the riverbed below me. I fired and shouted for my platoon to follow suit; however, few had as clear a view to the riverbed as I did.

During this engagement, I was in radio contact with the company CO, keeping him informed. I made the point that the NVA wasn't encamped but on the move, so he radioed battalion advising them of the situation. However, they had already called in napalm and helicopter rocket support. He ordered me to hold my position and wait for the air bombardment. From my position, I had a narrow view of the riverbed below. I noticed movement again and saw another column of NVA passing to the south. The brush and trees limited my view, so I could only see heads passing through this small opening. I saw one pass, then another. I opened fire and heard noises echoing from below. I informed the CO again that an enemy column was moving south and toward our rear. I asked if we should pursue them and suggested he consider sending one or two platoons down to block the riverbed. He reported this to battalion, who ordered us to stay put and wait for the air support. I think we missed a chance at the enemy right there.

Soon I heard the aircraft approaching our position, and the radio contact between the CO and pilots commenced. I saw red smoke about fifteen meters down the ridge from my position, and I heard the pilots identifying the target as about fifty meters beyond the red smoke. The CO acknowledged the target, but my point man was between thirty and forty meters beyond the red smoke. I called the CO and asked for clarification of the target and the payload. He replied, "Napalm is to be dropped fifty meters beyond the red smoke." "My men are too near the target!" I exclaimed and asked him to abort the mission or tell them to identify green smoke, which I was popping. The CO said, "Don't pop another smoke," but it was too late. The pilots identified two colors of smoke and requested clarification. I asked the CO to tell the pilots to target fifty meters beyond the green smoke. I don't remember him making any comment, but he complied. I called out to the point man to retreat toward my position ASAP, which he did.

I knew that my actions were disobedient, but under the circumstances I was prepared to take the punishment. The napalm hit, and the upper ridge looked like the sun had fallen from the sky. I could feel the heat, and the sound was deafening. The once forested ridge was a huge ball of fire and would soon be barren. Even with the target changed to fifty meters beyond the green smoke, the napalm blast leveled the area where my point man had been.

After the napalm, the battalion ordered our company to abort our current mission and locate a landing zone as fast as possible. The CO put the company in an about-face, and we moved to an LZ in the valley below. He set a very fast pace downhill, and we made it to the valley before our sortie of helicopters arrived. As the last helicopter lifted off, other aircraft flew over the ridge and pounded it, the creek bed, and surrounding mountains with a large arsenal of munitions. We had our sights on NVA that day, and I hoped that the bombardment took some of them. However, the NVA column was moving away from the targeted area, and I knew we had missed another opportunity by not blocking the riverbed to our south.

We made our fifth air assault of the day near another mountain to our northeast but still in the same mountain range. At the new LZ, the CO called the officers together to explain our next mission. I waited to be dressed down by the CO for disobeying orders. He did address me but only ordered me to once again take my platoon on point up the ridge. He said that battalion wanted us to move as quickly as possible and that another company was already moving up the ridge south of our position. An NVA column was on the mountain, and we were to give quick pursuit.

A well-worn path snaked up a defoliated ridge and showed signs of recent, heavy traffic. The forest line didn't begin until the top quarter of the mountain. This would've been a great place for the NVA to lie in ambush. I had the platoon spread out so that, should we come under fire, we'd have room to maneuver and not provide easy targets. We reached the trees and continued to follow the well-worn path through the thick forest and underbrush. The trail flattened as we reached the top of the ridge. I now cautioned my point man to move a bit slower and watch carefully for booby traps and signs of ambush, and I then relayed this order to the rest of the company. Soon we came upon a dead NVA on the trail. Since his body position didn't look natural to me, I instructed my men not touch or move the body. He was probably booby-trapped to entice souvenir-seeking American soldiers. The CO passed the word back throughout the company not to touch the body. We continued along the trail, seeing signs where people had been, but we found no one.

The sun was beginning to drop low in the western sky, and soon it would be dark. The CO received another call from battalion with orders to return quickly to our previous LZ and prepare to be airlifted to the east side of the mountains onto the Bong Son Plain. We were all very hungry and looking forward to setting up camp for the night. Soon the choppers arrived to take us to the new LZ, our sixth air assault of the day. Our hunger would continue a while longer.

CHAPTER 17

Night Patrol

Nighttime can be creepy when you're in a dark, unfamiliar place, but in a war zone in a dark, unfamiliar place, the creepiness can be nightmarish.

Very little sunlight was available as we approached our new LZ on the Bong Son Plain. This would be our last air assault for the day since it was nearing dusk and too dark to move a full company by air. However, the entire battalion was encamped and waiting for our arrival; I figured something big must be planned. Alpha and Bravo Companies were camped side by side at the north part of the plain, and Delta Company was in the south with an empty space in between. That space was for Charlie Company, and we headed directly there. The CO had informed all his officers of the layout by radio and told us that battalion headquarters and a battery of artillery were also in place. The LZ was battalion strength, well protected, and offered an impressive sight from the sky. The camps were aglow with campfires, and I could see soldiers digging in, tents set up, and mortar and artillery placements. As we descended, a chow line was waiting in our camp perimeter, a welcome sight. I hadn't heard a word, not even scuttlebutt, about our purpose here, and all of us were curious and anxious to know why so many troops and so much firepower had been assembled. As we flew into the area at dusk, the camps looked like a vast Civil War battle line, as seen in the movies. It was rare to bring artillery to a temporary LZ, so we knew the battalion was serious about this mission,

and we were anxious to know more about our role in the major assemblage
of troops and armaments.

After landing, information came to me in bits and pieces. Battalion
called the four company commanders to the field HQ to get orders. We
ate our dinner, prepared our LZ, and waited for the CO to return with our
orders. Because of the large number of troops on the plain, the helicopter
activity, and the myriad of campfires, our presence was certainly no secret
to anyone. However, battalion issued orders by radio for silence, and the
plain suddenly became surprisingly and eerily quiet. The CO returned from
his briefing to inform his officers that Army Intelligence had information
and sightings of a very large contingent of NVA. They reported that the
NVA was gathering along the lower mountains on the eastern edge of the
plain. The battalion's plan was to send out a small night patrol to the base
of the mountain to search for signs of the enemy. When and if contact
occurred, artillery would provide support, and the assembled companies
would begin moving to engage and block. Of all the officers present at that
encampment, the CO informed me that I'd lead the night patrol of one
squad of soldiers. I thought, "That'll teach me to disobey orders." However,
he volunteered that I had been handpicked by the battalion commander
to lead the mission. Although it hadn't been the CO's suggestion, he said
that he concurred with their recommendation. I was flattered to be leading
such a spotlighted mission, considering the number of officers available.
I was certainly not the senior lieutenant since I had only been in-country
three months. I was also apprehensive and aware of the danger; it could
become a death patrol.

I quickly assembled six men and my RTO. I chose SGT Lebron
Figueroa's squad and asked him to take the point. He was very experienced
at walking point—very observant and moved like a cat. The CO and
someone from battalion wanted to tag along. I thought, "All we need
now is a movie production crew." The CO was quick to say that I was in
command, and that neither he nor our battalion visitor would interfere
with the mission.

As we were preparing our gear, I noticed the radio echoes throughout
the camp. Someone would call, and I heard them on my radio as well

as echoes from other radios all around the camp. The previous order for silence hadn't been applied to radio communications. I called the CO and suggested that we ask folks to go to radio silence. I didn't want to advertise that I was on the way. The CO relayed my request to battalion, and they issued an order to silence the radios. Well, aren't I something! First, I disobey an order from my CO, and now I'm giving orders to the battalion. It's a lot easier to throw in humor after the fact, but at the time I had a feeling of helplessness as I looked out into the darkness and pictured that very large concentration of NVA lying in wait for my men and me. I recalled the first night in OCS when the senior candidates came to wake us at midnight. They created chaos, uncertainty, and a feeling of helplessness, and I was experiencing that once again. If we made contact with the NVA, we'd have little chance for survival. I remember being calm and confident as we checked our weapons and loaded up with ammo and grenades. We replenished our water then applied camouflage black to our exposed faces and hands. It was time to move out.

We left the camp, moving into the blackness. My radio was on silent mode, and my RTO kept the receiver to his ear to monitor communications from battalion. From our camp, we moved across an open rice paddy and soon were among palm trees and hedgerows with the lights of the camp gone from view. It was very dark, and I could see very little. The trees had a thick canopy, and only a little light from the sky shone through. We had to stay in close formation to avoid losing each other.

Sergeant Figueroa was true to form and moved catlike, stopping to listen frequently as he moved forward. We weren't on a trail but moving through bushes, ditches, and an occasional open area. Actually, being on a trail would have been more dangerous since it would have provided better ambush sites, and I had instructed Figueroa about that. There were north-south trails leading along our route, and we moved cautiously across several. US soldiers were notorious for walking the trails, often running into booby traps and ambushes.

The darkness was unsettling, and we were tired. I kept seeing things that weren't there. What looked like movement was a shadow. I could hear soft sounds when there was nothing to hear but a leaf or twig falling to the ground. I figured the first sound of contact would be the staccato sound of an AK47. I've stated this before, but this war wasn't like our fathers' war, where they came face to face with the enemy. That seldom happened in this war. The enemy made himself known when he had the advantage and often from ambush or as a sniper. We moved quietly and slowly, stopping frequently to listen. We heard nothing but our own breathing.

As we moved through the heavy brush, Figueroa stopped suddenly and motioned everyone to get down. I moved forward to his position. He was listening and observing a wide, well-used trail that ran north and south. The other side of the trail was thick with bush. According to my map (I carried an infrared flashlight), the mountains were about a hundred meters to the west. If the enemy was on the plain, this would be a good place to establish a camp—the trail provided a clearing, and the mountains protected the west flank. We waited there for several minutes, listening and watching for signs or sounds of activity. Finally, Figueroa moved across the trail, and we followed, one man at a time. On the other side of the trail, we again stopped to listen and watch. After several minutes, I ordered Figueroa to move out toward the mountain, slowly and quietly. We covered an additional seventy-five meters and were probably close to the base of the mountain range, but it was too dark to see. We hadn't had any sign or sound of the enemy, so I radioed battalion, gave them our approximate location, and asked for further instructions. Soon we'd begin climbing the rugged mountain slopes in the very, very dark night. If the enemy didn't get us, the treacherous night climb would probably take a casualty or two.

Battalion ordered us to return to the base camp and conclude our night mission. I offered to take a different route back to camp, but my orders were to retrace our steps as close as possible. I know we all felt relief, realizing that our chances of dying that night were now diminishing. Figueroa moved more quickly through the bush on the return trip. We did continue to stop and listen as we approached trails and in open areas, but we still made good time getting back to camp.

When we saw the lights of the camp, I could almost see smiles on the faces of my men, and I felt a new burst of energy moving me forward to safety and out of the dark. We will never know if the NVA was out there that night. I'm content that things worked out as they did, but we were prepared and willing to do our jobs that dark, dark night. Many missions were like this. We'd receive orders to pursue known or sighted enemy. We'd move cautiously and with trepidation without any enemy contact. This sometimes was a letdown, having built ourselves up for the big game, and our opponent didn't show up. My ancestors seldom had this problem. They knew where their enemy would be and moved to engage them. They had frequent encounters of close-range firing and hand-to-hand combat. I was expecting that experience and was prepared physically and mentally for it. My war did have some similarities to my ancestors'. My grandfathers who rode with J. E. B. Stuart had the luxury of horse mobility, which allowed them to move quickly, as I did with First Air Cav. We all were exposed to the elements, sniper fire, booby traps, ambush, night patrols, homesickness, wounds, death, and probably even an occasional faulty intelligence report.

We were thankful to be back in camp. Boy, I really could've used a beer about then! It was around 0100 hours, and I remember thankfully lying down on my air mattress, thinking of the rainbow and sleeping like a baby for what was left of the night. The next morning the companies went in different directions, resuming their normal search missions. We had the enemy in our sights earlier while in the mountains west of the plain, but we left to pursue other orders and strategies of the battalion.

We, especially the officers, frequently discussed Army Intelligence and wondered why we had so many misses while trying to make contact with large units of the NVA. The army trained us for close combat, and we expected to have that experience multiple times during our tours. We reacted quickly to pursue large enemy sightings and were able to move with great speed using the air mobility of the First Cav helicopters. Yet, we rarely found anything to confirm the reports by Intelligence.

CHAPTER 18

Highway One and the General

The main transportation artery going north and south was Highway One, a route heavily traveled by the US and South Vietnamese military and the civilian population. Occasionally, we conducted patrols near this road, searching nearby villages, ditches, culverts, and low or bushy areas in pursuit of Charlie or signs of his mischief. I mention Charlie/VC and not NVA since the VC tended to concentrate their efforts in the more populated areas. They mixed with the locals and even lived locally; it was impossible to tell the enemy from the friendly, in most cases. During one such mission along Highway One, the company was strung out on both sides of the road. The Third Platoon entered a village to conduct a search, and after being there for some time, a shot rang out, and then a burst of automatic-weapon fire erupted. The firing stopped very quickly. I monitored the radio communications between Captain Markham and Third Platoon, but about ten minutes lapsed before I was able to get clear information about the situation. My instinct was to move toward the village to support the Third Platoon, but I needed that order to come from the CO. Eventually he radioed me that a private had been wounded, but no one except the wounded soldier had seen anything of Charlie. The soldier was taken to the battalion medical unit by medevac, and the company continued to search the area.

*The Vietnamese three-wheel vehicle along
Highway One—Central Highlands*

Toward evening, we moved to another location in the highlands where we patrolled and set up camp for the evening. The company was abuzz with speculation about the wounded soldier. His platoon leader didn't have a high opinion of this soldier, stating that he did whatever he could to get out of work and out of harm's way. The platoon leader also told us about his investigation after the shooting. The platoon searched the area where the private was shot, looking for signs of the enemy and for spent rounds from an enemy weapon. They found nothing. The soldier's wound wasn't serious since the bullet entered and exited the fleshy side of his foot. The platoon leader thought the wound was self-inflicted and that the soldier fabricated the story about the enemy. The CO reported the platoon leader's suspicions and requested battalion conduct an investigation.

Some days after the shooting incident, battalion reported the findings of their investigation to the CO. The private finally admitted that he'd shot himself in the foot and that he'd made up the story to get out of the war. He thought he'd get to go to Japan for recuperation, and when ready for duty, he might get a rear-echelon job with light work. Instead, he was court-martialed and later dishonorably discharged from the army. During my year in-country, other army units reported incidences of self-inflicted wounds similar to this one. It's likely that wars from the beginning of time suffered casualties of this nature.

One morning, not far from Highway One, Captain Markham called his officers together to tell us that General Creighton Abrams had scheduled a tour of all military operations in Vietnam. During his visit with the First Cav, the division had selected Charlie Company, Second/Fifth for the general to observe infantry field operations. This was an honor for the company and the battalion. General Creighton Abrams was replacing General William Westmorland as commander of US forces in Vietnam, and that was the reason for the tour. The CO told us that the general would visit us the next day, and during his visit, battalion had laid out a sweep of the villages and plains south of our current location. We needed to look sharp but handle the sweep professionally and in a normal manner. TV crews would accompany the general's party, and we should look our best.

To ready ourselves for the visit, we were required to bathe, shave, and prepare to receive fresh uniforms. Off we went to a nearby river, where we took turns bathing, playing, and guarding the area. Our bathing location was in a moderately moving river, so leeches weren't a problem. We all joked about the visit, waiting for an order to spit-shine our jungle boots, which were mostly canvas. We also wondered if Charlie would be bathing; after all, he was in the general's area of military operations. I was more concerned that Charlie would take advantage of us during our baths; however, I'd welcome him tomorrow during patrol. A little combat would look good for the cameras.

It made more sense to me to have us looking as normal as possible to show the reality of being a combat soldier in Vietnam. If I were the general, that's what I'd have wanted and requested. However, the Vietnam War was the first war to be on television and constantly in news clips, and sometimes without regard to people and their feelings. In this case, if my mother and wife had seen me in the news, they would be pleased to see me neat and tidy.

On the day of the big event, we stayed in our base area waiting for instructions from battalion. We waited and waited. Finally, we started our mission without the general. It was difficult to take this mission seriously. The CO frequently reminded us not to get our uniforms soiled and gave updates concerning the general's whereabouts. We took many breaks, so that we wouldn't cover too much ground before his arrival. In the late afternoon, we were told that he wouldn't have time to visit Charlie Company since he'd been delayed at earlier stops on his schedule. With this announcement, several soldiers dropped to the ground and rolled in the dirt.

CHAPTER 19

Wow!

The countdown from March 6 to R & R was about 160 days, but it seemed like forever. August was the month for my R & R, and I was ready and anxious for it to arrive.

In mid-June, Captain Markham informed me that the battalion commander wanted me at LZ Uplift, battalion headquarters, to discuss a new job for me. They needed to replace the assistant S4, who was finishing his twelve-month tour. Captain Markham thought this would be a great opportunity and encouraged me. The next morning I took the early chopper back to LZ Uplift to meet the colonel. I was expecting a job interview, but that didn't happen. I was given a tour of the battalion facilities, introduced to all the officers and men of S4, and asked how soon I'd be ready to start work. That was a surprise, but I was excited to get the position. I'd start as soon as Captain Markham released me, which was within a week. By the way, Captain Markham had received a promotion to major, and he left Charlie Company within days after I did. I think he knew this when he sent me to battalion for the assistant S4 position. I think he wanted to help me before he left, and I really appreciated this opportunity and his confidence in me.

On June 15, I said good-bye to Second Platoon and Charlie Company. We had been together day and night for three months, and we were a family. Saying good-bye was tough since they would continue to be in harm's way while my new position would be less exposed to danger. My new position in battalion would allow me to visit the field from time to time, and I planned to visit Charlie Company as often as possible. Many men asked that I remember them when a position opened up in S4. I couldn't promise anything, but I hoped to bring a few men from the Second Platoon along with me.

The excitement about my new job and R & R just around the corner made the transition from the field easier. Being a rear-echelon officer lessened my daily exposure to harm, and Jeanie was elated with the news. Soon after I left the field, my replacement arrived. He was killed during an ambush in October 1967, the day after his twenty-first birthday. Lieutenants had a short life expectancy in the field, and I had been fortunate.

My departure day for R & R was August 4; I caught a chopper ride to the nearby airfield at LZ English. From there, I took a C130 flight to An Khe, where I handled necessary paperwork and left the next day via C130 to Cam Ranh Bay. For our area of operation, Cam Ranh Bay was the entry and exit point for Nam. From there, a US commercial airline flew me to Hawaii.

I left An Khe with several other officers from the division. Like me, one was heading to Hawaii to meet his wife, so, sharing a common destination and purpose, we struck up a conversation and became friends. He was a warrant officer (unfortunately, I don't remember his name) and a helicopter pilot for the medevac unit at LZ Uplift. We shared stories of our experiences and talked about plans while in Hawaii. We really connected during our trip, and we stayed friends after R & R. His medevac HQ was a short distance away from my battalion HQ, and we visited almost daily after we returned from Hawaii. For R & R we wore khakis, and it felt good to get out of jungle fatigues for a while. I was so very excited, knowing I'd soon be with my sweetheart. She was bringing civilian clothes for me, and I looked forward to the change.

Hawaii was a dream, and so was my lovely little wife, Jeanie. She'd booked us at the Polynesian Cultural Center Resort on the northeast side of Oahu. It was paradise, very quiet with fabulous food. After six months in Nam, I really wasn't a good judge of fabulous food, but Jeanie agreed the food was great. We had a grand time at the Cultural Center doing very little except lounging, swimming, dining, and enjoying each other. We thought about soaking up the culture of the center, but we decided to play and just hang out together instead. After several days there, we moved to Waikiki Beach to be closer to the action. We did plan to do more than stay in our room all day, and the south side of the island provided a lot more distractions and attractions.

We rented a small Toyota and drove all over the island; you can't hurt a rental car, and we proved it. At that time, the north point of the island didn't have a paved road to join the east and west along the coastline, but that didn't stop us. We drove around lava boulders and blazed our own trail, creating our own adventure in paradise. During our weeklong stay, we drove over the mountain pass many times and encountered rain showers at the top of the pass every time, very interesting and refreshing. At Waikiki, we got a pink hotel for six dollars a day, Jeanie's choice, with a balcony overlooking the beach and the ocean—quite romantic. We did some major tourist sights, such as the Don Ho show, Diamond Head, Polynesian entertainment, and most of the souvenir shops, and we ate a lot of good food. The days and nights went by fast, too fast, and soon it was time to say farewell until March 1968.

We discussed plans for when I returned from Nam, and we said our good-byes. That was really difficult, knowing that we wouldn't be together again for another six months. "Until then, I'll see you in my dreams."

CHAPTER 20

The S4

It was tough leaving my sweetheart behind in Hawaii. However, knowing that I had a new job with a lot less risk from combat made it easier. I greeted my new job with great enthusiasm, and I soon had the routines down well. In less than a month after I started as assistant S4, the S4 captain finished his tour and left for home, leaving me with both jobs. Priority for replacement captains went to field units, so they made me the acting S4 as well as the assistant S4, promoting me to first lieutenant. In September a captain arrived to take command, but in early October he left for the States to handle a personal matter. He returned in late October with a transfer to Army Intelligence. While waiting for his official transfer orders, the colonel made him battalion executive officer, and by November 1967 I was officially the S4 for the battalion. I guess they liked the job I was doing, so they didn't bother to fill the assistant's position. Instead, I held both positions until February 1968.

During my time in S4, I was able to make a positive impact on the job and on several people. The mess and supply sergeants didn't rotate to the States until early 1968, but everyone else in S4 left for home within two months of my assignment there. I was responsible for the mess hall, motor pool, and supply, with my main mission being to keep the field infantry companies supplied. It could take months to get a replacement from the States for S4 positions, so we got creative in filling vacancies.

Fortunately, I had a good mess sergeant and supply sergeant, two critical NCO positions. I filled most of the other job vacancies from within the battalion ranks. Since I knew the men in Second Platoon of Charlie Company and was familiar with some of their skills, I requested and got several men by name. Soon I had many more requesting jobs with me. I was able to accommodate some, especially those with skills for the motor pool. I specifically recruited my former RTO, Jim Henby, to run the S4 communications center. In September, I was pleasantly surprised when a soldier walked up to me, saluted, and shook my hand vigorously. There was Tom Jarrett, my first RTO in Charlie Company, back from his medical leave, and I immediately arranged for his assignment to S4. I eventually promoted both Henby and Jarrett to Sergeant E5. I also brought in Specialist McNealy from the Second Platoon for the motor pool. He proved his skills almost immediately, and I made him acting motor pool sergeant and later promoted him to sergeant. By the time I left Nam in March 1968, the entire motor pool contained former Charlie Company soldiers. Sergeant McNealy arrived in the Second Platoon during the summer of 1967 as a private. When I left Nam, he was a staff sergeant running the battalion motor pool, not bad for a country boy. Mac was from North Carolina and loved working on vehicles; he also demonstrated a lot of leadership and was an excellent fit for his job.

I visited Charlie Company in the field several times as the S4. While there, I got some ribbing about stealing all the good men from the company and received comments about visiting them only to recruit more men, but it all seemed to be in jest. The officers and sergeants of Charlie Company that I talked to thought it was great that I was able to offer deserving men opportunities.

As I mentioned earlier, the primary mission of S4 was to keep the infantry companies well supplied. That meant having a strong and reliable system for procurement and distribution. The motor pool provided transportation to procure supplies, but the distribution to the infantry companies required helicopters to resupply the field units. They were seldom in the same place for more than a day. I recruited a few soldiers from Charlie Company to handle this function as well. Every evening the infantry platoon sergeants took inventory for their respective platoons and developed a list of replenishment supplies. Their lists went to the company's first sergeant, who would radio the company's supply needs to battalion S4. Needs were identified as emergency or regular replenishment. The emergency needs, usually munitions and water, went out with the morning delivery; all others went with that evening's delivery. The S4 communications center collected all orders and dispatched them to the supply sergeant and to the S4 helicopter pad team. The latter assembled the orders, loaded them on mules (the mechanized supply transport flatbed vehicle that replaced the original army mules), and staged them by company on the helicopter pad. As the resupply helicopters arrived to pick up deliveries, the helicopter team loaded the choppers and gave an inventory list to the pilot to give to the receiving company. I gave the pilot the coordinates and call signs for each company and radioed the companies advising them that their supplies were on the way.

The S4 landing pad at LZ Uplift—Central Highlands

Jeanie had asked me to describe a typical day as the S4/assistant S4, and I offered the following: "My day begins at 0500 hours. My first task is to radio my assigned helicopters to determine their estimated time of arrival at my LZ and to insure that all company resupply orders are ready. Next, I contact battalion HQ to report my readiness and see if there are any additional or changed instructions for the day's operations. Then, I go to the landing pad to supervise the activities and communicate with the field companies. Choppers arrive at my landing pad around 0600 hours and generally drop off discards on their return around 1000 hours. After the resupply is finished, I do the rounds of my other operations (motor pool, mess, and supply). All during the day, my communications center is taking radio messages from the field companies and recording orders for the evening deliveries. Around 1330 hours, I begin preparing for the evening operations. On most days, all resupply activities conclude by 1830 hours. After which, it's time for dinner with the battalion commander, followed by a briefing in the battalion HQ. I'm generally free to take care of my personal matters by 2100 hours."

Although extended workdays for resupply weren't the norm, it was common when operational conditions called for full battalion support. In these instances, my duties and responsibilities were elevated to a critical level. In one instance, Bravo Company ran into NVA in the late afternoon. They were pinned down by automatic-weapons fire and were forced to stay in position until the next morning. I spent the afternoon and night on my landing pad with radio in hand directing helicopter supplies, relaying medevac instructions, and directing chopper crews. During that night, Bravo Company lost eleven men, five killed and six wounded. Alpha Company moved into the nearby mountains, and on the following day they encountered the same contingent of NVA. We continued operations from my chopper pad for three days, eating only three meals in that time. Alpha Company lost nine men, two killed and seven wounded.

On another day, the Second/Fifth was called to assist the First/Fifth, who encountered a large contingent of NVA about six miles south of LZ Uplift. I ran the S4 operations from the chopper pad from 1330 hours to 0030 hours during that action. During this enemy encounter, one of my OCS classmates and former roommate was killed, and another was wounded. We had other operational days and nights similar to the ones described here, but they were the expectation. Most days were routine.

As the S4, I had duties from time to time in An Khe. I had supply personnel and a motor pool there to support our battalion needs at Camp Radcliff, so occasional trip there were necessary. The options for going to An Khe were to fly in a C130 or drive in a jeep. For my first official visit, I decided to drive. Driving was a bit slower than taking a plane, but it was a good change of pace. To fly, I had to drive to LZ English (about fifty miles north of Uplift on Highway One) to catch a flight to An Khe. When I drove, I usually went with the supply or motor pool sergeants or the chaplain, sometimes sharing the driving duties. It was about a three-hour drive. I like to drive, and I took every opportunity to do the driving on these trips. The route was south from LZ Uplift on Highway One then west on Highway Nineteen. The roads were generally in good repair, and we could make good speed through the open countryside. At Uplift, I always carried my .45 on my hip, and on trips to An Khe, I had an M-16 and extra clips of ammo as well. Everyone leaving the camp by vehicle was issued weapons and munitions. When I was in Charlie Company, many of our missions weren't far from the base camps or roads that I now traveled. We always traveled the roads with caution, being alert for Charlie all around us.

Every morning, soldiers swept the major highways for mines, but we kept an eye out for suspicious people or activity as we drove. Highway One was busy with military and civilian traffic, but Highway Nineteen had sparse rural traffic. The last twenty miles of the journey was very desolate, and the road went through the lonely An Khe mountain pass. This pass had been the site of previous battles, most notably during the French army's time in Vietnam. I stayed extra vigilant through this pass since it would've been a good place for an ambush. With every turn in the road, I would lean out as far as I could to see what lay ahead, as if we could've turned the jeep around in time to make any difference. It was rather exciting but was no comparison to my first months in Nam. I probably made seven vehicle trips back and forth to An Khe and never encountered any enemy resistance.

Vehicles along Highway Nineteen with An Khe
pass in the distance—Central Highlands

During September, we received information concerning a move for the entire battalion to Camp Radcliff in An Khe as well as scuttlebutt about moving north near the DMZ. The first rumor came to fruition in early October, and I worked closely with Major William E. Murphy, my CO and the battalion executive officer, to develop and implement plans for the move. It was a lot of work, but the move was a success with the entire battalion in place at Camp Radcliff by early October. While there, we kept busy reorganizing the battalion facilities while the infantry companies conducted missions in the surrounding area. I had a few helicopter log operations to supply the infantry units, but most of my companies were encamped within Camp Radcliff and were supplied by truck. In late October, I got orders to develop plans to move north, so Major Murphy and I went to work again. We were to have everything ready within twenty-four hours. As we approached that time, orders came to move the next day, but instead of going to the DMZ, we went back to LZ Uplift to continue operations in the Central Highlands. It looked like I'd get to finish my tour at Uplift.

Shortly after returning, I had a visit from an ARVN company commander stationed at Phu My, south of Uplift. His name was Quan Hai (ARVN first lieutenant) Binh, and he spoke excellent English. The First Cav had approved his visit to learn more about the differences and similarities of our armies. I shared information with him about my time as a platoon leader and about the duties of the S4. He provided a scary picture of life in the South Vietnamese Army. ARVN officers had three men assigned to them twenty-four hours a day. The men would cook, clean, prepare uniforms, and serve as bodyguards. Now this sounded good, but there's more. All officers and higher-ranking NCOs were required to correct their subordinates, of course, but most often they used slapping or punching as the method for correction. Additionally, an officer could kill up to five of his men in a year, usually for insubordination or incompetence. They'd stab or shoot them rather than the court-martial system of the US Army. I'm not sure what would happen if more than five men needed killing in one year, but I'd guess that if you had that many problem men, the men might not be the problem. In that case, the officer would likely get a knife in his back or something like that. He told me of a sergeant ordered by his company commander to kill his lieutenant. During the night, he executed the lieutenant while he was sleeping. I like the American system much better.

CHAPTER 21

Those Magic NCOs

NCOs are the backbone of the army and the key ingredient for the success of S4. One of my responsibilities was the motor pool, which consisted of many jeeps, several supply trucks, and a number of mechanical mules, which were perfect for transporting resupply to the S4 landing pad. The motor pool responsibility included maintaining vehicles, tracking usage and expenses, refueling, etc. The battalion commander and his staff had permanently assigned vehicles. All other vehicle requests were issued based on need or by first come, first served.

Being located at LZ Uplift, we had excellent access to Highway One. To the north was the town of Bong Son, to the south were Phu Cat Air Force Base and then Phu My, and just south of that was Highway 441, which went southeast to Qui Nhon. Qui Nhon had a large naval presence and the army supply depot for our area of operations. Due to the daily mine sweeping, the well-traveled roads were considered safe to drive during the daylight hours. Occasionally, road mines or ambushes occurred, but this was a war. After the morning mine sweep of the highways, an all-clear message was radioed to the units along the roads. That was taken to mean, "Gentlemen, start your engines." Since the convoys would begin rolling, the NCOs could now head out to take care of business.

On one trip to Qui Nhon, several battalion NCOs had taken several jeeps. While the NCOs were taking care of business, someone stole a jeep belonging to the Second/Fifth. When they told me, I was very, very anxious since I was responsible for all the equipment of the battalion. I conducted an investigation and reported the findings to battalion HQ. I was expecting the worst. Instead, the reaction was nonchalant; no one seemed to be that concerned. However, their reaction really didn't bring much relief to my anxiety. It was still lost, and I was still responsible for the inventory. My mess and supply sergeants told me later that afternoon that they would return to Qui Nhon the next day and conduct a search. They told me that they had some leads and thought they could find the jeep.

The next day they left for the army depot, and by afternoon they returned with what they reported as the lost jeep. However, upon inspection, I found the jeep to be in showroom condition, whereas the lost jeep was old and well-worn. I checked the serial number and found it to be correct, so I said to myself, "Since my superiors don't seem to be concerned, don't look a gift horse in the mouth," and I moved on to more important matters. NCOs could perform magic, especially in a combat zone, and I had the proof.

On their many trips for resupply in Qui Nhon, the mess and supply sergeants frequently visited the air force and navy, in addition to visiting the army depot. The depot provided all the basic needs of the battalion, which included a good supply of beer and liquor. The sergeants would requisition their maximum with every trip, and then they'd shop with the air force and the navy, looking for unique items for trade. During the last half of 1967, the army began to receive some LRP food packs, and the air force and navy wanted all they could get. They also wanted C rations, and we had plenty, so trades were frequent. The army's food inventory was basic, but the other services ate higher up the food chain. My mess sergeant often brought back special items, such as T-bone steaks and lobster. What a deal, one case of C rations for one case of lobster. Now, that's magic!

The sergeants would make at least one resupply run a week. Before leaving, they would visit all the officers and NCOs at Uplift to see if they had any special needs. They'd always inquire about my personal supplies, and even if I told them that I didn't need anything, they always brought back something special in the way of alcohol for me. I had to give the stuff away due to my overstock. Ah, such was life in wartime support areas.

Sometimes trading worked to our disadvantage, as was the case with the army's new camouflage hats. The Department of the Army approved floppy-brimmed camouflage hats for field soldiers early during my tour. However, it wasn't until sometime in early fall 1967 that I received news that hats had been ordered for all of the First Cav. Field soldiers only had steel pots to wear, and rear-echelon troops wore the field or fatigue hat. The camouflage hat would be a welcome addition and more comfortable.

Every day we expected to receive information from the supply depot that our shipment had arrived. We waited and waited, and finally one day a report came that the hats for the division had arrived but were missing. How could you lose hats for a whole division? As time went by, we received reports of the camouflage hats showing up for sale at stores and by street peddlers in towns all over Vietnam. Several of my men even purchased them from merchants along Highway One. I had heard reports of the black market being lucrative, but this was my first personal experience with it. The official report from the depot was that they were missing, and we'd get hats when additional shipments arrived. When I left in March 1968, we still didn't have camouflage hats or any word about a future delivery. Someone benefited from these hats; unfortunately, it was not the soldiers who needed them.

CHAPTER 22

The Chick(s) and Egg Thing

The battalion doctor, CPT Douglas Fisk, visited Qui Nhon periodically to collect medical supplies and to visit his counterparts at the hospital there. One day in October, the doctor visited me to reserve a jeep for later in the week and invited the chaplain, CPT Malcolm Brummitt, and me to join him. The city was about an hour south of LZ Uplift. The doctor had been to Qui Nhon many times, and the chaplain and I hadn't been there at all. The doctor thought we might enjoy the sights as well as visiting villages and shops along the way to see how the town folk live, eat, and work in the larger cities and villages of Vietnam. I liked the idea and so did my boss, so off we went.

The three of us left first thing the next morning for Qui Nhon with me driving my jeep. On the way, we stopped at a small village store. The doctor was looking for something, maybe a local herb. The store was cluttered and smelly. While the doctor shopped, I stood near the door, since my infantry training made me cautious when among the civilians. The chaplain followed the doctor. On a chair near the door sat an old woman looking about the store. "Maybe she's the security guard," I thought. When she looked up at me, I greeted her with a nod, and she responded with a toothless smile. Soon, a child came to deliver a bowl of multicolored eggs to the old woman. When the child left, I watched the old woman take one egg, crack it, and peel off the top. To my amazement, a chick with embryonic feathers appeared, covered in a gooey mess of liquid and blood.

I thought, "She's not going to put that in her mouth. Holy mackerel! She's actually eating that thing, or rather gumming it. I sure wish they'd hurry up before I barf." I looked away, but my gaze kept returning to the old woman, and each time she was either chewing, sucking the fluid, taking another bite, or peeling another egg. It freaks me out just writing about it. At last, the doctor was ready to leave, and as we left the store, I pointed out the old woman and her lunch and asked if they'd eaten. I suggested that we could probably get a few for the road. The chaplain grimaced, but for a minute I thought the doctor was going to make a purchase.

In Qui Nhon, the doctor got his supplies quickly, took us to the officers' club for lunch and then showed us the sights of the city. It was the busiest place I'd seen in Nam since my arrival in Saigon back in March. Vendors were set up all along the sidewalks selling goods, and stores were all busy with customers. I kept looking for Charlie, but they all looked liked Charlie. What a war! The doctor had previously advised us not to eat the local food. Many army documents published this advice, since hepatitis was a possible by-product of inadequately prepared food. The doctor, however, didn't heed his own advice and snacked on fried bananas and other treats as we walked the streets. He said that it was a risk, but he was willing to take the chance in order to experience the culture. I couldn't get the image of the toothless old woman sucking on the egg out of my mind, so I abstained.

Looks like a Playboy Bunny Club—Qui Nhon, Central Highlands

Hotel in Qui Nhon——Central Highlands

Along the thoroughfare, we passed a dentist office. We had to look closely at the storefront since it looked more like a museum than an active practice. The office had what looked like a window display of antique dental equipment, mainly old-fashioned drills, pliers, hammers, and other stuff, some of which seemed more appropriate for a machine shop. I thought of the old comedy western movie *Paleface*, with Bob Hope playing a dentist named Painless Potter. I remember the antics of Mr. Hope as he worked on patients, and this dentist had similar equipment. Actually, I think Painless Potter had better equipment than this Vietnamese dentist had. The door to the office was ajar, so we went in to take a closer look. The dentist came out from the back to greet us and was very pleased to show us around his office. The display window turned out to be where he worked on patients. He had a patient waiting, so he gave us a demonstration of dental work in the third world. Scary! We didn't stay there long after he started his work, for fear he might insist on giving us some free dental attention. I did take a few photos, however.

The dentist in Qui Nhon—Central Highlands

We ended our trip by running into several other guys from Uplift. I began to wonder who was minding the store back there. They invited us to join them for a beer, and they knew just the place—an elaborately decorated bar that apparently catered to American soldiers. All branches and ranks of the US military were there along with an equal number of scantily attired young waitresses.

A waitress seated us at a large table in the rear of the bar and took our drink orders. We had about seven men at our table, and soon seven young waitresses delivered our drinks and then sat in our laps and tried to make conversation. You should've seen the expression, or rather grin, on the chaplain's face. This was a surprise to him and me, but the others seemed to have experienced this before—apparently, a normal event when you visited bars in Nam. Until then, I'd never had exposure to Vietnamese bars since the bars in An Khe were in the brothels, which I didn't patronize. It soon became clear that the girls weren't just waitresses. We didn't encourage them, and most of them left our table for the attention of other, more promising, patrons. We had several beers before beginning our journey home. This was a fun and informative trip; I'll never lose the mental image of the toothless old woman biting and sucking the chick out of the egg, and I doubt that the chaplain will forget the chick in the bar. Every time we made eye contact while driving back to LZ Uplift, he gave me a funny little grin.

CHAPTER 23

S4 Helicopters

The First Cav Huey helicopters were marvels of technology, and they were deadly to the enemy when they were equipped with rockets and machine guns. They also could be deadly to the soldiers who flew and rode in them. In my role as the assistant S4, I was responsible for the delivery of supplies to the four infantry companies in the field. I had one and sometimes two helicopters assigned to me for that purpose—one delivery in the morning and one in the evening. The number of helicopters was dependent on the distance of the units to the battalion HQ and to each other. I had a helipad specifically designated for S4, and two soldiers operated the helipad from early morning to early evening. Their quarters were adjacent to the pad so they could respond quickly in an emergency.

The new S4 landing pad at LZ Uplift—Central Highlands

The morning deliveries carried coffee, doughnuts, and emergency supplies. They also brought back trash, discarded clothing, and empty mess cans and utensils from the evening meal. The evening missions carried food and routine supply orders and returned items not needed by the field units. The objective in the evening was to have the last delivery finished before sundown. For most of my stay in S4, I had a captain and a lieutenant assigned to fly the helicopter for daily deliveries. They were nice guys and a pleasure to work with. The chopper(s) would arrive on the S4 LZ at dawn for the morning deliveries. When the operational orders for the day allowed it, battalion personnel could catch a ride on a supply chopper with their early morning delivery and return on their trash pickup trip later in the morning. I'd occasionally go out to survey a company about our services, to determine if they had any needs, and to visit a few friends. Everything generally went well, and it was good for the companies to see support staff and vice versa.

On one occasion when I visited Charlie Company, our return trip was almost a disaster. The chopper captain had complained to me earlier in the week about mechanical issues with his and other Hueys. It seemed that they had had a big turnover of mechanics, and it took more than one visit for repairs to get the job done right. While we were on the ground with Charlie Company, he told me that he'd had his machine in for maintenance several times during the week, yet he continued to have concerns and problems. These comments made me feel a bit insecure since I'd be his passenger on the return trip to Uplift. I suggested that he take his chopper in for additional maintenance at his home base at LZ English as soon as he dropped me off at Uplift. If they couldn't fix the problems, they should send a replacement for the evening deliveries. He said he'd probably finish out the day and put it in for maintenance the next day.

After we left the company site, we flew at several thousand feet over the valley heading toward LZ Uplift. Suddenly, the engine shut down, and the helicopter started to drop from the sky. At first, I thought he was showing off, but then I remembered the conversation we had earlier about the mechanical problems and saw the frantic movements of the pilot and copilot trying to maintain control and restart the engine. I knew we were in trouble. I saw the fast-approaching valley floor below and prayed that they could get the engine going again. It was a rapid and scary descent, but the pilot did a great job controlling the chopper; it dropped straight down without spinning. As the ground was quickly approaching, the engine suddenly started up, and we continued on toward LZ Uplift. The pilot glanced over his shoulder at me with a look of relief on his face. Wow! The First Cav had its own amusement rides, and I'd just had a turn. The drop lasted for seconds but seemed much longer.

At Uplift, I once again strongly encouraged the pilot to put the chopper in for maintenance and shut his operations down for the day. He commented that they were short of pilots, but he'd have someone look at it when he got back to LZ English. He also said that we were lucky to have made it back at all. He had tried several times to restart the engine with no reaction from the engine, and then suddenly it restarted. He couldn't explain the why or how, but we made it. At 1600 hours, they were back on my LZ in the same chopper. Maintenance couldn't find anything wrong, but they were going to give it a thorough going over the next day. They were getting a loaner ready for them to use until their bird was back in service.

That evening they completed their usual deliveries to three of the companies without incident. Their final delivery was to the company on security duty at the Bong Son Bridge. From there, they would fly directly to LZ English, which was a short distance away. They dropped off the resupply at the bridge and took off toward home. I received a radio report from the company guarding the bridge that the resupply chopper had simply fallen from the sky, crashing near the town below. The fire and smoke were visible from LZ Uplift. An element of the company at the bridge went to secure the site of the crash, allowing medical personnel to land and treat the injured. Both pilots had died upon impact; two more friends lost.

On another occasion, Alpha Company ran into an NVA ambush as they patrolled along the coastal mountains. The actions resulted in a number of US soldiers killed and wounded. This happened late one afternoon with most everyone in the battalion monitoring the activities on their radios. A platoon had walked into the ambush, was pinned down, and had stayed in their position throughout the night. Some wounded were medevaced that night, but many remained in place until the morning. During the night, the NVA slipped away, as usual. At dawn, medevac carried the other wounded to the medical unit.

That morning the S4 helicopters made their usual deliveries, giving Alpha Company priority. Because of the encounter with the NVA, I sent two choppers loaded with plenty of supplies and, of course, hot food. After off-loading at Alpha Company, the two choppers returned to Uplift. One of the choppers landed on my S4 helipad, and my men called me to come and help decide what to do with the chopper's load. I arrived at the pad to see a four-foot-high pile of dead soldiers, carelessly tossed, one on top of the other, in the center of the chopper's deck. The captain flying the chopper was new and was insisting that my crew off-load the bodies, but they wouldn't, so he wanted me to order them to do so.

My childhood imaginary killing and being killed is a far cry from the real thing. These men weren't going to jump up and continue playing war.

I'll never forget the sight of those lifeless, bloodied, youthful-looking faces with eyes staring blankly into nowhere. I directed the pilot to the medevac pad, where graves registration was located. He argued a bit, so I told him that he could take them there or carry them with him to his home base, but he couldn't leave them here. He left quickly, in a huff. The other chopper, with our regular crew, had had a load of bodies as well, but they'd gone directly to the medevac pad. After off-loading the bodies, both helicopters returned to my pad to drop off supply discards and pick up supplies for the other companies. The image of those young soldiers piled in the helicopter is permanently etched in my memory.

Earlier I mentioned the warrant officer that was with me on the flight to and from Hawaii and his duties as a medevac pilot at Uplift. We visited often, and in early September he talked to me about a new major assigned as his commander. The major was cocky and had a know-it-all attitude and approach to his job. The major had recently graduated from helicopter school, and this was his first assignment in Nam. Almost every day my friend visited and talked of his experiences with his new commander. He was most concerned about the major taking unnecessary, daredevil risks while my friend was copiloting. The risk-taking was just to show off while flying to and from missions that weren't even combat related. His favorite stunt was to buzz palm trees and other such structures, playing chicken. He'd asked the major to stop, but to no avail. I asked if it was appropriate for him to request a transfer. He responded that he was in the process of doing just that and hoped to get a new assignment within a month.

Several days went by, and I hadn't seen my friend. I decided to visit him at his unit. There, I discovered that he and the major had died a few days earlier while returning from a night medevac mission. Their chopper clipped a palm tree and exploded. The most difficult part of war for me was placing my life in the hands of others, especially the incompetent. In this case, my friend's life wasn't in his owns hands, but in those of a reckless major. They both died needlessly along with their injured passengers.

CHAPTER 24

Love and the Officers of the Round Table

Under normal situations, the duties in a battalion HQ were routine. My daily duties included overseeing the loading and unloading of S4 helicopters in the mornings and evenings, reviewing the status of operations (supply, motor pool, mess, and communications) by visiting with my sergeants and men, reviewing plans and any difficulties that may have arisen, and then having dinner with the battalion commander followed by a staff briefing session. It was a major change from the field, but I stayed busy, although I missed the field duties and the camaraderie with other infantry soldiers.

LTC Joseph B. Love was the battalion commander during most of my stay at LZ Uplift. He was very regular army and played his role similar to the strong commander types that everyone has seen in the movies. Lieutenant Colonel Love had been an infantry private in World War II and received a battlefield commission to lieutenant during the war in Europe. After the war, he received an appointment to West Point and, subsequently, made the military his career.

Our battalion officers' mess tent was standard field grade issue with folding, rectangle, metal tables lined up in rows to fit the dimensions of the tent. The colonel wanted everyone to be face-to-face with him, so he ordered a large, round, wooden table to be made for the mess tent. It was well made and spacious and reminded me of the story of King Arthur and the Knights of the Round Table.

The colonel liked his staff officers to eat the evening meal with him. He used that time to communicate about operations and world events, and he called upon officers at the table and encouraged everyone to participate in the discussions. He was always at the center of the conversation and handled the meal discussions the same way he discussed military matters, with authority and superiority. He often put officers on the spot and embarrassed them. When he called on a person to talk, he expected you to talk knowledgably and logically. If you didn't, he'd sometimes offer an insult or a mild reprimand, like an authoritarian father of the nineteenth century. I dreaded the evening meal, fearful that he'd ask me to talk about something I knew nothing about. In later years, I would welcome the chance to speak in public, but at that time in my life, I was a bit insecure with only a little higher education behind me.

I'd take a little time each day to read, swapping books and magazines with others. I particularly liked to read *Time* magazine, studying articles in case the colonel called on me to talk on some topic. It sounds silly now, but that's the way it was. He inspired fear of humiliation, but he did get me to read a lot about world events, and he was a good combat commander. When guests were coming to dinner, HQ would ask for volunteers to eat with the troops and give up their place at the table. The military teaches you never to volunteer (e.g., the incident from basic training that got me KP duty), but when the call went out to give up a place at the Round Table, I was in line with a lot of company.

Colonel Love added other personal touches to LZ Uplift and the battalion. He ordered the motto, *Ready Sir,* painted with black lettering on a yellow background on stationary objects such as, rocks, barrels, and all vehicles. It did make it easy to recognize our battalion vehicles. If you saluted, you were to respond, "Ready, sir," sounding a bit like OCS. Salutes were not protocol in the field, but in the forward base camps, senior officers expected them. I was personally a bit more relaxed about that policy. One morning, Colonel Love radioed me while I was at the helipad tending to the resupply. He informed me of a tree near his landing pad that he felt was a hazard and ordered me to remove the tree before he returned in an hour. I assembled a few men and told them of the challenge. We removed the tree, leaving a stump big enough to paint yellow and inscribe *Ready Sir* in black. We completed this task and returned to our normal duties long before the colonel returned. The next time I saw him, he smiled and said, "Well done."

Normally, infantry officers wore the insignia of crossed rifles. Colonel Love added his touch by replacing the crossed rifles with crossed sabers, which was the traditional emblem for the US Cavalry. He had the saber patches sewn on all officer fatigues and gave us brass sabers to wear on our khakis and formal uniforms when we returned stateside. It made the Second/Fifth distinct from other units, and everyone liked them. On occasion, people have asked me about that insignia, and it made a good story since I couldn't resist telling about Colonel Love and my adventures with him. He did another nice, unique thing for his officers. He sent an inscribed bugle to our residence in the United States with a card to each family telling about the gift. It was a good idea, and I still have it as a memento from the war.

Lieutenant Colonel Love sometimes seems like a fictional character from the movies. He did then and especially does now as I recall some of the stories. During the fall of 1967, the battalion returned to An Khe for duty, retraining, and a little R & R. The colonel had many plans to train and entertain us since he had his entire battalion all together as his audience. One evening, he ordered all officers and senior NCOs to join him to view an old movie, *Beau Gest*. It's about the French Foreign Legion in the Sahara. The legion encounters conflicts and danger, and, of course, a few heroes emerge. Actually, that could be a description of most movies made about the legion. The colonel gave an overview to highlight some key points about the main hero and the tactics he employed, and then he showed the film. I don't recall anything in particular about it, except the popcorn, even though I'd tried to watch it on TV before I entered the army. It was boring. The colonel praised the movie and seemed to expect us to share his enthusiasm. There was no enthusiasm other than the colonel's, but the event was a topic of conversation for some time afterward.

The colonel also admired GEN George S. Patton and even emulated him. While in An Khe, the colonel visited the sick and wounded in the hospital, and, shortly afterward, a story spread throughout the battalion about his visit to one soldier. The colonel, along with his executive officer and sergeant major, visited a soldier who had no wounds. He inquired why the soldier was there. The soldier replied something about stress, and the colonel lost it. The story goes that he called the soldier a coward, severely dressed him down, and ordered him to report to his company immediately. That incident generated a lot of buzz among the officers and men of the battalion. General Patton was reprimanded for a similar outburst during World War II, but I don't know if Colonel Love was.

While we were in An Khe, the colonel held a court-martial for one particular soldier from Third Platoon of Charlie Company. The soldier was being prosecuted for marijuana use and possession. I wasn't a part of the court-martial board, but I remembered the soldier during his time with Charlie Company. His platoon leader and sergeants indicated that he was frequently insubordinate. He did his own thing while on missions, going into homes and searching villagers' personal items and generally not following directions well. In addition, I think he was the soldier involved in the incident when a VC supposedly tossed a grenade into the camp. I was always suspicious about that incident. I didn't know him personally, but I'd seen him around the battalion, all glassy-eyed and smiling a lot. I knew something was strange and different about him. He was sent to military prison and later dishonorably discharged.

CHAPTER 25

The Chaplain, the Latrines, and a Hot Shower

My best friend at LZ Uplift was Chaplain Malcolm (Mal) Brummitt. He was about thirty and, like me, was married without children. He arrived in Vietnam several months after I did, so he always referred to me as a short-timer. Soldiers started to count days early during their tours in Nam, and short-timers tended to brag to the newer arrivals about how many days they had left. Everyone counted days, and I never came across anyone who couldn't tell you instantly how many days they had left. We all had a year to serve in Vietnam and knew it wouldn't exceed that unless you chose to extend. I looked forward to day zero when I'd return to the source of my rainbow in early March 1968.

I ate breakfast in the mess hall and the command supper with the colonel. The mess hall served a full lunch every day, but after a while I got tired of the heavy lunches, and so did Mal. His wife and former parishioners frequently sent him jars of peanut butter, saltine crackers, snacks, and sweets. He had more than one man could eat, and he graciously invited me to join him for lunch. Actually, he had more than two men could eat. A few crackers with peanut butter and a cookie or two topped off with a beer did the trick for lunch. His quarters were next door to mine, and we visited often, talking of the war, home, and plans for the future. His tent was clearly identifiable by a flag containing a white cross on a blue background.

Chaplain's quarters at LZ Uplift—Central Highlands

When Mal returned from his R & R in Thailand, he brought back a solution to the unused pipe tobacco problem that I mentioned earlier. He had purchased several pipes and gave one to me; so we smoked our pipes, joked, drank a few beers, and enjoyed good conversation almost every evening.

The chaplain used the mess hall tent for his nondenominational church services at Uplift. He also visited the companies in the field to hold services out in the open. One of my former classmates from OCS, 1LT Roger Miller, was in the battalion S2 and had been in construction in civilian life. He wanted to build the chaplain a chapel; however, we had very little room for new construction. Shortly after Colonel Love arrived in the battalion, we moved to Camp Radcliff, and another battalion took over our spot at Uplift. We only stayed one month there, then returned to Uplift. Since it had gotten a bit crowded, we moved to a hill just east of and outside the perimeter of the LZ. This provided a good change of scenery from our previous site as well as the adventure of creating an HQ from scratch. Our former quarters were well-worn, and the bunkers were heavily infested with rats. The rats in my bunker were the size of small cats! Fortunately, we only had one mortar attack while I was in those quarters, so I only had to fight the rats once. Frankly, I preferred fighting Charlie.

Our new home at Uplift was outside the current perimeter, so the companies of the battalion rotated perimeter guard duty until construction of the camp expansion was complete. The Corps of Engineers built the roads and strung the barbed wire. I supervised the layout and building of our new S4 facilities. Rather than dig foxholes for all bunkers, we built an aboveground, sandbagged bunker for the S4 communications center. It also served as my bunker during attacks and as sleeping quarters for my communications team.

Building the new HQ was an enjoyable change of pace, and it came together remarkably fast. Construction included rudimentary latrines and showers, but we added a luxurious, kerosene heater to the S4 shower, which was just behind my quarters (convenient planning). I soon became very popular and the envy of everyone at LZ Uplift. Of course, the colonel had a heated shower as well. One of the first things a soldier coming in from the field wanted was a shower, so, of course, we made the hot shower available to them. My supply sergeant developed a schedule for showering so everyone in S4 got a daily turn. The sergeant traded unscheduled hours for goods and services with other soldiers in the battalion HQ. It wasn't long before other hot water showers begin to appear around the LZ.

The wonderful S4 hot water shower at LZ Uplift—Central Highlands

As anyone who has served in the military and has experienced a field latrine will attest, they stink. They were functional and were constructed and torn down quickly, but the stench could become overwhelming. The cleaning of latrines occurred daily, and periodically the waste required burning. I tried to schedule trips away from the LZ at that time. To accomplish the burning chore, soldiers doused the containers of waste with kerosene and burned the waste to the last bit, which could take many hours, depending on the menu served by the mess hall in the recent past. Burning kerosene alone smells bad, but burning kerosene with human waste would offend a skunk. Smoke clouds developed around the containers. The wind and helicopter activity on the LZ made it virtually impossible to escape the odoriferous bouquet completely. This definitely wasn't a time to be downwind of the containers or to be eating. In addition, it wasn't dignified to see sergeants and officers run screaming and flailing in search of safe air. That was stinky stuff!

Field latrines at LZ Uplift—Central Highlands

The final architectural touch at LZ Uplift came when Lieutenant Miller finished construction of the chapel. Everyone in the battalion contributed in some way but mostly by allowing soldiers to help with construction when they completed their routine duties. The standard infantry battalion chapel is a tent, but since ours was made of wood, our chapel was special and was a very nice addition to the LZ. It was ready on Christmas Eve 1967.

Our chapel at LZ Uplift—Central Highlands

CHAPTER 26

Thanksgiving and Christmas 1967

Thanksgiving and Christmas have always been special times for me. My wonderful family made it that way. Jeanie and I were married on December 30, 1966, so we hadn't spent a Thanksgiving or Christmas as man and wife, but we did spend those holidays together, and that provided wonderful memories. To be in the land of Charlie in wartime didn't make for a fun holiday season, but I did the best I could under the circumstances.

All troops in Vietnam celebrated in one way or another. My battalion was back at LZ Uplift, and for the holidays the field troops in the Second/Fifth were ordered to stand-down, so no missions were ordered on Thanksgiving or Christmas. We flew out special meals to the troops in the field, and at battalion we had traditional dinners, award ceremonies, and other celebrations. We talked, shared stories, and enjoyed our holidays as much as possible.

Nothing particular stands out in my memory about the Thanksgiving week, but just before Christmas, Martha Raye headlined a USO (United Service Organizations) tour at Camp Radcliff. The USO tours are great for morale and are a wonderful change of pace, bringing the familiarity of home to a faraway land. However, in most cases, the troops who were able to attend these events were the rear echelon. The field troops were too busy taking care of business and were rarely in a location to attend. I was in An Khe on business when the show came through, so I attended with several other officers from my battalion. The performance was in the evening, and we decided to get there about forty-five minutes before the start time, thinking we'd get good seats. Boy, were we wrong! We should've gotten there at noon. Our seats were on the grass and were three football fields away from the stage. All I could see were specks on the stage, but the sound was loud and could be heard all around the camp. Apparently, most of the An Khe troops showed up early to claim the good seats. We listened and watched the specks move about on the stage. Oh, well!

We left the show a bit early to get a seat at the O club bar. We didn't want grass seats there too. The cast members and senior officers of the division would visit the club after the show to be wined, dined, and entertained. We got good seats at the bar, and shortly thereafter the entourage arrived with smiles and handshakes all around. We ate a bit, had a few beers, and watched the entertainers eat and drink. Doesn't that sound like fun? It wasn't, but the food, beer, and music were good. The club had a band, and the colonel and Ms. Raye danced a few times. In 1967, Martha Raye was old enough to be my grandmother, so no one seemed to mind that the colonel dominated her attention. At least I had seen a live USO show, and I had seen Martha Raye, a big star from the 1940s and 1950s, and it was something to write home about.

During the week before Christmas, the battalion organized a crew to visit a village near LZ Uplift to spread the Christmas spirit with the people there. The villagers seemed to like the goodies we distributed, but I'm not sure what they thought of our Santa Claus. He arrived at the village sitting on a half-ton truck, tossing candy and waving at the crowd. He also had a few infantry soldiers carrying guns nearby, not the traditional image for Santa's elves. On Christmas Day, we took turns having pictures made around a Christmas tree. A soldier in the battalion had managed to get his hands on a few Christmas decorations and put up a nice-looking tree outside his tent. He also volunteered his Polaroid camera and film for the photos. Mal gave me a small tree, and one of my men gave me some decorations. I put the tree in my tent, and as relatives sent presents and goodies, I placed them under the tree, waiting for the big day. On Christmas Eve, we had a very nice service at our new chapel and another on Christmas morning. The chaplain made his rounds of all the field companies, and late in the afternoon on Christmas Day, a few of us gathered in my tent. They brought the presents they'd received from home, and we all opened our gifts and shared a few liquid spirits, Christmas sweets, and good cheer.

Here comes Santa and his infantrymen, along
Highway One—Central Highlands

*The S4, Lieutenant Soyars, Christmastime at
LZ Uplift—Central Highlands*

During November and December 1967, I had a few personal decisions to make concerning my army career. All of the senior officers in the battalion were graduates of West Point, and, knowing that I hadn't finished college, Colonel Love and Major Murphy talked to me about my future. They wanted to know my plans for college, and I told them I was establishing my residence in Texas and planned to attend school there after I completed my service obligation. They asked if I'd considered a military career. I had, but a college degree was critical to my future, and with the war it would be difficult to complete a degree while still in the military. They asked me if I'd consider West Point. This caught me by surprise. They explained that as graduates, they could nominate promising young officers with good records of accomplishment, and they asked me to consider it.

As a married man, I didn't think a West Point lifestyle would work. After living with my wife for only a little over two months and then being in Vietnam for one year, I couldn't fathom four years of academy life. I was thinking about attending college at the University of Texas in Austin while Jeanie taught public school there. We could have our own place and spend as much time together as school and work permitted. In my letters, I sometimes mentioned that a military career might be worth considering, and her response wasn't favorable, so I decided not to mention this. I eventually thanked Major Murphy and the colonel for considering me worthy of an appointment, but I declined the offer. I did tell Jeanie about this after I returned from Nam, and she said that would have been exciting, and she would've encouraged me to apply. But that wasn't meant to be.

In November, I received advanced orders for my posting after Vietnam—Fort Belvoir, Virginia, to instruct infantry tactics at the Engineer Officer Candidate School there. With my residence established in Texas and plans to attend college there, I requested a change in assignment to Texas. After some time, they gave me new orders as an executive officer in a reserve unit in Waco. Jeanie and I were both satisfied with that, since Waco had a university and was a nice city. Colonel Love and Major Murphy wanted me to take the Fort Belvoir assignment. The colonel had been assigned there earlier in his career, and because of its close proximity to the Pentagon, the assignment was considered choice.

In December, the colonel asked me to consider a short assignment with General Urby as an aide. The position was for six months, which would require me to stay in Vietnam for an additional three months. The exposure and opportunity would be unique. I think they were trying to get me to reconsider my army career, but again I declined, wanting to get home to my wife. I told Jeanie about this, and she agreed that I should come home. Since then, I've thought about these opportunities and the decisions we made and have played the what-if game. While I have no regrets about the path we chose, I was a good officer and appreciated the opportunities offered to me.

CHAPTER 27

Tet 1968

The war was heating up, and I was winding down. At least my calendar of in-country days was getting shorter, and going home was constantly on my mind. The military had been abuzz for months with rumors of an offensive from the north. We now know that the NVA and VC had been building up troop strength all over the south for most of 1967. They were preparing for widespread assaults to coincide with the celebration of *Tet*, the Vietnamese new year, which begins on the second new moon after the winter solstice and is the most celebrated holiday for the Vietnamese people. In 1968, *Tet* began on January 30. We were instructed daily to be alert and prepare for attack at any time and place. The reports of VC and NVA activities were increasing, and skirmishes were more frequent in many parts of the south. On January 30, the NVA and VC launched their first attacks, and the *Tet* Offensive officially began.

At this point, I'd have preferred to be with Charlie Company rather than at battalion HQ. In the field, I'd be equipped, ready, and able to meet the enemy. However, at LZ Uplift the battalion wasn't well-equipped for combat and was questionably able to fight should the need arise. I did have a few combat veterans in my command and knew we could assemble quickly if necessary. I was counting days to go home and really didn't want to see the NVA right now. Jeanie was on my mind.

Chaplain Mal knew that a day or two away from LZ Uplift would be good for him and me, so he arranged for a two-day stay at Phu Cat Air

Force Base, a twenty-minute drive south of Uplift. We could get away from the rumors and the constant updates, and that seemed like a grand idea.

The air force base was known to have stateside-like facilities with plenty of R & R activities. They were also known for fine dining and a well-stocked bar. It really did look a bit like a stateside base, and the quarters were well furnished for a combat zone. We unpacked the few things we had brought with us and were getting ready to go out to find the officers' club when two of my men arrived with a message from Colonel Love to return immediately. Well, I bet that was the shortest R & R ever taken; we were on the road longer than at Phu Cat. The Second/Fifth received orders to relocate to the Quang Tri Province. Our new home would be Camp Evans, which was presently occupied by other units of the First Cav. The camp was about thirty-five miles south of the DMZ. Our major supply point would the city of Quang Tri, which was fifteen miles north of the camp. The city is located on Highway One about six miles west of the South China Sea.

I couldn't believe my eyes when we arrived back at Uplift; soldiers were scurrying around everywhere packing and loading trucks. We'd only been gone a little over an hour, and I thought I'd have a lot of work waiting for me when I returned. Instead, our moving plan had been put in place by my sergeants, and little remained for me to do except to meet with the colonel for a briefing about our deployment and plans once we arrived at Camp Evans.

October through April is monsoon season, so we stayed wet on most days. In preparation for our new assignment, my supply sergeant issued sweaters to everyone in the battalion since the temperature was much cooler in the north. We could only carry essential equipment, so we took one 2½-ton truck, a few mules, a mess tent, and the command HQ tents. The round table didn't make the cut; it stayed behind. Everyone else in HQ would camp infantry style, so we issued ponchos, liners, air mattresses, and other essential field gear. Everything else would be taken to Camp Radcliff and sent to us when military conditions in the north permitted. All of this was ready when I returned to Uplift. On February 18, the battalion was transported via vehicles in convoy to LZ English, where we took C130s loaded with equipment and personnel to Quang Tri City. From there we convoyed south to Camp Evans. The camp was strategically placed halfway between Quang Tri and Hue. As we convoyed, we passed US military vehicles littering the road, all damaged from booby traps or battles.

It was late in the evening when we arrived at Camp Evans. We set up a camp that night for the battalion HQ just outside the perimeter with orders to begin building a permanent HQ in that location the following day. I wrote Jeanie that night telling her of our situation and the weather. It was thirty-five degrees Fahrenheit and rainy. The temperature and weather never improved while I was there. The next day our HQ construction moved at a slow, soggy pace. We didn't have the same level of engineering support that we'd had at Uplift, so my men did much of this work by hand. Without tents, we built temporary poncho shelters and slept on air mattresses on the ground just as I had done in the field with Charlie Company. This new LZ wasn't as strategically located as Uplift, which was on hills next to Highway One with rice paddies all around. It was an ideal space. Our new location had hills in the distance and rolling terrain with a few small shrubs scattered about. We heard constant mortar and artillery shelling and occasional bursts from automatic weapons. The cold drizzle was constant, and the sweaters weren't enough to keep us warm. We drank a lot of hot coffee, layered clothing the best we could, and huddled around campfires. I couldn't stop thinking about my Jeanie and going home. I was too short on days left in-country to be here near the DMZ, but I didn't have a choice.

Supplies were difficult to come by because we had an entire division vying for the same things and only one location to procure them. With only one 2½-ton truck, we almost wore it out running back and forth to Quang Tri City for supplies. Clothing resupply was almost nonexistent; when I could get clothing, I sent it to the field soldiers. I knew from experience how important fresh, dry clothing was to an infantry unit. I stayed wet and muddy the entire time I was at Camp Evans, and many of us had constant sore throats and colds. While we had mess facilities, very few supplies were available, so we had C rations for most meals.

Within a week of our arrival at Camp Evans, the NVA destroyed the bridge over the Thach Han River between the camp and the city, and that shut down our ground supply route completely. The army had to airdrop essentials, such as ammo and C rations, into the camp. Without the bridge, other supplies would have to wait. The new bridge hadn't been completed by the time my orders arrived to return to An Khe. Around February 25, the division put out a call for volunteers to be a part of a ninety-man unit to raid Hue in the darkness to determine if American prisoners were there. The goal was to bring them out safely. If this call had come in early 1967, I wouldn't have hesitated to volunteer, but I only had a few days left in Nam, so my hand didn't go up. They probably wouldn't have let me go anyway due to my S4 status and time left in-country. I'm not sure if the raid took place or not, since I left for Camp Radcliff several days later.

My replacements joined me at Camp Evans to learn the duties and routine of S4. Both were pleased to be leaving the field during this uncertain time. They came from infantry companies in the Second/Fifth; one was a company commander and the other was a platoon leader. They were being rewarded for doing a good job in combat.

As my time to leave drew near, many visitors came to wish me well on my journey home and with my future life in the States. Most of the men expressed good-humored envy, especially because of the escalation of hostilities. I remembered all those who'd left before me and how I'd felt at that time, still counting the many days I had left in-country. I didn't rub it in, though. It was a grand feeling, knowing that my time there was ending, and a new chapter in my life would soon begin.

One evening, Chaplain Mal asked me to come with him while he visited one of my men concerning a problem he was having at home. Mal said he felt it was important that I be there while they talked. I thought this was odd but joined him anyway. Upon entering the soldier's tent, I was welcomed with a round of "For He's Jolly Good Fellow," a cake with many candles, and the smiles on the faces of the men who had followed me to S4 from Charlie Company. They'd bought a gift, which I cherish to this day. It's a plaque with the First Cav emblem, a combat infantry badge, flags of the United States and South Vietnam, and the following message:

"With high regard and deep affection, we present this plaque to LT T. R. Soyars our loyal leader and good friend. S4 Section, 2nd/5th Cav, 1st Air Cav Division." It was a wonderful surprise and event, which meant a lot to me and to my men as well. I could see the pleasure in their smiles and hear it in their voices. I hardly knew what to say, but everyone waited as if they expected a speech. I said a few words but not near enough. This event and these men were so very important to me. I hope I conveyed that to them. We enjoyed the party—eating cake, drinking a few beers, and talking about our plans when we returned to the States. It was fun but a little bittersweet since we were ending a significant chapter in our lives. All of them rotated back to the States intact within several months after I left, including Mal.

All of my men in Vietnam were special, but these men had become extra special comrades in the field and as workmates and friends in S4. We were young soldiers in combat, and that is a special bond. My experience in Nam was one of great pride and importance to my life and development, and I know that many of the men who served with me felt the same. The bond and emotion found among those who fight front line in any war is hard to comprehend by those who have never experienced it.

On the morning of February 28, 1968, I was ordered to return to Camp Radcliff and prepare for my departure to the States. *Tet* was in full swing, with elevated fighting occurring throughout Vietnam, and I was more than ready to get home. I went by helicopter to Quang Tri. From there I flew in a C130 south. I don't know where we landed, but I spent one night at a military installation near the South China Sea and departed for An Khe the next morning. When I landed at the camp, I felt a great relief; I was leaving the war behind. At Uplift and Evans, we were always under the threat of attack and were hit by mortars and small arms frequently. Camp Radcliff was established in 1965 and was very secure, with no enemy activity reported there in many months.

I had only a few days in An Khe. My first task was to process all paperwork with headquarters, turn-in my weapons, collect my duffle containing my few personal items, and get my orders to fly to Cam Ranh Bay. I stayed in the camp officers' quarters near the airfield and was within walking distance of the main O club. On the night before my departure for Cam Ranh Bay, I knew I wouldn't sleep much, so I teamed up with several other officers and spent the evening at the club. I'm sure we bored each other to death since all any of us talked about were our plans for when we got home, but the beer was cold, and it passed the time.

We didn't stay late at the club since our flight was early the next morning. Surprisingly, I went to sleep quickly. Around 0200 hours, I was awakened by sounds of a mortar attack on the airfield—yes, the one near my sleeping quarters. The same field my flight to Cam Ranh Bay was scheduled to use. The entire camp went on alert, and all officers in my quarters ran to a nearby bunker. None of us had weapons. We had turned them in to our battalions as part of our processing for departure, so we felt a bit helpless. The mortar attack lasted about a half hour, and then quiet engulfed the camp. We stayed in the bunker for several hours before the camp called off the alert, and we were allowed to go to our quarters for a few hours of sleep. We were told that the air field would be thoroughly inspected at first light, but a preliminary inspection indicated that the airfield hadn't received major damage. My flight left on schedule the next morning.

As I mentioned before, Cam Ranh Bay was a beautiful beach resort on the South China Sea, and the air force base there was a real showplace. It really looked like a stateside facility. Although it was an air force base, the army also had a presence there. My flight got to the Bay in the late morning. I checked in and got instructions for my early-morning flight and directions to the officers' quarters, mess hall, and base exchange. The rest of the day, I was on my own.

I got together with the other officers from An Khe, and several officers from other units joined us. We disposed of our remaining military script by first visiting the base exchange to spend as much script as we could. I bought luggage and some things for Jeanie, saved enough for the O club and as keepsakes, and converted the balance to US dollars. Most of the afternoon, we drank beer and played cards at the club. All of us were getting into the stateside attitude prevalent at the Bay and were looking forward to getting on the plane and going home.

Since all the An Khe men were lacking sleep because of the attack the night before, we didn't stay late at the club and turned in early. Again around 0200 hours, mortar fire jarred me awake. The base was put on alert and, once again, to the bunkers we ran. Cam Ranh Bay was a country club, and I couldn't imagine the place having a lot of combat gear around. Several of us were infantry, but there wasn't a weapon in sight. We talked about getting some weapons and a few enlisted men so we could help defend the bunker, if needed. We halfway joked about fully armed NVA storming the bunkers as we watched helplessly, armed only with a deck of cards and some US dollars.

One of the staff members in the bunker with us said this was the first attack ever on the military facilities at Cam Ranh Bay; however, because of *Tet*, military installations all over Vietnam were anticipating events like this. We never saw the enemy, and the attack ended as quickly as it started. Again, we slept very little.

Ready, set, get on the airplane, and hurry before Charlie sees me. I felt like I must be on their most wanted list, and they were chasing me down like bounty hunters. I really wasn't paranoid; I was just humoring myself, I think. I finally left Vietnam around 0600 hours on March 6, 1968. We had a good flight. I fell asleep shortly after takeoff and woke up as we were landing in Tokyo. Tokyo was our refueling stop before heading across the Pacific and was also the site of the large US military hospital. Our plane was carrying wounded who were destined for this hospital. I'm fortunate that I didn't have the hospital experience that so many other soldiers of that era had.

We deplaned for about an hour and only had time to explore the international in-transit terminal in Tokyo. It was dark when we landed, so I couldn't see much of the surrounding landscape. While in the terminal, I thought I saw Charlie and thought, "Good grief, he's everywhere." Again, I was just entertaining myself. These people were Japanese, not Vietnamese. Maybe I was paranoid!

I don't remember much about my long flight across the Pacific. It's no wonder, since the stewardesses pushed the drink carts continuously up and down the aisles, serving free alcoholic beverages, compliments of Uncle Sam. After a few drinks, I slept a long time on the flight home.

CHAPTER 28

Home at Last

Well, Seattle wasn't home, but at least I was on US soil, where my rainbow had begun in March 1967. I felt joy and excitement when we landed and deplaned. I wanted to kiss the ground as some soldiers did, but I preferred to save my kisses for Jeanie. The terminal was full of returning GIs from Vietnam, but we were largely ignored by the public—the exception being a few family members greeting returning soldiers and a few war protestors carrying signs saying "Baby Killers" and "Stop the War." I only stayed in Seattle long enough to catch another flight south to Los Angeles.

Jeanie and her dad had driven from San Antonio to Los Angeles in her Sunbeam Alpine sports car. She and her dad had stayed a couple days with a friend of his from the military; her dad was a World War II and Korean War veteran and was retired from the air force. I flew from Seattle to LA, where Jeanie and her dad were waiting for me at the airport. I can't express the way I felt when I saw and embraced her. This was the first chapter of the rest of my life, and I knew that by the final chapter it was going to be a best seller. My first desire, after many kisses and other such hanky-panky, was a cold glass of milk. The army only had powdered milk in Nam, and, to me, it wasn't drinkable. I don't remember anything special about that first day other than seeing Jeanie and drinking my fill of milk. We were young, in love, ready for some fun, and making up for lost time. We played in LA for a few days, visiting Disneyland, Universal Studios, Knott's Berry Farm, Beverly Hills, and many fine restaurants.

After LA, we headed east. We visited many sites along the way, but our next major destination was Sierra Blanca, New Mexico. Jeanie had rented a chalet at a ski resort there, and since neither of us had skied before, we were in for another adventure. On our way to Sierra Blanca, we drove through the White Sands National Park and couldn't resist stopping and playing awhile. If we could ski the sand dunes, the snow should be a piece of cake.

Fourth honeymoon, at White Sands, New Mexico

Sierra Blanca was a picture postcard, including a very large Saint Bernard who greeted us at the lodge office. However, he was not friendly and barked and growled a lot. I wonder if he was Cujo's grandfather since he had a similar attitude. Our chalet was cold, but once we got the fire in the fireplace going strong, it was comfortable. For the rest of that day we played inside and outside and enjoyed ourselves very much.

The next day we signed up for ski lessons. They showed us all the correct things to do with those long pieces of wood and eventually turned us loose on the baby slope. Yes, baby slope. I was glad my men from Charlie

Company couldn't see me. My first major obstacle was to ride the lift. Jeanie got on and headed up the slope. I got on and fell off. The instructions were to place the skis in the previous ski tracks and let the lift push you to the top. Somehow, I misunderstood and sat on the push bar, which immediately tipped and dumped me into the snowbank. Next, I tried to manhandle the ski tracks, and that forced me back into the snowbank once again. I fought that thing several times before finally getting to the top of the baby slope, my clothes covered with snow. I wanted to go back to the chalet to get my medals so people wouldn't think I was a wimp. Boy, the baby slope was high up, at least to us. Jeanie took off slowly, and I followed. A bit of a daredevil, she decided to give it some gas and took off down … I wish I could say down the slope, but she didn't go far before her skis and legs got into an argument. The skis won. Poor Jeanie looked like a pretzel, all twisted and in pain on the ground, unable to move. A Good Samaritan with skiing experience came to help her untangle. I moved as fast as I could, which wasn't very fast at all, to her side. I kept looking for that Saint Bernard with the keg of whiskey around his neck, but he never came. That was probably a good thing since he would have eaten her instead of rescuing her. Poor Jeanie hobbled down the slope as if she had something large stuck up her rear. It's a funny memory, but it wasn't so funny at the time—no more hanky-panky for a while! Our skiing was over for this trip. We lounged around the chalet and lodge a bit then decided to hit the road since Jeanie couldn't ski, and I didn't want to go without her.

Our next stop was Fort Bliss in El Paso, Texas, to visit one of my friends from Vietnam. He was working, and we were unannounced. We didn't stay long, but it was good to see him and to catch up. The drive from El Paso to San Antonio is lo-o-ong and boring, but we had fun talking, singing, sharing, and stopping along the way to see the flora and fauna. We were anxious to begin our life together wherever military, college, or civilian life took us. Thus, one journey ended and another began.

One of the first things Jeanie and I did when we got back to San Antonio was drive to Waco to visit my new unit, to get teaching applications for Jeanie, and to check out available living arrangements. We visited the reserve unit first so I could introduce myself to the commander, and I'm glad we did that first. He greeted me with, "Didn't the Pentagon reach you?" Surprised, I responded, "No, sir." They had consolidated reserve units and no longer had a position for an XO. In fact, they had a number of surplus positions, including the CO's. The Pentagon wanted to talk to me about assignments in other parts of Texas. So back we went to San Antonio.

When we arrived at Jeanie's parents' home, her mom gave me a message to call the Pentagon; a major had called a number of times trying to reach me. I knew what it was about and called immediately. The major explained the situation at Waco and was very accommodating. He asked where I'd like to be assigned. I told him of my desire to attend school in Texas, and school location would depend on where my wife could obtain a teaching position. Talking through the locations of major universities in Texas, he asked, "What about San Antonio?" I replied, "Why not; I'm already here." Therefore, I became an executive officer at the Fourth United States Army Headquarters at Fort Sam Houston. Jeanie and I were relieved to finally settle on an assignment and looked forward to the last months of military life. My military obligation would end in September 1968.

Adjusting to life back in America was an easy and exciting transition. Before I went to Vietnam, I slept very deeply and was difficult to wake up. Vietnam cured me of that. Jeanie tells of a lazy morning in San Antonio shortly after I returned home. We'd slept late, and some kids in the neighborhood set off some firecrackers. I rolled from the bed and to the floor in one fluid motion. Looking down at me from the bed, she had a good laugh. Sheepishly, I realized I wasn't in Nam anymore; some habits are hard to break. I had a few other incidences, but they diminished with time.

While I was overseas, Jeanie purchased a Kodak Carousal slide projector and many slide trays in which to organize my photographs as they came to her. I was anxious for a peek. Jeanie and her family had already viewed the slides but wanted to hear the stories that went with them. We spent several evenings going through the slides and talking about the events related to each one. It was difficult to talk about certain stories and people without some emotion. I thought as time went by it would be easier, but it seems to have gotten worse, especially around Memorial Day and Veterans Day.

My visit to the Vietnam Veterans Memorial in Washington, DC, was particularly emotional, but I noticed that I wasn't the only one affected. I think writing this book has helped; I've somehow released some of the pressure from within by putting my memories on paper. However, there will always be the emotional memories of those I knew and lost in combat.

While stationed at Fort Sam, Jeanie taught English at a junior high school, and I played administrator to a headquarters company. Of course, stateside duty was no comparison to my Vietnam experiences, but I enjoyed the assignment. During the spring and summer of 1968, Jeanie and I talked a lot about having a family. We wanted a child, but with me leaving the military and starting school full time in the fall, a child would be difficult for us. The army came to the rescue during late summer by dangling a promotion to captain and guaranteeing my stay in San Antonio if I'd extend and stay in the army for one more year. I accepted the offer and took command of the Twenty-fifth Transportation Company (back to the motor pool again). Our first child was born in April 1969. She cost us a total of seven dollars for the civilian birth registration. You can't beat those military medical benefits. In addition, during that period, I attended a community college in San Antonio, accumulating some core curriculum requirements for a degree.

I resigned my commission from the army in September 1969 to attend college full time. Before graduation, Mobil Oil Corporation recruited me to work in its Dallas office. After graduation, we moved to Dallas, where I worked in the old Magnolia Petroleum Building (home of the flying red horse). My Mobil career provided many great career and personal growth opportunities as well as some very interesting assignments. I held positions in Dallas, New York, Virginia, and Africa. We had two more children, a boy and a girl, and my family moved and lived with me in all those work locations. Our adventures and travels were extensive, and we have fond memories of my career with Mobil.

I retired from Mobil in 1995. I ran my own business for a while but didn't enjoy it, so I got out of that. Shortly afterward, I obtained a position with a local college in Dallas, where I plan to stay until I cease having fun.

EPILOGUE

When my country called me to serve in 1965, America was committed to the cause of freedom in Vietnam and to helping the people there achieve it. The United States military draft was the law then, and the Vietnam War was part of US policy at that time. We were drafted or volunteered, were exempt or sought ways to be exempt, or left the country. Most took the first option. Ironically, many of those who served weren't even eligible to vote for the lawmakers or the laws that governed them. We merely answered the call as our fathers before us had done.

The first combat soldiers arrived in Vietnam in 1965, so when my tour begin, the American sentiment about the war was mixed but not volatile. During my year in Vietnam, the tide of American opinion deteriorated, and the media and the American people, at least the most vocal, began demanding an end to the war. I've read that our government never saw its role in Vietnam as one to achieve a victory for the United States. Its role was to help the South Vietnamese forces achieve their victory, and that proved to be impossible. During my tour and interaction with the South Vietnamese military, I never saw the passion, confidence, or rhetoric that demonstrated a commitment to win the war. The US military demonstrated far more passion and commitment, and the South Vietnamese seemed content to let the United States lead the way. When Congress and the president ended US involvement in Vietnam in 1975, the South Vietnamese military was left to fight alone, and the fight was short-lived.

The American casualties during the war were significant. Over fifty-eight thousand were killed and over three hundred thousand were wounded.

Of the more than 2.5 million who served, trauma and stress have marked some forever. Those who lost their lives, those loved ones left behind, and those who have suffered from the experience deserve a nation's thanks and prayers. I lost classmates and friends during the war and know the sorrow well. I have wept for the lives they gave and for the lives they never lived, cut short by their sacrifices in war.

Unlike prior wars, Vietnam veterans returned home without accolades. The following is from an e-mail I sent to the student programs director at Mountain View College after she invited me to attend a Veterans Day celebration at the college in 2007. The message sums up the feelings shared by me and other veterans of the era:

> As a thank-you for today's event, I want to share a few thoughts about being a combat veteran of Vietnam.
>
> A Vietnam War veteran never got anything but boos and hisses back in the 1960s, and somehow our efforts and sacrifices seemed to be looked upon differently than veterans from other wars. Our pride and patriotism during Vietnam equaled that of other wars; we were brave and some died, and we sacrificed; yet we never heard the cheers or got the thank-you.
>
> My experience in Nam was one of great pride and importance to my life and development, and I know that many of the men who served with me felt the same. The bond and emotion found among those who fight front-line in combat in any war is hard to comprehend by those who have never experienced it. And we often share a never-ending tear for those we left behind.
>
> Events like this one today help ease some of the pain of the past as well as serve to motivate pride and patriotism in everyone participating.
>
> I received a 'Thank-You' today! I thank you for this event, and most importantly, for extending a personal invitation to me.

We received an unwelcome upon returning home; we were pitied, even looked down on, by protesters. This must never happen again. We who serve should be honored. There is no shame in serving when your country calls. By the way, you may notice that I refer to the *war*. Congress calls the US involvement in Vietnam a *conflict* rather than a war. This may have been a logical and necessary approach in international politics. Nevertheless, for those who fought there, it was a war, and we all called it that and still do.

When I returned to the United States, I found the atmosphere shocking. I'd read the news reports about the growing antagonism and the escalating costs of the war, but I was disheartened by the general reception I personally received when in uniform and on the streets of America. The looks weren't of respect or awe for my uniform and the medals I wore but of disdain and repugnance. Many negative stories about the war have been spread throughout America; the positive stories were neither wanted nor believed. Most of the negative experiences I encountered because of the Vietnam War came after I returned to the United States, and that was from the public and the news media. Think about that! I was fortunate to have family and friends to honor me, and that made all the difference.

People sometimes asked me if I felt I'd wasted my time by serving in the army and spending a year in Vietnam. I quickly replied, "Absolutely not." I'm proud of my service, and it was my duty then as it had been the duty of my forefathers. Most people didn't think or care about the duty of young men during the Vietnam War era. I am amazed at how the media influenced people of that era and how some people influenced the media. Loudly and clearly, we heard the negative side of the Vietnam War, but I'm pleased that I can share a realistic and more positive side to this conflict.

My wife and I had another experience with the news media and its inflammatory influence on the public while living in Zimbabwe during my career with Mobil Oil Corporation. We met many wonderful people there, but sometimes they would ask about living in such a dangerous place as the United States. The news in Africa about America was of crime, gangs, shootings, drugs, car chases, etc. They were fearful about vacationing in the United States. My wife and I shared with them what our friends and family expressed to us before coming to live in Zimbabwe. We all paid close attention to the media coverage about that area of Africa. The only news was political turmoil, war, crime, shootings, and kidnappings. This is the news that sells. The US media painted a negative image of life in Zimbabwe, and the African news offered a negative image of life in the United States. We had only positive experiences in Zimbabwe and assured our African friends that life in America was wonderful and safe. Anywhere you go you can find what you look for. It's largely dependent on your attitude and perspective. The media can and has influenced public opinion, as did some authors who wrote about the Vietnam War.

My military training provided a great foundation for my future. US military training is the best! It emphasizes discipline, dedication to tasks, teamwork, loyalty, and leadership. What a good foundation for college, career, and life. I've continued to develop and use skills learned from the army in every job and aspect of my life. I also learned to take better care of my underwear—actually, Jeanie gets the credit for that. While I inherently seemed to understand leadership, my OCS training and real-life experiences in Vietnam taught me how to be successful as a leader. I encourage every young adult to consider the opportunities offered by the military. They should read chapters three and four of this book to get a feel for life during military training. Actually, when they read my book they might think the army is the only option available, but it's acceptable to consider other branches. I also recognize that military life isn't for everyone, but for those who give it their all, it can make a big difference in their lives and in their futures.

I offer my best wishes for a safe journey to American servicemen and servicewomen everywhere. Always remember to honor and respect those who serve on active duty, those who are veterans, and especially those who gave their lives for the cause of freedom.

Peace. It does not mean to be in a place where there is no noise, trouble or hard work. It means to be in the midst of those things and still be calm in your heart—Unknown

APPENDIX A

Excerpts from Letters

Jeanie wrote to me daily, and I reciprocated when conditions permitted. She lived for mail delivery and I for mail call. In the summer of 1967, Jeanie and her family were at her parents' lake property for a long weekend. The property was between Austin and San Antonio, but Jeanie drove to her parents' house in San Antonio on mail days to collect the mail and then return to join the family. We both became depressed when several days would pass with no mail, and we reflected this despondence in our letters. Of course, the melancholy was temporary since soon three to five letters would arrive, and our morale went sky high. As time passed, we both knew that letters were on the way, and we learned to have more patience. We had only been married for a couple of months before I left for Vietnam and it was a tough year for both of us.

In many of my letters, I tried to give Jeanie descriptive information concerning my location. She had a map of Vietnam and attempted to track my location and movement the best she could. I was prohibited from writing about operational topics, but I tried to give her a flavor of my daily experiences and my location. I do not include excerpts from all my letters. I have used only those that I believe add to my war stories and the more poignant story of Tim and Jeanie. Periodically, I insert excerpts from Jeanie's letters to me to show the perspective of war from the home front. While her letters do not contain war stories, they do tell the story of a young wife left to wait for her husband's safe return. Jeanie was the most important part of my life while I was in Vietnam, and she was always on my mind. As you will see from the letters, she felt the same.

The following excerpts were reproduced faithfully as they were written. The regular font excerpts are from my letters, and the italic font excerpts are from Jeanie's letters:

10 March 67–Arrived in Hawaii 7:30 am … only one-third of the way to Nam. Almost caught the sun, but while we were landed there, it got away…. I'll write you soon. Be good. I love you bunches, Timmy

10 March 67–This year's going to be awful, and this is only the first day…. I miss you so…. This afternoon I re-arranged my room and packed your clothes…. Daddy's brother will visit soon and the whole family is going to Houston to see a pre-season game against the Yankees…. Everyone says they wish you were here to go with us…. My love is always around you. I cherish every little memory and possession of yours…. I love you, your Gigi

12 March 67–I arrived in Vietnam at 0500 hrs. The temperature was a humid 90°. We exchanged our U.S. currency for military script, and next went to the officer's quarters at the 90th Replacement Battalion, Bien Hoa, forty miles northwest of Saigon and ten miles west of Long Bien…. I was told it would be about two and one-half days before I get an assignment…. I haven't slept much and this letter is sloppy and rambling…. If you thought driving in New York City was bad, you should have been in the convoy to Bien Hoa. There are no traffic rules, and everyone drives offensively. The place looks like a huge junkyard…. I'm tired and sleepy…. The hardest part of the whole trip was trying to stop thinking about you–impossible. Gigi, I love you more than I can express in words.

12 March 67–You only have been gone three days, but it feels like a year…. I'm really an infantry wife. I've got a large detailed map from National Geographic on the wall, bordered by smaller colored maps, the Infantryman's Prayer and The Man with the Rifle. Of course, your pictures, mug and grenade are set out too. Someone said that being separated so early in our marriage would be easier to take than if we'd gotten use to each other longer. They sure didn't know what they were talking about.... It wasn't Sherman who said, War is hell; it was Sherman's wife.... I love you and I'm at your side constantly.

13 March 67–Yesterday I told you I was sleepy. I went to sleep around 1600 hours and woke at 2400 hours. I was covered with mosquito bites.

13 March 67–I got your postcard from Hawaii. Wish I was there with you.... I can hardly wait till your letters start arriving.... I am so proud of my combat platoon leader, my husband who is fighting for me and for the things that we believe in.... My never ending love.

14 March 67–Yesterday afternoon I got my orders. I am scheduled to leave at 1445 hours today for An Khe to be assigned to the 1st Cavalry. I don't know what I'll be doing, but it's not hard to guess. Let me tell you what happened when we left Hawaii. I fell asleep. There were three seats on each side of the plane. I was sitting in the center between two Signal Corps second lieutenants. I guess I slept for about seven hours. When I woke, they told me that I kept trying to cuddle. One said he almost woke me when he thought I was going to kiss him. See, you taught me bad habits.... We left for Bien Hoa airfield at 1445 hours, but did not take off until 1815 hours. We flew a cargo plane (luxury seats on the floor) to An Khe.

14 March 67–Got my first letter today and it was wonderful.... I had ten calls about buying your GTO today.... Keep your fingers crossed.

15 March 67–I will be platoon leader second platoon. I met my CO last night here in An Khe. He's a West Point graduate, and he seems all right.... We will be working in northeast Vietnam in the rice paddies, villages and mountains. The operation is called Pershing.... The CO said it would take about thirty days for your letters to catch-up with me, so please keep sending them. I love you and miss you. Be good. I'll write again soon. Love you bunches.

16 March 67–Wrote a letter to my mother and sister yesterday. I told them that I would not have much time to write once I am in the field. So, the only letters I'll make time to write are to you. Please keep my mother and sister informed. I've taken pictures at Bien Hoa and here in An Khe. I'll finish the role today and send them off to Kodak.... Last night at the officers club, Captain Markham showed slides he bought in Hong Kong ... nude slides with captions.... This place is not that bad! He told me I should plan R&R after I've been here six months. Let's start making those plans. I love you bunches. Your favorite husband.

17 March 67–How are you today Sweetie Britches? So far, I haven't had a rainy day. The temperature is in the 80s during the day and 60s at night.... I'll join my company soon. They are operating around Bong Son and in a few weeks will move into the An Lo Valley. Bong Son is northeast of An Khe on the South China Sea. In my Fort Polk papers I have a map of Vietnam if you would like to keep track of my movements.... No letter yet.... Maybe Uncle Sam will find me soon.... Love you bunches, Timmy

18 March 67–Another day without a letter.... I know you will have very busy days, but please try to drop a card or short message. No news from you is miserable.

18 March 67–In January the 5th Cav was operating in the An Lo Valley. During their first week of operations they found a small VC PX. It included four sewing machines and thousands of black pajamas and khaki uniforms. The labels on the uniforms said made in Saigon and San Antonio, Texas. Intelligence believes that they came from a black market source in Texas.... It looks like you've got VC in San Antonio.

19 March 67–Last night I went to the main Officers Club at An Khe with two other officers.... We had steak & baked potato, a real fine meal. They had a band and floorshow. The floorshow was really great ... the Korean Rockets.... The only officers that really get to use the club are doctors,

warrants and other officers assigned to the fort in An Khe... I hope you got the Easter flowers and card. I love you more and more every second. Be sweet and send me some kisses.

20 March 67–I went through my second day of Remount Training yesterday, and we rappelled from helicopters. The first time I didn't jump right, and the non-commissioned officer in charge said, "Sir, you didn't do that right. Drop and give me ten and try it again, Sir." One-two-three-four-five, etc. I said, "Thank you for the push-ups, Sergeant." It was fun.... Tomorrow we go on patrol in the territory around An Khe and spend tomorrow night camped out in the bush.

20 March 67–I love you so much; I'm in pure misery without you. Your safety is all I think about. You can't image how comforting it was just to sit near you in the car or the movies.... It's amazing how fast you take these small things for granted. You never realize they exist until they're taken away. Be careful and love me.

22 March 67–We finished Remount training last night. Thirty-four other green troops and I camped out under the stars and played war.... While we were putting out trip flares and claymore mines, one of my squad leaders spotted a VC. I took six men with me to look over the situation but found nothing. It's a good thing we didn't search further for the VC last evening since in the morning we found booby traps that he had left for us.... No one was hurt.... I'm still waiting for your letters ... maybe soon.... I love you and miss you.

22 March 67–You don't know how happy you made me today. I got four letters. I hope my letters reach you soon. I write everyday.... I finally have you pinpointed on my map. It took time to find Bong Son and the An Lao Valley.... You are the most wonderful thing that ever happened to me.... All I think about is you and me in Hawaii.

23 March 67–I arrived at LZ English at 0900 hours this morning, and I am sitting around waiting for the battalion commander to fly with me to join Charlie Company.... I don't think I'll be able to buy too many items native to the country. I'll probably be in the field until R&R, and there really isn't anything to buy.... Send cookies and pictures.... Boy, oh boy, I can't wait until R&R.... Love you bunches.

24 March 67–Shortly after I finished yesterday's letter, the battalion commander arrived to fly with me to join my company ... arrived around 1800 hours.... I have a fine platoon sergeant and excellent squad leaders.... The platoon has thirty-three men; a bit under strength, but it will be easier to control.... Today we conducted a mission into the valley ... covered only about three hundred fifty meters, but we found three tunnels and a well with a cave in it. Believe it or not, but I really enjoyed today.... I'm told that you don't find Charlie until he wants you to.... We are busy tonight, so I'll write you tomorrow. Be good. I love you bunches.

25 March 67–Well, I'm really having a swinging Saturday night. I'm lying on an air mattress in my platoon command post (two ponchos fastened together on sticks and tied to the ground) on a hill overlooking a village and rice patties, swatting mosquitoes, using a flashlight, and writing my Gigi a letter. How's that for excitement.... This morning we made an air assault three miles from our previous location. After we landed, the company went in one direction and I took my platoon on another air assault into the mountains. We didn't find any VC, but we found a number of booby traps.... 1st Cav is a great assignment because the air mobility seems to be only a call away.... These are the greatest bunch of guys I have worked with. Each man knows his job and does it.... Tomorrow is Easter. I hope you got the flowers I sent.... Happy Easter ... bunches of love and kisses.

25 March 67–It's so hard to live on memories. Of course, your letters help tremendously; that's what will get me through this year. But they just aren't a sufficient substitute for my Timmy.... I know you are with me in mind and soul, but I sure am partial to having your body around as well.… I love you, sweetheart.

26 March 67–Good morning Baby, I hope the Easter Bunny came to see you. He brought me two Easter eggs. Every morning the battalion tries to bring us coffee and donuts. This morning we had colored hard-boiled eggs.… I am usually in a hurry when I write, so I don't get to really explain everything. This morning we don't leave on a mission until 1030 hours, so I have a little more time. Most mornings we try to start patrolling around 0800 hours and finish up about 1600 hours, if all goes well. We do very little night patrolling. The night before last I took my platoon out just before dark and set-up an ambush. It was an ideal ambush site, but Charlie didn't come by.… This command really makes me feel great. Already the men, most with a lot more experience and age than me, look to me for guidance and leadership. It's really great.… When I am patrolling, the time goes fast, but my thoughts are first with you and second on the safety of my men … eleven and a half months to go but only five and a half to R&R.… I haven't had a shower in five days now–I should be really ripe in five and one-half months … getting close to assault time.… Be good, stay sweet and pretty. I love you bunches and bunches.

27 March 67–Well, our air assault didn't turn out bad. We thought we were going into the area to cordon and search. Instead we went back to LZ English to secure the base.… I set up a command post, and we all had a little beer party, compliments of the battalion.… This morning I received an order to take fifteen men to patrol an area where the Air Force lost two 750 lb. bombs. We found one, and I sent six men to look for the other while I waited for a Chinook to come and lift the bomb out. This afternoon, we are scheduled to assault back into the mountains of the An Lo Valley to act as a backing force.… Hoping today I'll get a letter.

28 March 67–Today, we are operating in the mountains and serving as a blocking force for other companies of the battalion operating in the An Lo Valley below.… No mail yet.

28 March 67–I visited the school district today to apply for a substitute position and they want me to teach 5th grade, and the elementary school is near Mama and Daddy's house.... I think I'm going to take it.... I worry about you so much, but I guess that's the plight of an infantry wife. I'd rather be a rich executive's wife. But I'd be your wife if you collected garbage. Write soon and love me.

29 March 67–My morale is really sky high today. This afternoon we walked from the mountains to the valley below, about three thousand meters. The temperature is in the 100s, but when our supplies arrived, I got my first two letters.

30 March 67–Last night we had a hectic night. We were set-up in a two-platoon perimeter. At 2200 hours a VC snuck up on third platoon's position and threw a hand grenade. No one was hurt. The third platoon was jumpy and fired for almost two hours. I put out an order to my men that if anyone fired, they better have a dead VC at the end of the bullet. There was no more firing from the second platoon, and finally the third platoon caught on and ceased firing.... This morning we moved to a mountain, which provided an excellent location to observe the valley, but it was covered with brush so we had to clear it. We chopped for about four hours to create a half-ass LZ and perimeter.... I received two letters today. They were great, simply great.

30 March 67–This getting up at 7:00 am is for the birds. I came home from school today and went to sleep until 7:00 p.m. I'm a person who needs lots of sleep.

31 Mar 67–Only three weeks—it's unreal.... It seems like years ago that we said goodbye at the airport.... I had no idea that being away from you would be so awful. When I get you back, I'll never let you leave again.... I brought home stacks of books and papers.... I have lesson plans and three sets of spelling papers to grade.... I took over three six grade classes as well.... It may sound trite, but I never really lived until I fell in love with you ... the most wonderful thing that has ever happened to me.

1 April 67–No letter today.... I was talking to the CO's RTO today. He said the other night when the grenade was tossed on the third platoon, the CO said I was so calm and cool and handled things very well. Got word today we are headed to An Khe for a while for relaxation and training.

1 April 67–Guess what! I'm pregnant–April Fools, so don't panic.... I finally got your letters that tell me what you are doing and where you are.... Your pictures are great.... Are you losing weight? Don't lose too much. I won't recognize you in Hawaii.... I've been reading The Green Berets *and I'm glad I am or I wouldn't understand half the things you say. Your terminology is right out of the book–LZ, Huey, beer (oops, I heard that one before), but don't worry, I'm a hard-core infantry wife.*

2 & 3 April 67–I received two wonderful letters from you today. I went in to Ah Khe today and bought a few things. I can't tell you what, but I'll mail them soon.

2 Apr 67–I simply thank God at the end of each day that you've made it one more day. The first day that the 1st Cav has a major action, I'm going to be pitiful until I get a letter from you telling me you are okay.

4 April 67–I bought a Minolta SR7 camera today at the PX for $99.25; they cost almost $300 in the States. I don't want to take it to the field, so I'll give it to the sergeant major for safekeeping and give it to you during R&R. We had a battalion meeting at the officers club tonight. The battalion commander congratulated me in front of the group on the job I was doing. That was a real surprise. I think my CO likes me. Tomorrow I get my Combat Infantrymen's Badge. Time goes slow in An Khe, but fast in the field.

5 April 67—I don't think we'll need a lot of money for R&R, unless they charge by the hour to use the bed.... Received two letters today.... Send peanuts.

6 April 67—We go back to the field tomorrow and I'm looking forward to going. Time moves really fast in the field, but slow here. Stay sweet. I love and miss you very much.

8 April 67—We are in Duc Pho in the north near the DMZ taking over for the Marines.

9 April 67—Today, five men and I went to a village near our base camp. The village had a well, and a little boy drew water for us, and we all bathed/showered as best we could. It was refreshing. Tomorrow we move to a beach near Khanh Nam where we are to secure the beach for Army Engineers to bring heavy equipment ashore.

9 April 67—I really enjoyed the Astros vs. Yankees game and the Astrodome is fantastic.... We got home at 3:00 am this morning.... I was so tired, but I read your letter before passing out in bed.... I miss you so much and I feel so empty.... At the game, I kept saying to myself, "Timmy would like this or that." I am always thinking that you should be here.... My life won't be complete until you are here with me.

10 & 11 April 67—We are on the beach. After setting up the perimeter, we took turns skinny-dipping in the ocean this morning. Late morning I took a tank squad and a Navy diving team south along the beach to look for another landing site for heavy equipment.

10 April 67—I don't understand this dumb mail system.... Your letters take four or five days and mine are taking eight to ten.

11 April 67—Received some of your slides and they are wonderful.... I also picked up pictures made from your slides and will send the pictures of me to you in future letters. Please have more pictures taken of you.... I'm not so sure I want you to stay in the Army.... You can't depend on staying in one place for long and especially when they need people like you in Vietnam.... I just couldn't bear to be apart from you for such a long time again.... A life apart is not living, only existing.... Be careful and love me.

11 April 67–Hi there! This is your cheerful gift girl. (This note was included in a package Jeanie sent)

Instructions:

1. *Fold-a-note–so you won't have to use GI postcards anymore (unless you want to, of course)*
2. *Mailers–sorry, I could only afford five this payday. I'll get you five more next month, okay?*
3. *Notebook–as ordered*
4. *The Green Beret–to fill in your idle hours and teach you about what's going on in Vietnam*
5. *Noxzema–as ordered*
6. *Plastic cigarette packs–who likes moldy, soggy cigarettes anyway?*
7. *Five ball points and five grease pencils–as ordered*
8. *Two Army men–for you to play war with–what else?*
9. *Water pistol–to protect yourself and is also good for taking showers*
10. *Darts–also to protect yourself, but also to throw at large nude picture of a Playboy Bunny*
11. *Various reading material*

I Love You

12 April 67–The mailman forgot Charlie Company again yesterday. This afternoon I got nine letters! I love the smell on the letters. It must be your bath powder. I keep all of your letters in a plastic bag in my side pocket. I take them out and smell them from time to time, so I always have the smell of my Gigi with me. I love you bunches.

13 April 67–I am enclosing two propaganda papers that are distributed and dropped from helicopters. One paper is from the 1st Cav and tells the people how the 1st Cav will help them, but warns the VC and NVA that the big birds will fly from the sky and destroy them if they are fired upon. The second paper is distributed by the NVA and tells how communism has helped the world and will help them.

14 April 67–All day my platoon walked with the engineers. We provided security as they built the road. Today we covered about six thousand meters of road from the beach inland. We were sniped at three different times, but no one was injured. I eventually called in artillery and tore-up the source of the enemy firing. We were ordered to burn villages and destroy hiding places. It was a long tiring day and I am glad for the rest. I sure miss you.

15 April 67–We are moving further north tomorrow near the Song Tra Cau River. I can't tell you anymore, but you can at least see the river on your map. This morning I was invited to go onto one of the Navy vessels. They didn't have a store, but they did have wonderful showers. I spent at least thirty minutes showering and it was great. I've not been this clean since San Antonio, but I'll get dirty again soon; the infantry way.... I will live for the day we are together again, and I'll love with words and memories until then. I'd like to sing you a love song, but I don't remember any of the words.... Send more pictures.

16 April 67–We finally changed locations and we're now at LZ Montezuma near the river I mentioned yesterday. While we enjoyed the beach, five days and nights of sand is enough for now. The Marines built this LZ and occupied it for about eighty days. They fixed it up nice during that time. Since my platoon is the only one here, I get the CP (Command Post), which is a large two-room bunker. All positions are well fortified. We are supposed to be here for five days, conducting small patrols in the surrounding area.

17 April 67–I don't have any place to put things. When I was in An Khe I did, but the CO told me that I'll likely not go there again until R&R in August. I appreciate whatever you send me…. I know how you feel when you want me to tell you how much I love you. That's what I look forward to in every one of your letters. Without those words, I get depressed. Baby, we know without any doubt how strong our love is for each other, and knowing this, we sometime take that for granted. My love for you is greater than I thought possible to love anyone. Day and night I'm thankful that I have you…. When God made you, he stamped you perfect and tagged you for Timmy…. You had told me I would see honey buckets when I got to Nam. These people don't use buckets. They squat and go when the urge comes. No inhibition at all.

17 April 67–Now, I see why I haven't received any mail. In the paper today it says 1st Cav moved north and is in some kind of action. In a situation like this, no news is good news…. The nights are so hard without you. I wish I could fall asleep as easily as you, but I just lie awake and think. This is the hardest to bear…. There's nothing to keep my mind off you…. I love you so very much.

18 April 67–This afternoon, we were notified to get ready to move further north. We were to be used as a ready reaction force further north…. When we landed at our destination, we moved quickly, sweeping through several villages, capturing four VC without firing a shot. No U.S. forces operated in that area and our fast movement was a surprise.

18 April 67–Second lieutenant; this is to inform you that your wife has not received any mail from you in over a week and is very upset. Please check the appropriate boxes on the enclosed card and return it. Sincerely, Mrs. Soyars…. Sweetheart, don't worry about the mail. I understand, but that doesn't mean I have to like it. I'll probably get a beautiful romantic letter tomorrow.

19 April 67–I got mail…. Just can't help being unhappy when I don't have any contact with you. You know I can't help but worry about you.

20 April 67–Could not write yesterday since we were on the move from dawn to dusk. We are now back in the Bong Son area.... Keep sending pictures.... On my next few rolls of film, I had my RTO take a few shots of me. One is of me in full combat gear as your brother requested.

20 April 67–Five wonderful letters today–wheeeeee! I have your film, stationary, nuts, and other goodies and will mail the box tomorrow.

21 April 67–Not enough time to write a lot today. The weather is 110° with high humidity ... wish I were spending the summer with you. Bye for now. I love you. See you in my dreams.

22 April 67–Thanks for the darts. This morning my men put a picture of a playboy bunny centerfold against a dirt bank and they took turns trying to hit selected places. You can imagine the point system used.... Right now I am sitting on a mountain looking out across the South China Sea. As I look, I can almost see San Antonio. Oh what I would give to be there right now. The streets are crowded, but I can see my Gigi, the most beautiful woman in the world. I know it's you. I see the beautiful hair, the twinkling eyes, and shapely sexy sway of your body.... See you in my dreams.

22 April 67–Gigi sure does miss her Timmy.... I went to the travel agency today and got prices and I picked a hotel on the beach I really like. It's the Reef on Waikiki Beach. It's $12 per night. The Fort Debussy cottages only cost $1.50 per night and they're on the beach.

23 April 67–Jackpot! Today I received seven letters from you. My letters should catch-up with you soon.... I carry the pictures you send with me at all times and I look at them often.

24 April 67–It has rained for five days straight now, and it's not even monsoon season.... The temperatures are cooler, but it's miserable to be wet all the time, especially in my sleep.... We get a change of socks daily

which helps.... As usual, it's getting late and I am tired from playing war ... goodnight.... I'll see you in my dreams.

25 April 67–I got to take a bath today. I took a squad on patrol in the mountains. We found a beautiful stream, so we took turns bathing.... No letters today.... I love you.

25 April 67–Got two letters today.... The one on the seventeenth made me feel so good, so warm inside, so loved, and secure; even from thousands of miles away, I feel your love reaching out to me and engulfing me in loving bliss.... I love you.

26 April 67–No mail again today, but I know you wrote to me. Letters will catch-up soon.... We are still climbing mountains. On your map, look for the tallest and steepest mountain east of the Bon Song Plain near the sea. That's where we are today.... Kisses and snakey licks.

Authors note: For those who may not know about snakey licks, Bill Cosby used the term in his *Wonderfulness* album, referring to the imaginary snakes surrounding his bed as a child. My wife used snakey licks as an affectionate way of kissing and being silly at the same time. She would put her face close to mine and flick her tong multiple times on my cheek; thus, the snakey lick.

27 April 67–Still climbing mountains ... still no letters ... maybe tomorrow.

27 April 67–No letter today, but I love you anyway. I'm able to take a few days without mail now much better than before. At first, it really tore me up. Now I know that I'll probably be getting a bunch in a couple of days.

28 April 67–I received two letters today and a package with all kinds of goodies ... the cookies were fresh and delicious. I ate my fill and shared with my men. They asked that you send more. I shared the peanuts with

my command group. They were great.... We are operating near Dam Tra
O Lake near the sea. We are now in the mountains following a stream
leading to the lake below.... One of squad leaders offered to give me a
haircut today.... I wish you could be in my next package. That would a
wonderful surprise.... Time for my haircut.... I love you bunches.

29 April 67–I found a Buddhist scarf and will send it to you when I can.
It's a bit soiled and frayed, but a great souvenir.... Thanks for the book, *Of
Mice and Men*. I finished it recently. Sergeant Sal is reading it now.... When
the mail arrives, one of my squad leaders collects the second platoon's mail
in a bundle prepared in An Khe. He always brings the bundle for me to
smell. The smell of your bath powder lets me know that I have a letter. My
men asked if they can smell my letters.... At night before going to sleep, I
look at the picture you sent me and smell my bag of letters.... It's the next
best thing to having you here ...We are supposed to wear our uniforms
until they tear. I try to find a way to tear my uniform at least weekly. Five
days of dirt and grime is enough.... I look forward to patrols that take us
near steams, and I try to give my men and myself a chance to wash-up
a bit.... We don't always smell that good.... Being separated from you is
harder than I thought it would be. When I return, I'll not let you out of
sight again.... I'll see you in my dreams.

*29 April 67–What do you mean you don't wear underwear? Doesn't that chafe?
Are you not wearing them because I'm not there to wash them? Ha ha! What
do you do with the dirty socks if you get new ones each day?*

*30 April 67–Happy four-month anniversary! We've been married four months
today and you've been gone half that time.... I miss you so. Everything seems
so empty without you.*

1 May 67–Received three letters today from a beautiful woman, and
each had a picture of her.... I look forward to R&R and our third
honeymoon.

1 May 67–Guess what? I got five letters returned to me from the 90th replacement battalion. I didn't put your SSN on the address. I guess they couldn't find you. I put them in one envelope and here they are.

2 May 67–We received an order that General Abrams will visit Charlie Company. He is to replace General Westmoreland as Vietnam Commander.... Today we were ordered to move to a river in our area of operation and take a bath.... The general must have a sensitive smeller.... Tomorrow night we are all to receive fresh uniforms.... Today my RTO put Kool Aide in coconut milk and it was really great.... No matter how hot it gets the coconut milk is cool.... My RTO told me to ask you to remember him in your prayers, since everywhere I go, he goes.... See you in my dreams.

2 May 67–I pray every night for your safety. I can meet any problem and handle my difficulties as long as you are there by my side. All I want is you.... Be careful and love me.

3 May 67–Received three beautiful letters today.... The general arrives tomorrow to watch us conduct a sweep of an area on the plains ... look for this in the news.... It's 2300 hours and I must go to sleep to look good for the general.... Million kisses and snakey licks.

3 May 67–They're playing Love Eyes *on the radio. Dedicated to my baby.... I love you.... Tell me everything you do. You will never bore me.... I live for your letters.*

4 May 67–I really needed you today.... We patrolled hard and long and I needed a hug.... By the way, the general never showed. He was delayed at other stops and did not have time for us.... Can I come home now?

5 May 67–We captured five more VC today.... This week my platoon killed three and captured twelve.... I don't always agree with my CO's tactics, and I offer my suggestions.... He often uses my suggestions, but I'm not

sure he likes to.... I always try to protect my men rather than setting them up as bait.

5 May 67–I've got you pin-pointed on my map.... You are giving very clear map instructions.... Anticipating August so much.... I want to see that special light in your eyes when you look at me.

6 May 67–I write you every day, even though you don't get mail. Writing is the only way I can let you know how much I love you and need you and miss you.

7 May 67–My watch died about a week ago.... One of men went to An Khe and there he bought a $10 watch ... nothing fancy, but it will do.... I sent a second letter to the 90th Replacement Battalion inquiring about the letters and package you mailed to me there.... hope to hear from them soon.

8 May 67–I had to cut last night's letter short.... I took men on a night patrol ... we didn't return until 0100 hours.... It really gets dark out there and I hope I don't have too many more of those.... Received five letters today and one large envelope with a bunch of letters forwarded from the 90th Replacement Battalion.... You asked about what happens to our dirty socks. We put them in a pot, add water and make stew; actually, battalion washes and returns them for re-use.

9 May 67–How is my beautiful little wife today...? Ten more months to go in Nam, and four until R&R.... Yesterday I found a guitar while searching an abandoned village. I sent it to An Khe for safekeeping.... We have a midnight amphibious raid scheduled tonight. We will surround the village on three sides. The fourth side is the ocean. At dawn we will sweep the area to the ocean. We hope to capture NVA there ... see you in my dreams.

10 May 67–Last night was interesting and successful.... The NVA heard us coming and prepared to leave.... I had my platoon stretched out for five

hundred meters from the ocean to the west. The NVA walked right into my platoon.... we killed five and captured twelve.... The whole company was there, but the battle belonged to the second platoon.... They came at 0400 hours.... It was pitch black and no moon.... They were on us very fast.... One of my men punched an NVA in the face before he shot him, they were that close.... I am so proud of my platoon.... They all like me and will do anything for me and me for them.

11 May 67–I had to cut my letter short yesterday and will finish it today ... At 1700 hours we made an air assault back to the mountains and it was 0200 hours before we got settled, and then we received orders for no noise and lights.... I am rushing to mail my letter this morning.... I'll write more this afternoon.... I love you.

12 May 67–Another day in the life of an infantry platoon leader....We climbed more mountains, pulled thorns out of arms, hands, and legs, ate a few C rations and looked for NVA.... Send pictures.... I got two letters this afternoon.... We climbed a bunch more hills and mountains today. I think about one hundred two. They went straight up and straight down.... I haven't been able to take pictures lately because of our missions.

12 May 67–Two more weeks of school and boy am I ready.

13 May 67–Received two letters today.... You are getting good at map reading and finding my location.... We move so frequently, it's hard to keep close track.... Today we are in the Bon Song area near Dam Tra O. We are west of the valley just before the mountains. Tonight we are set-up between the villages of Cuu Thanh and Cuw Thanh.... Today we traveled down the ridge line to the north west of here. Two days ago we air assaulted into the valley on the other side of the mountains near Tri Twong. The next morning we climbed the mountains to the north, Nui Daa Twong and today we ended up in the valley.... No twin beds in Hawaii, so stay away from the Army fort if that's all they have. We need to stay on the main part of the island where the action is and in a nice hotel. We may want

breakfast, lunch and supper in bed.... I don't want to worry about expenses there.... It's getting late.... Be good. I'll see you in my dreams.

13 May 67–I'm the luckiest girl in the whole world.... You are the most thoughtful and considerate man that I've ever known.... The Mother's Day flowers were delivered today. They are beautiful.... I heard the 1st Cav had action today south of Duc Pho. I don't think it was you. I sure hope not.

14 May 67–Happy Mother's Day to a mother to be sometime in the future.... I love you.

14 May 67–Missed you a lot today.... I felt lost and empty. I kept thinking about things we did together; especially I find myself thinking about walking down Broadway holding your hand. I miss the touch of your hand, the way you look at me, the pleasure and security of your mere presence.... I'm so afraid something will happen to you before I can get you back in my arms. Be careful and love me. I love you.

15 May 67–Yesterday we traded places with the 1/5 Cav. We're set-up in a blocking position at the mouth of the An Lao Valley.... In two days we are to move to LZ Uplift to provide security for the battalion base camp.... I have received compliments from my CO and other battalion officers about the job I am doing here.... I have had men in other platoons request reassignment to second platoon.... I feel good about all this.... Also, my men have a lot of pride and they show it.... I'm not really bragging, but if I didn't tell you this, you may never know.... I love you baby.

16 May 67–I got two letters today and two pictures.... My CO just returned from R&R in Hawaii. He rented a car there and paid $6 a day. He said a smaller car should cost $4 per day.... The nineteenth is Ho Chi Minh's birthday.... The 1st Cav is painting Happy Birthday Ho on all artillery rounds.

17 May 67–Received four letters today and four pictures.... Today's temperature was 125º, humid with no wind.... We went on patrol and I had to call in medevac for three men that were suffering from heat exhaustion.

18 May 67–Got one letter and a package with fudge. That's great stuff.... I want plenty of cold milk when we're in Hawaii, nothing but the powered stuff here.... Your research on places to stay in Hawaii is good and they all sound great.

18 May 67–I had a scare today.... On my way home from school I heard about a platoon being lost in the Central Highlands, but they didn't say from which outfit.... I worried until the paper came and it said it was the 4th Infantry.... Don't these dumb news people know that this kind of detail is vital.... Well, I visited you last night, but you were asleep and I didn't want to wake you. So I just sat near you and looked at you sleeping there on your air mattress in those grungy fatigues with stubble on your face and dirt on your hands and I love you.... I can't come often; it's too hard for me to leave. Isn't make believe nice? I need to hear your voice and see you move, that way your pictures can come to life.

20 May 67–You've only been gone three months.... This year will never end.

22 May 67–We leave LZ Uplift today and move to LZ Pony.... It's the same type base camp, but smaller.... We all have had enough of the security duty. It's boring and time moves slow.... I am ready to get back in the field and find NVA.

22 May 67–I am teaching elementary music next year and I already have a replacement lined up to take my place next February.

23 May 67–I really hate this security duty ... too much time to think and too boring.... Received two letters today.... I live to receive your letters....

I am really home sick for you.... I don't mean to depress you.... I'm writing what I feel.... See you in my dreams.

24 May 67–Tell your mother that I'll look for rocks.... When on patrol it's difficult to think about rocks.... My platoon made an air assault south of LZ Pony today and searched as we made our way back to the LZ.... We didn't find any signs of enemy activity, but it's great to get away from security duty.

25 May 67–My CO told me that he plans to recommend me for one of several jobs in battalion HQ.... In a way I don't want to leave the field.... I really love leading these men and I love the challenge.... A job in HQ is less risky and a good development opportunity.

26 May 67–Received three letters today.... Today I took my platoon to LZ Mead to provide security and conduct patrols in the surrounding area.... The rest of the company is at LZ Ollie.

27 May 67–This afternoon I leave for An Khe to handle paperwork for the CO. I'll return to re-join the company early tomorrow.... Today we are at LZ Mead, and I am the perimeter commander.... I need to close for now to coordinate a few things before I leave for An Khe.... I love you.

28 May 67–After I took care of business for the CO, I discovered that Camp Radcliff has a Mars station and soldiers are allowed to place calls beginning at 2300 hours in the evening, first-come-first-served.... I got there at 2300 hours and was twenty-first in line.... They place calls by region and Texas was in the last region.... At 0415 hours only three soldiers remained in line for calls to Texas and they lost contact and closed the station.... I am really tired now.... I sure miss you.... I'll see you in my dreams. I love you.

29 May 67–Don't be impatient with guard duty. Your mission could be much worse. Maybe you won't be so bored, but you also wouldn't be as safe.... I know that no matter what I do, it's no fun without you there to share in it.

30 May 67–Received five letters today.... The CO just left my CP. He came to tell me that he was recommending me for the Bronze Star for Valor for my actions during the amphibious landing we made on May 10.... I already told you what happened there.... The CIB (Combat Infantry Badge) was enough for me, but I'll take this, if approved.

1 June 67–Two hundred eight-two days to go before my tour ends.... We may have to take R&R in July, since nine men in the company are already scheduled for R&R in August.... I live for the day our lips touch once again.

1 June 67–Timmy, come home. Gigi was sick today and she wants her Timmy.... Now listen here, Tim Soyars, so help me, if I get another set of slides from you that has only one picture of you in it ... I'll send it back.... This is the second set like that.... The next set I get had better have at least half a roll of just you.... If you could only get an HQ job, I would feel so much better.

2 June 67–I really miss you and I am homesick.... We are on a beach relaxing at this time and preparing for another night amphibious assault on the village of Dieu Quang.... I'll need to end the letter since we are traveling light without a flashlight.... I'll write more tomorrow.

3 June 67–The assault went as planned, but not as successful as the last one.... My platoon killed two and captured one NVA. Another platoon captured one NVA.... This morning I have a bad sore throat.... I got a penicillin shot and hope that cures it.

4 June 67–I had a temperature of 101⁰ this morning.... My platoon was set up as a blocking force for the company as they swept the area, so I got to rest a bit.... I feel better this afternoon.

4 June 67–I never really expected love to be so wonderful, so fulfilling. That word wonderful keeps cropping up, but it applies to us and you so perfectly. Everything is wonderful (except being apart).

6 June 67–When I read the part about your nomination for the Bronze Star, I got all shaky and started to cry.... I'm very proud and happy, especially, now that it's all over with and you're safe.... I don't want you to get any medals. All I want is for you to be safe somewhere. I want you and not a bunch of ribbons and medals.... Just keep your head down, okay?

7 June 67–I received a beautiful letter from you today; it makes me homesick, but will keep me going for a long, long time.... For the past two days we have made air assaults in the early morning to conduct search missions, and then return to LZ Uplift to provide security there by early evening.

7 June 67–I daydream about you/us a lot.... I picture us in all kinds of beautiful and fun settings and your career in business.... I think of the past; Polk Officers Club, your BOQ, the house, a Mexican restaurant on the river, a rainy wedding, a perfect honeymoon even with twin beds, a Polynesian restaurant, a small but beautiful transit cottage, many lovely hours in those twin beds, driving to NY, of walking Broadway, a terrific musical, drive down the valley, many movies.... We both remember, don't we? And we'll always remember.... I love you.

8 June 67–I want to meet you at the airport in Hawaii if possible ... I want to be with you every second.

9 June 67–Received two letters and two pictures today.... I promise to ask my RTO to take pictures of me when we go on the next patrol, probably tomorrow.... Send any book you think I'll enjoy reading.... Stay sweet and beautiful. I'll see you in my dreams.

10 June 67–My CO gave my officer's review today and was it a surprise.... He said I was the most tactical and professional officer he had been associated with and he said I have done an outstanding job as platoon leader.... He said with his recommendation, the battalion wants me as assistant S4.... Captain Markham makes major on June 15 and is leaving the company.... I look forward to the opportunity.... The CO asked if I have plans for the future, he said I should rise fast in the military.... Something to think about, but the University of Texas sounds real good to me right now.... R&R will truly be the most beautiful seven days of our lives, until then, I'll see you in my dreams.

10 June 67–I don't feel like doing anything except writing you.

11 June 67–Received your letter of June 3 today.... We made an air assault this afternoon and I sent out a squad to locate a position for establishing a listening post for the night.... While returning to our base camp, they hit a booby trap and three men were wounded.... They were sent out by medevac.... This is the seventh man I've lost to booby traps since March 1967.... All of the booby traps we have encountered have been U.S. Air Force CBU bombs.... Sergeant Clanton was the leader and he was walking point.... His leg is messed-up and he had shrapnel all over his body, but the medic seems to think he'll be ok.... Clanton is one of my favorites and my buddy.... It's times like this that makes me want to stay in the field.... They are a great bunch of guys and they tell me they want me to stay with them as their leader.... The officers seem to get the breaks to get out of the field and enlisted men hump the hills for twelve months.... Doesn't seem fair.... Love you.

12 June 67–I got a report that my three wounded men should be ok.... Two will be sent to the States and one's returning after recuperation.... I can hardly wait till R&R.... I'll be like a seven-year-old at Christmas when I see you, but I won't act like a seven-year-old, so look out.... I love you, baby.

12 June 67—It's funny. I've been dreaming more and tossing, turning and waking up … must be ESP.… I miss you and want to see you badly.

13 June 67—Received three beautiful letters today.… I also got a real sexy picture … keep them coming.… We have a very special love. A love perfect for books and movies.… I love you so much.… Please try to love me too much and I'll just love you that much more. You could never love me too much, but you can try.

13 June 67—I think I have your Hawaii wardrobe complete.… Bought new stuff and re-soled your dress shoes.… I start teaching beginning swimming next Tuesday at Kelly AFB.

15 June 67—I couldn't write yesterday.… We conducted a very long patrol and didn't return until dark.… After dinner I laid on my air mattress and fell asleep.… The battalion called the CO to tell them I should return to LZ Uplift tonight to begin my assistant S4 position tomorrow.… Today is my last day in the field.… I feel honored getting this position in the battalion. There are many lieutenants more senior and with longer time in-country but they selected me.… The current S4 leaves for the States in seven days and the assistant S4 leaves in twenty-seven days.

15 June 67—I really hit the jackpot … three letters.… You are getting quite romantic. I sure like to get those kinds of letters.… I'm so proud of your recommendation to S4.… Exactly what does an S4 do…? Do the other men talk about their wives? You must be setting a very good example (being faithful), anyway I trust you completely … I'm much too possessive to want to share you no matter the circumstance. You are mine, body and soul, as I am only yours.… I love you so very much and it's knowing that you love me that keeps me going.

16 June 67—In addition to all the assistant S4 duties, I am also the platoon leader for all enlisted men in the battalion headquarters. Should we need to defend the LZ, I'll lead them.… I'll hardly have time to learn everything

the assistant S4 is responsible for and then I'll take over the S4 duties as well.... No mail today.... See you in my dreams.

16 June 67–I read in the Army Times that Al Rogers was killed in action.... It put a damper on me today.... His death really brought the danger too close, and I'm scared.... Please be extra careful. I want you home next March to stay forever.... I love you.

17 June 67–I ran into an OCS classmate who is assigned to Alpha Company, he says two more classmates are in the 2nd/1st.... He said LT Al Rogers was killed in action with the 25th Infantry Division.... Please try to verify that.... I'm enjoying my new job.

17 June 67–Please be cautious about booby traps, snipers and everything, for me.... When do you think they'll move you back to battalion? I wish they'd hurry up.... Make August hurry and come.

18 June 67–I am working long hours here at LZ Uplift. I start at 0500 hours and end around 2100 hours. Let's not plan our days in Hawaii. Let's do what catches our fancy each day.

19 June 67–You're getting more and more romantic and poetic all the time (I'm speaking of your letter dated the thirteenth).... I love you so much.

20 June 67–Hey, cool it lieutenant! I hate to put a damper on your CO's praise, but as soon as you extend and made captain they would send you right back to Nam. I couldn't go through this again; I'd go mad.... We'll talk in Hawaii, but my vote is no!! Hawaii seems to be all we talk about.... You know our chance to love each other will be so short and has to be perfect, so our reminiscing for years to come will be as romantic as the months before you left.... I'll love you so much that you'll really believe in fairy tales.

21 June 67–Sorry I haven't written in two days.... On the nineteenth, Company B ran into a company of NVA and was pinned down until late

that night. I spent the day and night on the log pad with radio in hand directing helicopter supplies, relaying medevac instructions, and directing chopper crews …. The company had five KIA and six WIA…. The next day Company A ran into the same NVA Company while patrolling in the mountains near company B's encounter. I continued operations on my helicopter pad…. I had three meals in three days, so you know I was busy to miss meals. Company A had two KIA and seven WIA…. I received three letters and three pictures…. Love you.

21 June 67–I am so happy that you are in battalion now … I'm proud that you have such an important job and glad you will be busy and safe … got your letters of fifteenth and sixteenth … I was glad to get those letters and to hear how much you love me. I'll never get tired of hearing or reading it…. The moon and sky is beautiful tonight … wish you were by my side.

22 June 67–The 1st/5th battalion ran into a battalion of NVA about six miles south of LZ Uplift and the 2nd/5th was called in to assist. I was on my landing pad from 1330 hours to 0030 hours…. This is not the norm…. I have four OCS classmates in the 1st/5th and I was told one of them was killed today…. I don't know a name.

23 June 67–Yesterday I mentioned the four OCS classmates in the 1st/5th. Lieutenant Cox was wounded and LT Bill Wagner was killed. Wagner had been one of my roommates.

23 June 67–You didn't hit the mailman hard enough. No letters today…. Gigi wants Timmy to come home and stop playing war with the other boys. Come home and let's play house…. I can come and get you. I'd say "Sorry General Baby. I know he's a valuable man and you need him, but I need him more. You understand these things. Good chap there–Talley ho and all that rot." Come dear. Then we'd board my private jet, AF1 on loan, and bring you to our Polynesian paradise and conveniently disappear for thirty years.

24 June 67–I got your sexy towel shot today. Oh Baby, it's so cute. Hey, wha wuz unda dat dere towl?... Forty kisses and four snakey licks.

25 June 67–One of my Charlie Company squad leaders visited me today. He just returned from R&R in Hawaii and gave me a lot of good information. He also brought me a bottle of Old Crow; how thoughtful.

26 June 67–I have arranged for my former RTO, Jim Henby, to join me in S4. He'll run my communications center and be my assistant.

28 June 67–LZ Uplift is southwest of Dam Tra O Lake on Highway One. Your map should show the highway and a railroad track. Uplift is between the two on a slightly higher elevation.

29 June 67–My day begins at 0500 hours. First off, I radio my assigned helicopters to determine their ETA and insure that all log orders are properly staged. I check with HQ to see if any additional/changed instructions are needed for the day's operations, and then I go to the landing pad to supervise the activities and communicate with the field companies. Over time, I'll delegate some of these duties. Choppers generally drop off discards on my pad and are finished around 1000 hours. After the re-supply is finished, I do the rounds of my other operations (motor pool, mess, supply). Around 1330 hours, I begin preparing for the evening log operations. They end around 1830 hours.

30 June 67–Companies B and D were ambushed last night and they had six KIA and thirty-two WIA. It was another very busy night and day.... Look forward to a good night's sleep.... Love you.

4 July 67–Happy 4th of July...! How did you celebrate? Here, we had the usual amount of local fireworks.... I watched Mutiny on the Bounty with Charles Laughton and Clark Gable.... I tried to locate you on the map below Dam Tra O and I'm listing the villages down to Phu Cat. I'm not sure where you are, but if you are not at any of these, you're hopelessly lost and will never find your way out! In such case, call me and I'll come and get you.... You're a great gourmet. You know good cookies when you eat one—besides you still need to work on my newlywed ego.... I'll send a truck load of peanuts in the next box.... If there was only some way to keep from missing you so badly.... I need to see you just to make sure that you're not a figment of my romantic imagination.... I love you.

6 July 67–The S4 left for the States two days ago, so I now have the assistant S4 and S4 job. The HQ CO has agreed to take over my S4 duties while I go on R&R. The target date is August 5.

8 July 67–My R&R has been approved to begin August 4 and end August 11.... I'm scheduled to arrive in Hawaii at 0400 hours on the fourth.... I am soooooo anxious and ready.

10 July 67–Exactly four months now.... It seems like years.... There's nothing I wouldn't give to have you home. And there's no price that could induce me to go through these last four months again. I love you.... The mail man was wonderful today. Four letters from my husband.... I want more than just a pen-pal. I want to fulfill my life as your wife and mate.

11 July 67–Our Fourth of July was just another day. The company guarding the perimeter here at Uplift got hold of flares and put on a display of sorts. I understand they got into trouble since it was unauthorized.... I can't wait till August 4.

13 July 67–They're having a photo contest here, and I've picked some of your photos to enter.... Just wait till Hawaii! Man-oh-man! I'm going to grab you and not let go for seven days.

15 July 67–Just two weeks and I'll start packing for Hawaii.... The time is dragging now.... It's going to be so hard giving you up again at the end of that week.... I do love you so very much.

17 July 67—Bring your duffle bag with you to Hawaii. I'll bring it home with me and imagine my surprise when I open it in San Antonio and out jumps Tim.

20 July 67—Happy birthday sweetie.... I got my orders for R&R today.

20 July 67—Happy Birthday to me! Got your letter of the fifteenth.... You seem to have only two things on your mind ... me and Hawaii.

23 July 67—Oh Baby, if the days don't start passing faster, I'm going to go crazy.... I want to feel your arms around me and hear your voice so badly. And, yet I know those seven days will fly by because we want them to last forever.

25 July 67—I made my reservations today.... I'll arrive in Hawaii at 0005 hours on the fourth.... I'll try to drop off luggage at the hotel; otherwise, I'll just sit and wait at the airport.

26 July 67—No kisses, hugs, snakey licks ... I'm saving them for Aug 4, at which time I shall drown you with them.

28 July 67—Happy birthday to me.... Just another work day.... I am so ready for Hawaii.... See you soon.

1 August 67—Had Mexican food tonight. I wish you had been there to help eat up the hot sauce, hee hee! I'm at a loss to say something different or at least in a different way. I'm feeling so keyed up that I'm not thinking much about words. I'll try something different.... I don't love you—except all the time. I can't stand you—to be away from me.... I don't want you near me—except constantly.... I love you more.

2 August 67—Tomorrow I'll leave to join my husband in paradise.

11 August 67– I had a beautiful dream.... I spent six wonderful days and nights with you in Hawaii.... We hardly kissed hello when it was time to kiss goodbye.... Seven months and I'll be home for good.... Until then, I'll see you in my dreams.

11 August 67–This is awful! I don't want to have to write you anymore. I don't like writing when I can say it so much better. I love you so much, Baby.... Leaving you yesterday was really bad.... One of your pictures won an award.... Six wonderful days with you and now I'm sitting in my little room writing you as usual. It all seems like a dream.... As long as I think about fun, excitement, ecstasy, I'm alright. I avoid thinking of the last moments of anguish before you were actually gone and how alone I felt. If I dwell too long on how badly I want you, I get upset and cry. I just think about how your eyes softened whenever you looked at me and how very warm and secure I felt being near you. About the satisfaction of doing something for you. About the happiness of just being together. My entire happiness lies in our love for each other. Thank God for that love!

12 August 67–Tomorrow, my OCS classmate, Roger Miller and I are being promoted to first lieutenant. My sergeants are throwing a party. My mess sergeant is grilling steaks and shrimp and he procured a bunch of beer.... Wish you could join us.

14 August 67–I'll check out the PX catalogue prices as we discussed in Hawaii.... All the silver seems to be plated.... You might check prices there for sterling.... The Buick Special Deluxe we talked about has a 210 HP V8 Engine, two door hardtop and costs $2,327.57.... Ask your dad if he can get a quote locally for comparison.

14 August 67–I filled one more carousel and most of another with your slides.... You know we're going to have eight carousels when I finish with the one I'm working on.

15 August 67–I was just thinking about how long I have left in-country and I focused on Thanksgiving, Christmas, our anniversary and New Year's.... I'll not be with you on any of these special days.

15 August 67–Gee, but I miss you. I daydream about our future all the time. Our trailer, your college, our children, your rise in business, our beautiful home–our future together, I'm so anxious to get started.... I love you.

17 August 67–I love you so much.... Do you know I have a picture of you in my mind from Hawaii.... It's permanently etched.... It's the morning of August 10 and you were sitting in the airport with me waiting for my plane.... You weren't feeling well but you looked beautiful ... you were wearing your muumuu and sandals and staring at the floor and walls.... Your beautiful hair hanging so still and neat ... you had a look on your face of sweet innocence.... It would have made a masterpiece painting.... All of the loveliness, kindness, and warmth are captured in my mind of the woman I love more than anything else in the world.... until March.

18 August 67–Got several letters.... The one dated the eleventh was beautiful and leaves no doubt of your love for me.... I've read it five times so far today.... I love you my beautiful and wonderful little wife.

18 August 67–My daddy, Chuck and I went to see The Dirty Dozen. It's great!!! You'd love it ... You're not always aware of how much love goes into a simple gesture. Like reaching across a table to squeeze your hand or looking at you through candle light or laying my face against your neck or kissing your lips lightly as you sleep. When I do these things, I don't need to say I love you; you know it without any doubt. I love you so, my darling Tim.... Be careful and love me.

19 August 67–Another OCS classmate, Dan Starns, Jr. was killed in action recently.... You may not remember him, but I introduced you to him at Fort Polk.

19 August 67—Is there anything you want that I can make you? You've never asked for anything except can stuff.... I'm already thinking about meeting you in California and our long drive back to San Antonio.... Make these months go fast.

20 August 67—So you bought a toy soldier that looks like me.... He's a bit shorter I bet ... I'm ready to come home and be with you.... I'm ready to stop playing war.

21 August 67—I'm in An Khe.... The battalion commander is unhappy with a warrant officer assigned to the battalion.... He's in charge of property and is Mister Regulation.... In war time some rules need to bend and the CO wants me to straighten him out.... I'll be here for a few days.

22 August 67—Things are going well with the warrant officer.... I found that he was not ordering things as requested by battalion.... He was ordering what he thought we needed.... I found some of my orders to him that he ignored.... He stammered as I questioned him.... I'll stay on his case, but I think he gets the picture.... I should be able to return to Uplift tomorrow.

23 August 67—It's 1100 hours and I am waiting for my supply truck to arrive.... I'm riding back to Uplift with the supply truck.... I really get depressed here at Camp Radcliff.... It's so distant from the happenings of the war.... It also reminds me of my first entry to the war and the waiting is maddening.

24 August 67—I think about how fun it was driving those crazy roads in Hawaii.... We giggled and laughed and enjoyed being together, all alone. I wish we had stopped and stayed there longer. Climbed around on the rocks, sat close and talked ... very intimate and loving, and in no hurry. It's strange that we're always in a hurry, and when we look back, we wish we hadn't wasted those moments consumed in the rush.... When I meet you in LA, let's take our own sweet time in driving back and forget the rest of the world.

26 August 67–It's Saturday.... Let's sleep late and then watch TV all morning.... In the afternoon we'll take a leisurely ride in your sports car.... Tonight we'll go dancing and return home late.... I bet we'll find more to do later at home.

26 August 67–Right now I'm with the family at their place near Canyon Lake.... It will be nice for us to come here as an escape from whatever post you're at.... Chuck says I shouldn't write such long letters to you; cause you might get attacked by the VC in the middle of reading and wouldn't have your mind on the fighting.... I drove fifty miles back home to get the mail.... Can you look at me and see how much I love you? Can you feel my love around you when I'm near? Can you read between the lines what I can't find words to say? I can.... You show me in so many wonderful ways.... I think the way I like best is when I catch you looking at me with that look on your face. You're love for me shows on your face.

30 August 67–First day of school was awful.... I love you more.... Not many men get a girl who loves them as much as I love you.

3 September 67–All I do is dream of us–past and future. I find it easier to think of the future than to reminisce about the past. Thinking of the past makes me lonely for you ... the future makes me excited.

4 September 67–I'm standing at an R&R reception center in Honolulu. I've been up for twenty-seven hours already and don't feel very good and can't sleep. Besides, you'll be arriving any minute now from the airport–your plane was late. The place is really crowding up with waiting wives and men who are going back and their wives. There are the buses! I saw them turn the corner. What is taking them so long? Here comes one! Oh God, I'll die if you're not on one of them! Well, that one's empty. Where is that other bus? I'd better get out of the street. It's too crowded here and I can see better over there. It's here! I know I'll recognize you; you can't have changed that much. Well, she got her's, where's mine? Hey, I've got the cutest husband of all the girls I met. How about that.

I'd better not spend so much time watching others kissing. Gotta look for you. Oh, my God! Not three feet away. That beautiful smile. I'm in your arms now, and we will have six days to live. I love you!

9 September 67–Do you remember the warrant officer that was with me on the flight to and from Hawaii? I just found out that he was killed while flying a medevac mission at 0200 hours this morning.… Last night he visited me for several hours … we drank a few beers and talked about Hawaii, work and plans.… Life is precious and can be all too short.… I'll miss him.

13 September 67–My morale is extremely high today.… I received five letters and pictures from my favorite wife.… I love you. See you in my dreams.

17 September 67–I'm still assistant S4 and S4 and I'm staying very busy.… Do you remember me telling you about my first RTO, Tom Jarrett…? I thought he was sent to the States due to malaria, but he walked up to me today, saluted and shook hands … he's recovered.… I immediately visited Major Murphy and Jarrett is now assigned to S4.… This afternoon I got another sore throat and I'm not feeling well.… The ear infection of a week ago is better.

18 September 67–I'm feeling lousy again today.… The monsoon season is fast approaching.… Most afternoons around 1500 hours we get a long rain shower.… I'm told that in about two weeks the monsoon season will be here, and it will rain continuously.

19 September 67–Gee, I miss you. I'll be so glad when we have our own home.… Things get hectic here with Chuck sometimes.… I think you are a very calming influence on me. I need you.… March seems so far away.… Be careful and love me.

21 September 67–All San Antonio schools were closed today because of hurricane Beulah and her accompanying tornadoes.... Wish it happened tomorrow, so we'd all have gotten a three-day weekend.... Twenty inches of rain in places and forty-four tornados reported.

23 September 67–Today I decided to make a visit to Camp Radcliff and check up on operations there.... I was pleasantly surprised to find everything running well.

24 September 67–Our battalion commander, Colonel McDonough, is being promoted and will leave soon for a new job in Brigade.... His replacement is Lieutenant Colonel Love.... I haven't heard good reports on him from the grapevine.... We'll see.

25 September 67–Be careful ... I don't want you being sick.... I'm glad time is passing fast.... Wish you could get an assistant to help with the load.... I long to hold you tight in my arms–to feel secure and loved.

26 September 67–Rain, rain, rain.... I'm getting sick of continuous rain ... rivers flow through our tents.... I had dinner with the new battalion commander and his staff tonight.... The new commander told me that Colonel McDonough has requested I make a presentation on my assistant S4 helicopter log operations to the brigade commanders.... It seems that the division aviation units have offered compliments about my operations.... That's an honor.

28 September 67–We were told to pack and prepare to move to Camp Radcliff, An Khe.... I'll get things organized here and then I'll be part of the advance party to Radcliff.... I don't know how long we will be there, but we are to get new orders later for another area of operations.

30 September 67–No word on when we leave for An Khe.... The new battalion commander is a lot different from Colonel McDonough.... LTC Love insists on eating dinner with his officers and requires china and

silverware for the evening meal.… After dinner, he holds a briefing and tells war stories and jokes and calls on officers to answer questions from time-to-time.

2 October 67–It has rained solid for two days.… We were to move by truck in convoy to An Khe today, but it's too wet.

4 October 67–We got a break and were able to load trucks.… We convoyed to An Khe today … all arrived safe and sound.

5 October 67–We think we'll be in An Khe for thirty days and then go north to Chu Lia, but that's not definite.… Don't let anyone send Christmas presents to me here.… They can send food goodies if they want.

7 October 67–Rain, rain, and rain twenty-four hours a day.… Everything is wet and muddy.… If I were a king, I'd give you my kingdom. If I were a millionaire, I'd give you my millions. If I were a prince, I'd give you my crown. But, I am only a man and I give you the only special thing I have … my love, all my love, all my life.

8 October 67–I 'm going to have to stop listening to The King and I album. I really break down during the finale. The song reminds me of how much I love you. The song describes how I feel so well that I just cry every time I hear it.… I hope my emotion is just because you're away and in danger.

9 October 67–Hit the jackpot today. Four letters.… My heart kinda stopped when you mentioned the scuttlebutt about Chu Lai.… I wish they would leave you at Uplift. Ya'll seem to really have that area under control.… Our love is holding up beautifully against this test, and we know it'll stand up against anything.… We have security in our love that some people never achieve.… It's a wonderful thing.

11 October 67–Can't wait to get away from Camp Radcliff and back closer to the action.… The S4, Captain Ward just got orders for Army

Intelligence and is being reassigned.... I'll be both assistant S4 and S4 again.... I'm not sure how I'll like interacting with LTC Love on a daily basis.... Major Murphy, my boss, is an ok guy.

16 October 67–I've been assigned to rebuild the S4 warehouse, motor pool, and ammo dump for 2nd/5th here at Radcliff ... another opportunity.

18 October 67–Making great progress on the re-build projects.... Lieutenant Zambinio who replaced me as platoon leader for second platoon, Charlie Company was killed yesterday from an enemy grenade.

21 October 67–LTC Love lost his cool when a company walked into a booby trap.... I was told he called the soldier a g-- d--- stupid b------.... Word on the vine is that the colonel is under the microscope ... hopefully, he'll change positively.... This evening I looked at all the pictures you have sent me. I spent thirty minutes looking at them, then an hour trying to walk. *Boy*, what you do to me.... I love you so much. Be good and stay sweet.

22 October 67–I don't like to think about Christmas. I get homesick. I remember last Christmas as if it were yesterday. It was so beautiful. I love you so much.

27 October 67–I got your letters of the twenty-first and twenty-second.... I know how you feel about looking at my pictures.... I pull out all of yours and look at them. It's a poor substitute for the real thing, but it's sure better than nothing.... I know what you mean about Christmas. Last year was so beautiful for us.... I remember before Christmas you came over to my house and you brought two new record albums.... I decorated the tree as we listened to the music.

30 October 67–I had a late night.... Major Murphy kept me up till 0315 hours making plans for the up-coming move we will make.... It looks like we are going to Chu Lai.

31 October 67–I got your package filled with Halloween goodies today.... Good timing.

2 November 67–Most of the battalion is in An Khe and I am at LZ Uplift to arrange for the dismantling of all tents.... trucks are due this afternoon to transport them to An Khe.

3 November 67–I got to An Khe around 1730 hours yesterday.... Upon arrival Major Murphy was waiting to inform me that we are moving out of An Khe in a few days.... We spent most of the night reviewing plans.

3 November 67–No mail from you again–five days now.... Oh, I hope you're not moving! I like you right where you are.... You're the most important thing in my life–you are my life, and I will always worry about you.... The news has very little about the 1st Cav, all we hear about is the Marines; they must have their own press agent.... I just love you.

4 November 67–We have everything ready to move and tonight I was informed to put the move on hold for twenty-four hours.... Just advised that we are moving tomorrow.... I think someone is messing with me.

6 November 67–Last night at 2000 hours we received trucks to move the battalion.... We moved today.... Guess where ... back to Uplift.... We aren't in the same place at Uplift. We are building a new location on a hill ... a lot of work and coordination still ahead for me.... I love you.

6 November 67–Got five letters today, a set of slides and a book.... I pray that you don't move to Chu Lai.... I wish you were back at Uplift.

10 November 67–You know what means even more to me is that look of love and pride on your face when we're in a public place, the praise you bestow when I've done something wisely or good, the value you put on my ideas, your wonderful tolerance, your appreciation when I strive to please you, your faith

*in my love and your faithfulness, and most of all the mutual joy we share in
knowing our great love for each other.*

12 November 67–We had an awards ceremony here at Uplift yesterday.…
I received a Bronze Star for valor and the Air Metal.… The Air Medal is
awarded for flying twenty combat missions. The Sergeant Major told me I
flew more than ninety combat air missions, but I wasn't counting.… The
Bronze Star is for the raid on the village of Lo Dieu.… I long to be near
you, to look at you, to touch you, to talk to you.… Until then, I'll see you
in my dreams.

*13 November 67–I'm glad you're at Uplift.… I want them to leave you
there.… I stay continually busy with school and I seem to work all the time.…
I'm miserable without you, so I work hard to compensate.*

14 November 67–I tried to take pictures, but the weather has damaged
the camera.… The advance will not function.… I'll work on it, until then
I have my small 16mm.

16 November 67–One hundred fourteen days to go.… See you in my
dreams.

19 November 67–I spent most of yesterday investigating an accident.…
One of my jeeps was hit broad-side on Highway One by a Vietnamese
bread truck.… The soldier is ok, but the driver of the bread truck was
killed.… Last night I finished writing my report on the accident.… I wish
I had the time to write about everything that happens here, but there's not
enough time.

20 November 67–The battalion CO radioed me while he was making a
helicopter trip to visit one of the companies. He said, "There's a tree on the
northwest end of my landing pad that presents a hazard for my chopper.
I'll be coming back to the LZ in twenty minutes. Let's see how fast you
can react."… I gathered a few men, an ax and two buckets of paint. We

chopped down the tree, painted it yellow and in black we painted "Ready Sir" on the stump.... I don't know if I told you, but I am the battalion S4 and assistant S4. I've really held those positions for most of my time here, but now it's official.

21 November 67–Here is the Thanksgiving menu, compliments of Uncle Sam and my mess sergeant: Shrimp Cocktail, Crackers, Roast Turkey, Gravy, Cornbread Dressing, Cranberry Sauce, Mashed Potatoes, Glazed Sweet Potatoes, Buttered Mixed Vegetables, Assorted Crisp Relishes, Hot Rolls, Butter, Fruit Cake, Mincemeat Pie, Pumpkin Pie with Whipped Topping, Assorted Nuts, Assorted Candy, Assorted Fresh Fruits, Tea w/ Lemon, and Milk ... not bad for a combat zone.... The men in the field will receive a similar meal.... I have attached a listing of all officers of the 2nd/5th Battalion. As you can see I am officially the S4.... I am also the assistant S4. No plans to replace that position in the near future.... I think they are content with me doing both jobs.

21 November 67–I'm so tired of doing grades.... I'm almost finished, but when you have five hundred fifty students, it takes a long time.... We worked almost exclusively on "Jeanette Isabella" in choir today. It's really giving them problems, since it's in three parts.

24 November 67–Delta Company is at LZ Two-Bits and today their mortar munitions blew-up.... Their supplies came from three locations and Uplift was one supplier.... It's not clear what or how, but it will be investigated.

24 November 67–Happy Thanksgiving, Honey and I have so much to be thankful for. I have the most wonderful man in the world in love with only me, and I love that man so, so much.

26 November 67–I may try to take an in-country R&R just to get some sleep.... I enjoy my job, but we work weekends and holidays.... I'm on duty twenty-four hours a day, seven days a week.

28 November 67–I want to be your husband. Not your pen pal. I'm tired of writing letters.... I've done a good job here. Can I come home now? Please! Can't wait to be home. I love you so much. Stay sweet. I'll see you in my dreams.

29 November 67–Roses are red, violets are blue, I'm your husband and I should be home with you.... Every evening the battalion staff officers are required to join the battalion CO for dinner.... We eat and listen to him talk.... At 1900 hours we leave the mess tent and go to the battalion command post for the daily briefing.... Each staff member is required to give a briefing on their activities.... The briefing is usually finished around 2100 hours.... Since my day starts at 0500 hours, my personal time begins at 2100 hours, and I'm ready for bed by 2200 hours.... Good night.

30 November 67–Got a package with pepperoni and cheese and several letters, but no pictures.... Take more pictures.

4 December 67–I miss you so much. I wish I could just skip Christmas this year and pretend that I don't see everyone else having fun with those they love. This time of the year is going to be next to unbearable.

6 December 67–LTC Love asked me to extend for three months to become General Urby's aide.... Naturally, I said no.... This year must be longer than other years. It seems as if it will never end....

10 December 67–It's getting cooler here on the Bong Son Plains and the rain only makes it feel colder.... The monsoon season in the highlands begins in October and ends in April.

11 December 67–Last night the mess supply tent burned to the ground. We salvaged what we could and the mess sergeant borrowed what we needed to handle this morning's breakfast.... Not sure of the cause, but I'll investigate.

11 December 67—You tell Lieutenant Colonel Love that I put a hex on him for even suggesting a three-month extension. I mean, after all I am a Jeanie.... You didn't send me copies of your awards orders. I'm real excited about the medals.

13 December 67—I received packages from my sister today. Several were wrapped so I've saved those for Christmas Day. I also got three stockings filled with candy and games.... I'll share those with my men.... I also got several Christmas cards and a package from you.... I struck it rich today.... The chaplain gave me a Christmas tree and one of my men gave me decorations. I put it on a box in my hooch and placed the presents under it.... It will do, but there's no place like home and being with you.... I'll see you in my dreams.

13 December 67—I got a very pleasant and heartwarming surprise ... a Christmas card and letter from Captain Brummett. He had some wonderful things to say about you. Things that I already know of course, but I'm glad others see these qualities too. I'm also glad to see the company you keep.

14 December 67—I hit the jackpot again today.... I received two letters from you, a letter and Christmas card from your parents, a present from my Mom (I put it under my tree), candy from my sister and a large box of candy from Aunt Stella and Uncle Carson.... It has really been cold.... Rain and high winds make it feel even colder.... I spent the morning visiting the infantry companies in the field.... They are complaining about the cold, wet weather as well.... After my visits today, I'm glad that I have a warm, dry place at Uplift for tonight.

15 December 67—Two hundred eighty days of writing you to tell you how much I love you; I'm ready to tell and show you in person.... I received seven Christmas cards today and one from you.... I really hated to hear about Chuck Pitts. He was really the greatest guy.... I remember running into him in the woods on a map reading course while in OCS.... We sat

and talked about being in combat in Vietnam and he talked about running into enemy fire and being hit and falling to the ground to die in battle.... We agreed to do our best and fate would take its course, and for him, it did.... A great friend lost.... I love to read your letters.... You sound like you love life and you make things sound so interesting and enjoyable.... Till March, I'll see you in my dreams.

16 December 67–Eighty-five days left.... This afternoon, I went to my tent and noticed a large paper sack under my tree. It had a note and was from Chaplain Mal Brummitt. Since it wasn't wrapped, I opened it.... It contained cans and jars of enchiladas, tamales, chili, tortillas, refried beans, taco sauce, and green chili.... Will you join me for dinner this Saturday night?

17 December 67–I drove to An Khe today with Sergeant McNeely, my motor pool sergeant. I received reports that none of the 2nd/5th vehicles there are running.... We needed to put a boot in the right place to get things straightened out.

17 December 67–When you get off the plane in LA, I'm going to fly into your arms and nothing will ever take me away from you again.

18 December 67–My choir sang great tonight and I was very pleased as were the parents. My boss was there and he was quite satisfied and pleased. But, I'm the most pleased of all, it's over.

19 December 67–Hi Sweetheart, This time last year it was a weekend; a very memorable weekend–you were here in San Antonio with me. You were so amazed at Texas–your first time here, but not your last. We had such a wonderful time, going places together. You say that that weekend made your mind up for you.... You know what I remember enjoying the most? The drive back to Polk. I remember driving along in silence, no one speaking, and thinking how unusual it was that I didn't feel uncomfortable in that silence. I wanted you to love me so much and was so ecstatic when you finally honestly

admitted it. You'll never know how happy I was when you asked me to marry
you. I love you so.

20 December 67–Received five Christmas cards today.... I also received a
call from Army personnel informing me that my new assignment will be
at Fort Belvoir, VA.... I'll talk to the CO and see what I need to do to get
stationed in Texas.

24 December 67–T'was the night before Christmas when all through the
LZ, not a creature was stirring, not even a VC. All the weapons were hung
by the foxholes with care, in hopes that Saint Nick soon would be there.
All of the men were snuggled on air mattresses with care, with visions
of mortar rounds dancing in the air. I in my OD sweater and Ma in her
picture frame had just settled down for a long monsoon's night. When out
on the log pad there arose such a clatter. I sprung from my air mattress to
see what was the matter. I zipped open the flap and threw up the poncho,
when what to my wondering eyes did appear–can't think of the rest of the
words, but you get the message.... We had our usual dinner and briefing
with the colonel, and around 1900 hours we all went to our new chapel.
It was completed this afternoon and really looks great.... We sang carols
and Chaplain Mal gave a good sermon, all by candle light.... Till March
... I love you bunches.... Merry Christmas and have a wonderful day
tomorrow.... I'll see you in my dreams.

25 December 67–Merry Christmas Honey, I hope you had a wonderful
day. Mine was as expected.... We did have a nice dinner with turkey and
all the trimmings.... Around 1630 hours Mal and I gathered around the
Christmas tree and we opened presents.... Both of us got games, about
eight in all.... I spent a lot of time looking at your pictures, but I do that
everyday.... I received three letters from my favorite gal this morning....
The Bob Hope show is visiting Chu Lia and is scheduled to be at the Phu
Cat Air Force base, twenty miles south of Uplift, tomorrow..... I would
love to attend, but that's not possible.

25 December 67—Merry Christmas.... I love my pearls and bracelet. They are beautiful.... I try to think about this time next year when we will be together for Christmas.

26 December 67—I feel down and very homesick; I miss you so much.... I'll need to work on my attitude.... I should be feeling great as March is now just around the corner.

27 December 67—I received a package filled with delicious Christmas cookies and peanuts.... Mal and I cooked Mexican food tonight.... We followed directions on the labels and it was good.... Seventy-two days left and my excitement is building.... Stay sweet and love me bunches.... I love you. See you in my dreams.

28 December 67—The U.S. Army is finally putting the ARVN in the fight.... An ARVN battalion is being assigned to the 1st Cav and they will be included in missions.... In the past two months the ARVN have had a few battles in our area of operations.

30 December 67—Happy first anniversary ... I love you with all my heart.... Today I've missed you more than other days as I thought of last year this time and relived the day over and over in my mind.

30 December 67—Happy Anniversary!

31 December 67—Happy New Year.... I've been working on a report for my boss this holiday.... The Cowboys lost the NFL Championship to Green Bay in the last few seconds of the game.

1 January 68—Happy New Year, Received two letters today.... Sounds like we both had a sad, lonely Christmas Day.... We'll make up for it over the next one hundred years.

2 January 68–I wrote the Department of the Army yesterday requesting a change in assignment from Fort Belvoir to Texas. The CO and everyone I talk to say it's a prestige assignment. LTC Love was there early in his career. There are only nine infantry officers at Belvoir and it's close to the Pentagon.… I'll not think of it anymore.… I should have a reply in about fifteen days.

3 January 68–Yesterday I had a visit from the ARVN company commander at Phu My. His name is Quan Hai (first lieutenant) Bihn.… He spoke good English and I found out a lot about the South Vietnamese Army.… Bihn grew up in Saigon and his father is a professor at the University in Saigon.… He has three years of university study to go before he becomes a doctor of medicine.… ARVN officers have three men assigned to them twenty-four hours a day. They cook, clean, prepare uniforms and serve as body guards.… An officer is allowed to kill up to five of his men in a year, rather than court marshals, they shoot or stab them for insubordination or incompetence.… He told of one sergeant who was ordered by his company commander to kill his lieutenant, so that night he killed him in his sleep.… The higher ranking officer or NCO is required to correct their subordinates and it's usually carried out by slapping or punching.… I like the American system much better.

7 January 68–The weather has been really nice lately … a break in the monsoons.… I plan to visit An Khe in the next few weeks. There, I'll pack all my personal items to mail to you.… When I leave for home, all I'll have are the clothes I wear, military papers and a shaving kit.

8 January 68–CPT Ward hasn't left for the States. He's been working on projects for the battalion commander.… The battalion commander told him recently to prepare to take over Alpha Company as their commander.… He doesn't seem enthused.… The colonel told me to start thinking about replacements for my positions.… He said when I leave, he plans to fill the captain and lieutenant positions.… Since it takes a captain and lieutenant

to replace me, they should make me a major. What do you think? Until we are together again, I'll see you in my dreams.

9 January 68–We might move north later this month, but nothing firm.

10 January 68–Due to enemy build-up of troops, all in-country R&R to resorts has been canceled, so I'm going to An Khe for a few days of relaxation.... You will read about units of the 1st Cav moving near the DMZ ... 2nd/5th to remain in Bong Son for now.... We will be the last infantry unit of the division to go north.... You should stop teaching in January; you'll need time to prepare for your trip to LA and to make plans for our fourth honeymoon.... I'll have thirty-five days leave and we still don't know where we'll be assigned, but I'm betting on Texas.

11 January 68–No mail again today. It's getting wishy-washy again.... I love you and need you sweetheart.

12 January 68–Left Uplift at 1100 hours and arrived An Khe 1600 hour.... Mal and I visited the officers club for drinks and a hamburger.... We saw a movie and turned in early.... It's nice to not be constantly called and interrupted for a while.

13 January 68–R&R is great! I got up at 1100 hours, got a haircut and read a bit.... I drove Mal to the airport.... He has services to hold in the field on Sunday.... The battalion is grilling steaks tonight, so I'll eat, read and catch up on sleep.... Tomorrow I'll leave for Uplift around noon.... Fifty-five days to go.

15 January 68–I made it back to Uplift and entered a mess.... Two companies were ambushed by NVA and I've spent most of my time on the radio and on the chopper pad directing re-supply.... My supply sergeant, Windham, leaves for the states tomorrow.... We had a small celebration for him.... He was completely surprised and even shed a tear.... While I was

in An Khe, I had a plaque made with comments from his men and me. It's really nice.... We'll miss him and I won't be far behind in my departure.

16 January 68–I got three letters and a package with some goodies from you today.... I didn't mail my personal things while in An Khe.... I'll handle that in Feb.... For the past two weeks I haven't slept well. I wake up often and look around for you.... You are on my mind twenty-four hours a day.... I love you so much. See you in my dreams.

19 January 68–Happy General Robert E. Lee's birthday.... He is LCT's hero and we had a celebration in the general's honor.... We had award ceremonies, a number of speeches and we grilled steaks.... Captain Ward leaves for the States soon and is having a party in An Khe. He's requested the chaplain and I attend, so I may go back to An Khe. The chaplain is leaving for R&R on Monday, so he'll just stay in An Khe after the party.... Sgt Windham will attend since he is in An Khe preparing to leave for home.

20 January 68–I flew to Camp Radcliff, An Khe for the party.... We had grilled chicken and a lot of beer.... My party was interrupted at 2300 hours with a call from LZ Uplift. I have to be back at LZ English by 1000 hours tomorrow for a meeting of all S4s in the Bong Son area.

21 January 68–The meeting lasted for almost two hours, covering strategies for moving a battalion.... They didn't cover anything new to me.

22 January 68–I love you so.... I want to see the love in your face. And, what is so wonderful is that it's really there and you never hide it. I hope you always look for it in my eyes, because it will always be there.... Be careful and love me.

23 January 68–Slowly, but surely An Khe is losing the 1st Cav.... All the main operational elements of the Cav have gone north.... I have forty-five days left in country; maybe the 2nd/5th will stay at Uplift.

24 January 68–You asked about my replacement for the assistant S4 position. I recommended Lieutenant Salzar and the battalion commander has approved him. I've had twelve lieutenants ask me about the position. It's a sought after job here.... I know I've enjoyed it.

26 January 68–Lieutenant Salzar joined me today as assistant S4.... You must really be sick. Your last letter had mentholatum all over it.... Get well soon.

26 January 68–I'm looking forward to that long drive home from LA so much. You and I all alone. We have so much to discuss.

27 January 68–NOW–concerning your idea of going naked for thirty-five days. It sounds great to me, but it will have to be someplace very private and warm.

29 January 68–You remember my first RTO, Tom Jarrett? He's Sgt Jarrett now and he leaves Vietnam twenty days before me.... He's going to Ft. Hood.... I love you. Stay sweet. I'll see you in my dreams.

30 January 68–The war news was very disturbing today. Although they didn't actually say it, I'm sure the 2nd/5th had action. It was either LZ Uplift or English that got mortared.

31 January 68–I didn't get to write yesterday.... All major LZs along the east coast of Vietnam were mortared in the early morning hours.... We also received word to prepare to move north in about two weeks.... This morning around 0200 hours, we were hit with 75mm recoilless rifle fire.... The 2nd/5th was not damaged.... The Vietnamese New Year, *Tet* has begun and enemy activity is increasing.... I got two letters from you and one from the Department of the Army. They said I have given them sufficient time to change my orders and they have assigned me to duty in Waco, Texas. How about that?

3 February 68–I got the Japanese Hakata doll and the Wisteria Maiden doll today. They are lovely, Sweetheart, and yes, they are what I wanted.... Thank you most honorable husband.

5 February 68–Got four letters today. One especially hit me rather hard. First, I was disturbed with Uplift being hit and you moving north.... Then I was exhilarated with your new assignment to Waco!

9 February 68–Four more weeks! Soon I'll be in your arms. It seems more like a dream than reality. This whole year has been one long nightmare, except for the week of paradise.... This time last year we were in NYC. We had some tense moments driving there, and lots of fun ones. I'd sure love to be walking down Broadway holding your hand right now.

12 February 68–I got six letters today.... With the move of the operational functions of the division north, the division APO was included, so mail is slow for those left behind.

14 February 68–Happy Valentine's Day! Got your letter of Feb 9. I want to hear that you're getting your mail. Knowing that you're unhappy only makes me unhappy too.... The days are really dragging ... worst than before Hawaii.

18 February 68–The chaplain and I got to Phu Cat Air Force Base mid-afternoon yesterday for a short R&R.... Around 1630 hours, two of my men walked-up to me, a surprise, and they told me that the colonel wanted us back at Uplift ASAP.... The 2nd/5th is moving north tomorrow.... I am writing this letter from a make-shift tent at 2000 hours at Camp Evans.... The camp is twenty miles northwest of Hue and seventeen miles south of the DMZ near Quang Tri.... Everything seems rather confused here.... We are in make-shift sleeping arrangements tonight and should get a more permanent battalion location tomorrow.... The big build-up in the north is on and I have twenty days left in-country.... I would have welcomed this in early 1967, but now all I think about is coming home to you.... It's really

cold here, 35° as I write.... We flew to Quang Tri by C130 and loaded into vehicles and convoyed to Camp Evans.... Disabled U.S. vehicles were strewn all over the road.... I love you.

19 February 68–It's been a busy, wet and cold day.... It will take a long time to get this battalion operating in a normal way.... Supplies are difficult to get, clothes are non-existent, and C rations are the only food available to us.... We are beginning to establish our battalion headquarters outside the existing perimeter of Camp Evan, so it will take time to establish a secure and comfortable camp.... I'm too short to be this close to the DMZ.

20 February 68–We left most of our heavy equipment at LZ Uplift. It's to follow us later.... We have a few mules and one 2½ ton truck.... We are working these vehicles to death trying to get supplies and handle the construction.... We don't have the support facilities like we did at Uplift.... The terrain is very different than the Central Highlands ... rolling hills and small shrubs make up our surrounding landscape.... It's great tank country, except for the rain and mud and we don't have tanks.... I'm really busy both day and night, so the time is moving fast.

20 February 68–It's so easy to get wrapped up in daydreaming now. I daydream about everything–LA, our trip, living in Waco, your schooling, getting pregnant.... There's so very much to do with our lives, and yet I know that time will fly by and that all too soon we'll be old and looking at the past instead of the future. We've got to make that past really beautiful to look back on. I know it couldn't be anything else but beautiful.... I love you.

21 February 68–I got six letters today.... They are finally catching-up with me.... I received a report today that the 1st Cav has located the NVA command post controlling the battle of Hue.... The 7th Cav has been put in place and is preparing for an attack.

23 February 68–I don't know if I told you, but we don't have tents. They were left behind at Uplift and were to follow with other heavy equipment. We

are making poncho tents and sleeping on the ground as I did with Charlie Company.... It's cold and wet and the sun never shines.... As best I can tell, I have eleven days left in the field and then I'll return to An Khe to clear papers and prepare to leave for the U.S.A.–An Khe still has a few non-operational Cav units left there.... I really look forward to our reunion in LA.

24 February 68–We are still building bunkers and other fortification.... Today NVA blew up the bridge to Quang Tri, so our supply lines are cut off ... estimated seven days to re-open the bridge.... Supplies are now being dropped from airplanes and they only include essentials such as ammo and C rations.... Without new clothing, we stay wet and muddy.... When we do get clothing, I send it to the field units.... I have a sore throat and I seem to be getting a cold, but I'll recover before LA.... I'll see you in a little while.

25 February 68–I keep writing you, but you will most likely be on your way with your dad to LA by the time this letter arrives. I'll write a few more to keep you posted anyway. I'll see you in a little while. I love you.

26 February 68–Got your letters fourteenth, fifteenth, eighteenth and nineteenth.... What's worse is the 1st Cav's big action north of Hue was after these letters were written.... I 'm so worried.... I love you so very much. Be careful and love me.

27 February 68–I received a call from An Khe today advising me that my flight to the U.S. is on March 5.... I can hardly believe that my day of departure is so near.... I've been told to prepare to leave Camp Evans tomorrow.... It takes two days to get to An Khe.

Charlie Company, Second Battalion, Fifth Cavalry Regiment Operational Reports, March 1967 to March 1968

The following are monthly summaries of operations for the Second/Fifth Cav from March 1967 through March 1968. The summaries are taken from the following site: http://www.tallcomanche.org/March_1967.htm. The site references the following sources: © 2000 Ken Burington, source, Operation Pershing Combat After Action Report with additional material from the 1967 Second/Fifth Cav History.

Summary – March 1967

The Second/Fifth Cavalry continued search and destroy operations among the crowded villages of the southern plains during the first six days of March 1967. The third week of Operation Pershing passed with C Company, often working with D Company, investigating wells, tunnels, and other hiding places east of Highway One around My An village during the day and setting out ambushes at night. The week was characterized by light contact and problems with snipers and various types of booby traps. At the end of this period, the battalion moved south a few miles to another AO: the area known as The Crescent.

Like the plains the battalion had just left, The Crescent was a coastal flatland bordered by mountains. It stretched north from Nui Mieu

(Mountain) to the Cay Giep mountain group and from the South China Sea beach west about twelve to fifteen kilometers to the coastal mountain ranges. The center of The Crescent was dominated by a large, shallow lake, Dam Tra O, and the entire area was very productive with sea and fresh-water fishing and rice growing. The fishing and farming in the area made it important to the Communists and the mountains provided convenient base areas. The Second/Fifth Cav had the same mission in The Crescent that it had on the plains to the north: to search for enemy troops, their hiding places and storage areas, to capture or destroy any Communist resources, and to disrupt any Communist organization in the villages.

With the company performing perimeter security for the new battalion CP at LZ Anchor, individual platoons searched villages and the foothills at the northern end of the plains for several days. C Company was then airlifted further south and placed to act as a blocking force while the Fortieth ARVN Regiment beat the bushes for VC around the southern end of Dam Tra O. C Company made contact, leading to the Battle of Phu Ninh near a village of that name located astride Highway 505 at the base of the Nui Mieu (Mountain). Despite having suffered severe casualties during the battle, C Company remained in control of the ground and continued to search and clear the hills of enemy for another six days, taking several prisoners, before moving their operations back to the northern part of the plains for two days. After this, C Company left the crowded villages of The Crescent and spent the last third of the month alternately searching the river valleys and slopes of the mountains west of LZ English and acting as a blocking force near Highway One north of LZ English while the Fortieth ARVN Regiment worked the area.

Summary - April 1967

The first day of April 1967 marked the last day of C Company's participation in Operation Pershing for a while. The company, with the rest of the Second/Fifth Cav, left the coastal region and returned to the First Cav base camp at An Khe for a stand-down to be followed by security operations in the highlands around Camp Radcliff. These plans were soon to be changed.

Due to increasing communist activity in Northern Quang Tri Province near the DMZ, the Marines had been forced to move resources out of coastal Quang Ngai Province just north of the Plains. This created a situation in which many of the VC and NVA who had been forced out of eastern Binh Dinh Province by the First Cav's Operation Pershing were able to move fairly safely into the area around the Marines' base at Duc Pho. In fact, it was estimated that 90% of the land area and population of Quang Ngai Province were communist controlled; the Marines held only the area immediately around Duc Pho. Obviously, help was needed and on April 6 MACV selected the First Cavalry Division to send it.

Relieved of their assignment at An Khe, C Company and the rest of the Second/Fifth Cav were airlifted into LZ English on April 7 and then made an air assault thirty-five kilometers north to Duc Pho to initiate Operation Lejeune. C Company and the battalion CP established a base at an old, abandoned, French, dirt airstrip, which was then named LZ Frenchy. The company spent the next twelve days helping to provide security for the LZ and for units of the 39th Engineer Battalion and at the same time, performing search and destroy operations around some of the hamlets of the coastal rice-growing area. The company suffered casualties from booby traps during this period.

The battalion's participation in Operation Lejeune ended on April 19 and on that day, C Company returned south to LZ Uplift in eastern Binh Dinh Province. The balance of the month was spent with the four companies of the second battalion, again part of Operation Pershing, searching for the enemy but having little contact in the flatlands near Dam Tra O and south of LZ Uplift

Summary - May 1967

As summer approached, the Second/Fifth Cav continued its participation in Operation Pershing in eastern Binh Dinh Province. The Communists' organization and command structure in the province had been disrupted during the preceding three months and the enemy was attempting to infiltrate troops into the coastal plains in an effort to regain strength and control over the many hamlets and villages. Since the civilian population of the mountain valleys had been evacuated and resettled, the lowland rice-growing areas near the coast became even more important to the VC and NVA soldiers; they had no other easy source of food supplies.

C Company's usual daily operations during May consisted of surrounding and searching villages in The Crescent, the flatlands in the vicinity of Dam Tra O (lake). This was a rich, agricultural area of rice paddies, with the large fresh-water lake and the nearby sea providing substantial additional resources. Infiltrators entered the area both from the western mountains and by sea. The Viet Cong attempted to blend into the legitimate populace of the many hamlets while the NVA troops generally seemed to stay in the two mountain groups; the Cay Giep to the north of The Crescent and the Nui Mieu to the south.

The cordon and search missions could be tedious and slow. The practice was to surround a hamlet early in the morning and then physically search the ground and the houses while Vietnamese police or ARVNs questioned the inhabitants, with particular attention being paid to military-aged males. Often nothing significant was found, but every so often a violent firefight would suddenly flare up. The usual method of approach was by helicopter but on one occasion, May 9, 1967, C Company made an amphibious assault on the village of Lo Dieu in a combined forces operation with the U.S. Navy. The unpredictable appearance of the cavalry troopers at scattered villages contributed to area security and helped keep the enemy off-balance and unable to establish political control over the population.

Summary - June 1967

June 1967 was a pretty busy month. The efforts by the Communists to bolster local forces and re-establish a military presence in the coastal area of Binh Dinh Province (the area known as The Crescent) continued with troops attempting to infiltrate both on foot and by boat, working their way south along the coast. The Nui Mieu (mountain) with its caves and rock formations and the Cay Giep (mountain), heavily wooded, were located south and north of the Dam Tra O Lake and adjacent to the South China Sea, and provided excellent terrain for concealment of the Communist base areas, but food supplies had to come from the villages below, and this meant coming out into the open.

In the beginning of the month, operations conducted with the South Vietnamese National Police in the northern Cay Giep uncovered weapons caches and the Second/Fifth Cav, working with ARVN troops and the Korean First ROK Regiment, searched the Nui Mieu. The constant presence of the Allied troops had the effect of forcing some of the Communist forces out into the lowlands where they were easier to find.

The companies of the Second/Fifth Cav sometimes made air assaults several times a day to investigate evidence of enemy activity and to assist each other. During the second week of June, numerous discoveries of weapons, new and hastily-built bunkers, and ammunition and food caches pointed to an increasing Communist presence. About the thirteenth of the month C Company captured three VC who had infiltrated by boat from the north. Their mission was to join local forces in preparation for an upcoming offensive in the Nui Mieu. This planned offensive was soon to be disrupted.

During the middle of the month, C Company established its night positions along the beach and moved to cordon and search nearby coastal fishing and rice-growing villages on foot each morning before first light. Those who were there during this period will remember the excellent swimming on that beautiful stretch of water, and the wind-blown sand getting into every weapon and meal. And they will remember the Huey helicopter, possibly part of a Night Hunter Team, that fired on the company the night of June 17, making two passes firing M-60s and wounding one man.

On the morning of June 19, C Company secured and searched a village just south of the Dam Tra O. Meanwhile B Company had run into a large NVA presence further south in a small village located along Highway 505 between the shore and the base of the Nui Mieu. Company A, Second/

Fifth Cav, made an air assault into the mountains behind the village to act as a blocking force and at 1600 hours C Company made a combat assault and joined B Company and tanks from the First/Sixty-ninth Armor in pushing into the village. The next day, after air strikes and an artillery fire mission, C and B Companies swept through and secured the battlefield. The two-day battle left thirty-one NVA soldiers dead. American losses were eight KIA and seventeen WIA.

Action then shifted west, to the other side of Highway One and the mountains there that formed the boundary of the coastal plain. The next day, June 21, an NVA prisoner led Company B, First/Fifth Cav into occupied fortifications in the hamlet of Van Thien (3) where they made contact with part of the Eighteenth Regiment of the Third NVA Division. C Company was picked up from their location south of the Dam Tra O, made OPCON to First/Fifth Cav and air assaulted into the area, setting up a blocking position to the south and linking up with elements of the 40th ARVN Regiment. Again, tanks from the First/Sixty-ninth Armor assisted the infantry in sweeping through the village. One hundred-one enemy were killed and one WIA captured. American losses in the Van Thien (3) battle were eleven KIA and eighteen WIA.

After this battle, C Company, along with the rest of the Second/Fifth Cav was tasked to remain in the beach and Nui Mieu areas to prevent another NVA build-up. It was while the Company was searching caves in the mountains that PFC Larry S. Byford was killed on June 23. A Psyops officer, Major Edwin W. Martin, Jr., was shot and killed while trying to talk NVA out of holes in a small mountain known as the Rockpile. Private First Class Byford was killed while attempting to assist the major.

C Company continued patrolling the Nui Mieu and searching villages along the coast as the month drew to an end. The last, large battle of the month took place on the twenty-eight and twenty-ninth. It became known as the Battle of Dam Tra O, and this time C Company was not involved. The fight began when the First/Ninth Cav stirred up a hornets nest in two villages, An Hoa and An Quang, located near the northern end of the lake between the Dam Tra O and the beach. Elements from the Second/Fifth Cav and the First/Fifth Cav, assisted by armored vehicles of the First/

Sixty-ninth Armor and the Fourth/Sixtieth Artillery (Dusters), attacked the villages, killing eighty-six NVA and capturing three. In addition, some NVA tried to escape across the lake by boat and were caught out on the water.

By the end of June, the Cav's aggressive and fast-moving operations had disrupted the communists' plans and efforts to build up a substantial force in the coastal part of Binh Dinh Province. The subsequent discovery from time to time of many previously unaccounted-for enemy bodies hidden among the rocks in the southern mountains showed the NVA losses to be even greater than first believed. The Crescent would be a little quieter for a time.

Summary - July 1967

Following the active month of June with its successful search operations and several large-unit clashes, the Second/Fifth Cav was assigned to provide security for the Bridge and several of the firebases along the Highway One portion of the coastal plains. While the first battalion, Fifth Cavalry assumed the responsibility for aggressive patrolling in the mountains and villages of eastern Binh Dinh Province, the companies of the second battalion took on a less mobile and generally less active function at Landing Zones, such as Uplift and Two-Bits and at the complex of bridges over the Bong Son (Lai Gang River) at the town of Bong Son.

Duties included stopping and inspecting civilian vehicles traveling over the bridges during the day (nothing legitimate moved at night) and a walking guard post over the steel bridge at night during which grenades were dropped into the water at random times and locations to discourage enemy swimmers who might attempt to mine the bridge piers. Concussion grenades were supposed to be used but, like many other items, were often in short supply so M-26 frags were substituted and caused a lot of damage to the wiring for the claymores and flares under the bridge as well as the telephone cables.

Most of C Company's guard assignments during July lasted one week. When that period was over, the Company would move on to another location such as LZ Uplift, replacing another second battalion company in providing security.

Duty at LZ Uplift meant a chance to see some old friends now working in the rear, a chance to catch a ride down Highway One to the Air Force base at Phu Cat to buy cartons of cigarettes in their Base Exchange, even a chance to get some replacement field gear or clean clothing. One of the disadvantages was that the visiting infantry companies were required to provide KP for the mess tents, but even that had a good side. Since most infantrymen are accomplished scroungers, a day working around the mess area meant a load of goodies to haul back to the bunker that night.

After a week at Uplift, it would be time for C Company to move on. Security duty at Two-Bits had a completely different feel to it, perhaps because of its location west of and nearer the entrance to the An Lao Valley area. It was located adjacent to a secondary road (Route 514) and a trading and black-market village had formed right at the entrance to the LZ. It was a good place to buy a case of American beer (ten MPC or 1000 Dong) or a fifth of Japanese whiskey for the same price, but the local patrols the Company ran in the area had to work in a busy and populous environment; it might have felt more comfortable to be a little more isolated.

English Airfield, also known as LZ English, was another large American base C Company guarded at times. Two others, LZ Ollie and LZ Pony, were small firebases that generally required less than a full company for their perimeters.

There were no significant incidents at any of the locations C Company occupied during the month of July. The entire area of operations from the western mountains to the coastline seemed subdued compared to the activity of the previous month, with even the first battalion not making contact in the mountains until the twenty-fifth. The next day, all of the second battalion companies were relieved of their security missions and returned to the Cay Giep (mountain) region to resume the search for enemy base camps but found no action, and July 1967 quietly came to an end.

Summary - August 1967

Charlie Company tried something different–again. As they had done before in May 1967, the company did a night amphibious assault.

The plains in Binh Dinh Province had long been a haven for Communist forces, dating back to the 1940s when the Vietnamese fought the French. The First Cav fought both Viet Cong and North Vietnamese units, and the Communists were often supported by the local population. CPT John "Jack" Yeagley was the Commanding Officer of C Second/Fifth Cav. He sent this e-mail:

This was during a phase in operations when we were interdicting infiltrating NVA to keep them from massing for an attack on a major objective. Intelligence wasn't very good. Basically, we seemed to be searching villages at random. Our normal mission for this type of operation was to cordon off a village to prevent NVA or VC in the village from escaping. After we would establish a cordon, the RVN National Police, the "white mice," would chopper in and search the village. An American AID (Agency for International Development) advisor was always with them. The white mice would question villagers and search the area for evidence of NVA or VC presence or movement. We would often round up a few of the enemy using these tactics. But we weren't as effective in the cordon and search technique when we moved in during daylight hours, including air assaults at dawn. The enemy could see us coming and sometimes fled from the area before we could conduct effective operations in and around the villages. It seemed to make sense to move in before daylight and establish our cordon before dawn. The troops were not used to moving as a company at night, but after we did it a few times and were successful at surprising the enemy, it became routine. We got very good at it and could move into a position at night without even causing a dog to bark.

That morning (August 2), we moved out about 0300 hours from a position about two or three km from our objective, a village on the plain near, as I recall. We moved on a direct azimuth to the objective with platoons in column, ranger style, leaving the weapons platoon with one mortar at our previous position for indirect fire support. I remember that it was an uneventful operation, and the white mice had come and gone when we began to move out of the area in early afternoon. As an aside, that morning our headquarters medic treated a little girl and a couple of women who had been injured a day or two before, unrelated to our operation. Our company docs helped where they could.

While we were moving out of that position, a burst of AK 47 fire killed Stottler and wounded two others. We immediately set up an LZ and medevaced the wounded while two platoons searched the village for the weapon, its owner, and any other enemy. We did not find anything, unfortunately. We continued for several days with the cordon and search operations in and around that area using the same tactics of moving at night. We had some successes and, thankfully, had no more casualties during that phase.

Ray Long was with the mortar platoon and recalls the company returned to LZ English on Chinooks after the operation was over. William Hawver was WIA with a wound to the shoulder, Monte Zierke was hit in the cargo pocket of his pants, and Ray Stottler, an M79 grenadier, was killed by a bullet to the head.

Summary - September 1967

With the Vietnamese national elections scheduled to take place on September 3, 1967, it was expected that the Communist forces would make very strong and serious attempts to intimidate the populace and interfere with the conduct of the polling. Therefore, during the first part of September, C Company, along with other U.S. and allied units, was tasked to help provide a secure environment for the voting. Many of the Cav units in the area around were pulled in from the western mountains and deployed near population centers to provide a sense of security. On election day itself, American forces were strictly held out of the towns where polling was taking place in order not to give any suggestion of U.S. interference with the electoral process. C Company was set up near and there was no trouble or major problems.

Having kept the lowlands of Binh Dinh Province quiet during the first several days of September, the Cav then took the war back into the mountains along the coast. From September 6 through September 13, as part of Operation Join Hands, companies from Second/Fifth, First/Fifth, First/Eighth, and Second/Twelfth Cav as well as the First Battalion, 40th ARVN Regiment searched for the NVA and VC hiding places in the Nui Mieu Mountains and the nearby Rockpile, resulting in three hundred ninety-two enemy KIA and seventy-four prisoners. At the same time, on September 6, the 227th Assault Helicopter Battalion conducted an air assault using forty-eight Huey slicks and eight Chinooks to land elements of five different infantry battalions on and around the Cay Giep Mountain to pin down an NVA regimental headquarters and support unit.

About the middle of September, C Company next moved into a relatively quiet period of providing security for an Engineer unit clearing ground for a new LZ near Route 1 and a couple of miles north of LZ Uplift. It was to be named LZ Ichibon and was planned to be the base for the 1st/50th Mechanized Infantry which was then on its way to Vietnam ("Ichibon" means "First" or "Number One" in Japanese). One of the duties was to "walk shotgun" for bulldozer operators since they were not able to hear the sound of gunfire over the noise of their machines. The Engineers used their equipment to dig positions on C Company's perimeter. During the day, platoon-sized patrols went out, usually west toward the mountains, and ambush patrols and LP's were set out at night. The week passed relatively quietly with one incident being the confiscation of about two pounds of C4 from a young girl who was carrying it in a basket.

With the completion of the clearing work at LZ Ichibon C Company was moved to LZ Uplift on September 21 to provide security, with part of the second platoon being positioned on top of Duster Hill where tracked vehicles ("Dusters") with twin 40-mm gun mounts were stationed. They were assigned to C Battery, Fourth Battalion and Sixtieth Artillery and were often used to fire harassment and interdiction missions into the mountains around Uplift.

This security interlude did not last long - C Company was back out on the beach on September 24 and spent the balance of the month performing cordon and search missions in the villages located along the coast.

The First/Fiftieth Mechanized Infantry began moving into their new home on September 27 and were permanently assigned to the First Cavalry Division. They would stay at LZ Ichibon less than two weeks; finding the location "unsuitable" and difficult to defend, they moved to LZ Uplift on October 9 and made that their base.

Summary - October 1967

The beginning of October 1967 saw C Company pulling out of the eastern portion of Binh Dinh Province and returning with the rest of the battalion to Camp Radcliff at An Khe. The Second/Fifth Cav was to assume the security of the Division's base camp and the four field companies left the coastal mountains, paddies and beaches on October 2 for what would turn out to be just over a month in the Central Highlands.

One of the first missions for C Company was patrolling north of Camp Radcliff in the "Y-Ring", a zone about five to seven kilometers out from the Camp's perimeter. Although the vegetation, the villages and the terrain all were different on the plateau, the operations were familiar: company and platoon patrols, platoon and squad ambushes and combat assaults.

Leaving the protection of the base camp to the other companies of the battalion, C Company took its turn providing security at various locations along Highway Nineteen, including posting squads at the many small bridges on the road and stationing a couple of platoons at LZ Schueller, a fire support base located alongside the road about eleven kilometers west of An Khe. The month ended with C Company back at An Khe.

2LT Quentin Dennis Zambona, the second platoon leader, was killed when a VC threw a grenade in Binh Dinh Province. It was the day after his twenty-first birthday—he had been in-country two months.

C Company remained at An Khe during the first week of November performing security duties for the Camp Radcliff base camp. On the 7th, the company returned to the area with the rest of the battalion ready to begin a new round of searches for the enemy in the mountains and valleys west of the coastal flatlands.

Following up on a LRRP team ambush on the 8th of November, C Company made light contact near 506 Valley, an area the company would spend much of the rest of the month in and around. The 506 and the Suoi Ca Valleys served as infiltration routes from the West toward the rich coastal plains, and the mountains enclosing the valleys were also rich hunting grounds concealing many Communist rest, training and base areas. There had been a noticeable increase in VC and NVA sightings here and the Second/Fifth Cav was tasked to halt the enemy movements.

Nature became the opponent on November 9 when Typhoon Freda made landfall at Tuy Hoa and headed toward the operational area. C Company established an FOB on a hilltop and was told to dig in deep and, by the way, "...there probably wouldn't be any helicopter support for three to four days." The company spent several quiet and wet days on the hill and then resumed normal patrol operations.

Pulled in from the field, C Company provided firebase security for several days before moving to the Bridge on Highway One about November 18th to guard that site. Bridge duty was always welcome and the four companies of the Second/Fifth Cav rotated responsibility for its protection, usually spending a week at a time at that location.

After a week at the Bong Son Bridge, the company returned to the mountains and the valleys to the west. The new Battalion Commander, LTC Joseph Love, had instituted a policy called the "mini-cav" in which a platoon from one of the field companies was kept airborne in Hueys while looking for targets of opportunity. If any suspicious activity or group of people was spotted, the platoon made an immediate assault to the location. This tactic proved very successful in catching VC who were trying to move in small groups during the daylight hours.

November passed with C Company working in the mountains and searching the small villages at the foot of the hills. The month ended badly with a friendly-fire incident on the twenty-ninth. While the company was working uphill toward suspected NVA positions, Lieutenant Arlington, Platoon Leader of the First Platoon, called for support from an ARA ship, which then mistakenly fired rockets into the platoon. There were several wounded and the platoon medic, Specialist Fifth Class Larry E. Shepherd, was killed.

Summary - December 1967

During December much of the enemy activity took place about eighteen miles to the north of the Second/Fifth Cav area of operations–the Second Battle of Tam Quan in the northern part of the Plains pitted the Division's First Brigade against the Seventh and Eighth Battalions of the Twenty-second NVA Regiment for over half the month. Consequently, the Crescent to the south and east was relatively quiet. C Company continued working in the mountains and river valleys west of the coastal plains, in particular around the southern end of 506 Valley. There was not much contact during this quiet period.

C Company, accompanied by A Company, returned to The Rockpile about the middle of the month. This small black mountain right at the edge of the sea and just east of the Nui Mieu (mountains) had been the scene of heavy combat during September of 1967, but the area was now quiet. After several days spent searching caves and rock shelters, C Company was pulled out of the field and given the task of guarding the Highway One bridge at Bong Son. With Christmas approaching this was a much-appreciated duty.

On Christmas Day CPT Dean Learish was replaced as Company Commander by CPT James Estep. The next day the company left the Bridge and resumed its search and clear operations in 506 Valley, Vinh Thanh Valley and the Suoi Ca Valley. 1967 came to an end with C Company making contact just hours before the New Year's Truce was to take effect.

Summary - January 1968

The first month of 1968 finds C Company heavily involved in operations in the coastal part of Binh Dinh Province. The company alternates providing security at various LZ's and Fire Support Bases with operations in the field. Patrolling in the mountains west of the coastal plains leads to frequent contact and searches in the villages near the South China Sea are equally profitable. Working with the First Battalion Fiftieth Mechanized Infantry, C Company helps develop heavy contact with the Ninety-fifth Battalion, Twenty-second Viet Cong Regiment in the Nui Mieu Mountains. The almost daily discovery of small groups of NVA and VC is due to Communist attempts to infiltrate troops in preparation for the planned *Tet* offensive, which begins prematurely in Binh Dinh Province one day ahead of schedule, on January 30.

Summary - March 1968

On March 1, 1968, the Second Brigade of the First Cav relieved the Second Brigade of the 101st Airborne and assumed the mission of clearing the enemy elements in the Hai Lang –My Chanh area. Hai Lang was the District Headquarters for the southernmost coastal district of Quang Tri Province. My Chanh, nine kilometers south along Highway One, was the location of an important bridge over the g Thac Ma (Thac Ma River) and also marked the boundary between Quang Tri and Thua Thien Provinces. After the First Cav took over responsibility for this area Second/Fifth Cav operations were widened in scope to the west and the east of the national highway. West of Highway One was the Hai Lang National Forest Reserve, a mountainous uninhabited area, heavily wooded with no roads and having very few trails. The Hai Lang Forest was a base area for infiltrators from the north. East of Highway One and stretching to the coast was the heavily inhabited area known by the French troops during the First Indochina War as the "Street Without Joy". Bernard Fall, in his book of the same name, described this flat area of rivers, canals, rice paddies, hamlets and cemeteries as "...fringed by a rather curious system of interlocking small villages separated one from the other by often less than 200 to 300 yards. Each village forms a veritable little labyrinth that measures barely more than 200 feet by 300 feet and is surrounded by bushes, hedges, or bamboo trees, and small fences, which made ground as well as aerial surveillance almost impossible." The villages are "protected in turn by a vast zone of swamps, sand holes and quicksand bogs, extending all the way to Road 1." There had been little change in "The Street" since the French had unsuccessfully attempted to eliminate the Viet Minh troops during Operation Camargue in July of 1953.

Large numbers of NVA had been gathering in the area with intentions of attacking Hai Lang, LZ Jane and the various highway bridges. C Company, along with the rest of Second/Fifth Cav, had been kept busy with search and destroy missions in the villages between Highway One and the coast as well as road and bridge security. The emphasis, according to the Second/Fifth Cav History (1968) "... was placed on the enemy's food supply; having taken away his fortress, the Cavalrymen were now attempting to starve him out of the area entirely."

On March 8, 1968 C Company was to search Pho Trach (1), Pho Trach (2) and Xom Dong My, villages in northern Thua Thien Province located about six kilometers east of the highway. It's an interesting fact that the NVA apparently knew we were coming. According to an intelligence alert that the second brigade received from the 101st Airborne, an NVA POW told his interrogators that 100 NVA had been in Sieu Quan hamlet and 70 had left early on March 7 and had gone to the vicinity of Pho Trach # 1 and #2. They were digging in and laying mines –they had four 60mm mortars with much ammunition, AK47 auto rifles, SKS rifles, and two fragmentation grenades per man. This information was received by Second/Fifth Cav at 0055 hours in the morning of March 8. At 1244 hours on March 8, the first elements of C Company making the CA touched down at a green LZ just two hundred meters southeast of Pho Trach (1). The Hueys then departed to pick up the second lift at the My Thanh bridge location.

While this second element was in the air, Brigade HQ ordered a mission change and diverted C Company to secure a Conex of "medical supplies" accidentally dropped from a CH-47 Chinook about one point four kilometers from LZ Jane near the north bank of the g Nhung. Remaining platoons were landed at the Conex site while the first group of men remained at Pho Trach (1) until 1400 hours when they were finally picked up. After the Conex was found and secured, first and third platoons were sent to clear the surrounding area and to find a good site for a NDP (Night Defensive Position). Meanwhile the following items were recovered around the downed Conex: one heavy duty engine; various chairs; three boxes of sundries; poncho liners; one safe; one broken gin bottle; "some beer." No classified material was found, and the safe was unopened. Pernel from LZ Jane arrived to inventory the contents and found there were no losses. Another CH-47 lifted out the Conex at 1720 hours and C Company moved to high ground about one klick to the west and set up their night perimeter, leaving a reinforced squad from first platoon at the site of the Conex impact. Both the ambush and the company spent a quiet night.

In the morning of March 9, 1968 C Company resumed the combat assault that had been aborted the previous day. At 0803 hours, the first lift of Hueys touched down to a green LZ at the same location used the previous day. The entire company was on the ground just southeast of Pho Trach (1) by 0841 hours, with the last lift receiving ground fire from a paddy area west of the hamlet during their insertion. An Intelligence Squad arrived at 0930 hours to assist in interrogations. The day started well enough. By 1000 hours Pho Trach (1) had been searched, two hundred pounds of rice found and the Intelligence Squad was beginning to question forty prisoners who had been detained. At 1100 hours, a helicopter was requested to pick up the rice and one detainee. An NVA uniform and over six hundred pounds of rice were turned up by noon and it looked as if the search operation was going to be successful. And then first platoon started receiving fire from Pho Trach (2), about three hundred meters to the north.

One man was killed and two wounded by the first rounds at about 1250 hours. The fire increased until by 1315 hours, first Platoon was pinned down behind a small embankment. As the platoon leader had received a serious neck wound and was not able to direct the men, the company commander, CPT James Estep, with the artillery forward observer, Lieutenant Maynard and his RTO Jack Pease, and several other members of the company headquarters section crawled across several paddies to the first Platoon location to take control of the situation. A scout helicopter and a Cobra gunship arrived at 1330 hours. Under the cover of the rockets and tube artillery, the casualties were pulled back. One of the wounded men died during this period; the lieutenant was medevaced at 1410 hours. Captain Estep was seriously wounded in the leg while first Platoon was pulling back and fell exposed in the last paddy before reaching cover. The Second Platoon Sergeant Mable, and a rifleman named Wesley, ran out under fire to carry him back behind a paddy dike. Captain Estep has said "... they worked together like they rehearsed it." Sergeant Mable, who would himself be seriously wounded five days later, received the Silver Star for this action.

After first Platoon rejoined the company, they continued working over the contact area. At 1429 hours, the first Platoon of D Company was placed under the operational control of C Company and landed at a large cemetery to the northwest of the Pho Trach hamlets to act as a blocking force. Small arms fire continued to come from the direction of Pho Trach (2), and gunships and ARA fired on targets there until 1614 hours while the company pulled back about two hundred meters and set up a perimeter. Battalion Commander LTC Joseph B. Love landed, bringing with him a replacement for Captain Estep, who was medevaced at 1628 hours. Effective at the time of the medevac, the Battalion S3 Air Officer, CPT Paul Ogg, took command of the company in the field. The first Platoon of D Company was released at 1734 hours and returned to the control of their company. C Company set up their NDP and placed an ambush between the company perimeter and Pho Trach (2) but there was no contact during the night.

At 2122 hours ARVN artillery at Phong Dien fired four WP (white phosphorous) rounds near the company perimeter, but there were no casualties. The search and clear operations in this area continued the next day, March 10, with the company receiving sporadic mortar and small arms fire throughout the day from 0830 hours until the late afternoon, resulting in two US WIA's. One detainee and two NVA KIA's (probably from ARA strikes) were reported.

APPENDIX C

Thanksgiving 1967

THANKSGIVING 1967
PHU MY, BINH DINH, REPUBLIC OF VIETNAM
2D BATTALION, 5TH CAVALRY

COMMANDING OFFICER: LTC JOSEPH B. LOVE
SERGEANT MAJOR: SGM JAY C. COPLEY
EXECUTIVE OFFICER: CPT HARRY J. WARD
S-1: CPT JAMES L. ESTEP
S-2: 1LT EDGAR L. SMITH III.
S-3: MAJ WILLIAM E. MURPHY III.
S-4: 1LT TIMOTHY R. SOYARS
SURGEON: CPT DOUGLAS FISK
CHAPLAIN: CPT MALCOLM J. BRUMMITT

"A" COMPANY

COMMANDING OFFICER: CPT CLAYTON A. PRATT
FIRST SERGEANT: 1SG RODNEY J. LAWSON

"B" COMPANY

COMMANDING OFFICER: CPT HUGH B. SPROUL.III.
FIRST SERGEANT: 1SG JERRY O. WATSON

"C" COMPANY

COMMANDING OFFICER: CPT DEAN LEARISH
FIRST SERGEANT: 1SG EDMUND FUNKHOUSER

"D" COMPANY

COMMANDING OFFICER: 1LT JOSE STEVENS
FIRST SERGEANT: SFC STEVEN CHARLEBOIS

"HEC"

COMMANDING OFFICER: 1LT CLARENCE W. KEHOE
FIRST SERGEANT: 1SG HERSHEL MULLINS

The first Thanksgiving was about 350 years ago. Each year
Americans have had more to be thankful for. In 1967, we are grate-
ful for our heritage, the support of the people of the United
States, and our other blessings. Along with other men of the FIRST
TEAM, the 5th Cavalry is READY for any mission assigned.

J.B. LOVE
LTC, 5th Cavalry
Commanding 2/5

THANKSGIVING DAY DINNER

Shrimp Cocktail

Crackers

Roast Turkey

Turkey Gravy   Cornbread Dressing   Cranberry Sauce

Mashed Potatoes   Glazed Sweet Potatoes

Buttered Mixed Vegetable

Assorted Crisp Relishes

Hot Rolls   Butter   Fruit Cake   Mincemeat Pie

Pumpkin Pie w/Whipped Topping

Assorted Nuts   Assorted Candy   Assorted Fresh Fruits

Tea w/Lemon   Milk

PRAYER

Father of mercies and giver of all good, by whose power we were created, by whose bounty we are sustained, and by whose spirit we are transformed, accept, we beseech Thee, our prayer of thanks.

For those who love us and of whose love we would be more worthy; for those who believe in us and whose hopes we cannot disappoint; for every good gift of healing and happiness and renewal, we bless Thy name, we thank Thee for our homeland, for all that is just and true, noble and right, wise and courageous in our history. We praise Thee for our place in the community of nations and we invoke Thy blessings on men of good will wherever they may be and who labor for a world of justice, freedom and fraternity.

Most of all, Eternal Father, we thank Thee for Thyself, the nearness of Thy presence and the warmth of Thy love, whereby our minds and hearts find joy and peace. Freely we have received, O God; freely let us give ourselves to Thy gracious purposes. For Thy love's sake. Amen.

COMMANDER'S MESSAGE

On this traditional Thanksgiving Day, as we find ourselves half way around the world from home, we should pause for a few moments to count our many blessings as Americans. We should never forget that in Vietnam, our actions are defending free men everywhere. We pray that peace will come to all the world and that all of us can return to our loved ones in the not too distant future.

W. C. WESTMORELAND
General, United States Army
Commanding

Thanksgiving Day
VIETNAM
1967

APPENDIX D

Christmas 1967

CHRISTMAS 1967
PHU MY, BINH DINH, REPUBLIC OF VIETNAM
2D BATTALION, 5TH CAVALRY

COMMANDING OFFICER: LTC JOSEPH B. LOVE
SERGEANT MAJOR: SGM JAY C. COPLEY
EXECUTIVE OFFICER: CPT HARRY J. WARD
S-1: CPT DEAN LEARISH
S-2: 1LT EDGAR L. SMITH III
S-3: MAJ WILLIAM E. MURPHY III
S-4: 1LT TIMOTHY R. SOYARS
SURGEON: CPT DOUGLAS FISK
CHAPLAIN: CPT MALCOLM J. BRUMMITT

"A" COMPANY

COMMANDING OFFICER: CPT CLAYTON A. PRATT
FIRST SERGEANT: 1SG RODNEY J. LAWSON

"B" COMPANY

COMMANDING OFFICER: CPT ROBERT H. CARROLL
FIRST SERGEANT: 1SG JERRY O. WATSON

"C" COMPANY

COMMANDING OFFICER: CPT JAMES L. ESTEP
FIRST SERGEANT: 1ST EDMUND FUNKHOUSER

"D" COMPANY

COMMANDING OFFICER: CPT JOSEPH M. CARPENTER
FIRST SERGEANT: SFC STEVEN CHARLEBOIS

"HHC"

COMMANDING OFFICER: 1LT C.W. KEHOE
FIRST SERGEANT: 1ST HERSHEL MULLINS

    Soldiers: Christmas Day is the birthday of the One called
the Prince of Peace. Let us do our duty in the way that will
bring true Peace. Health and good spirit to each of you.

                    J.B. LOVE
                    LTC, 5th Cavalry
                    Commanding 2/5

A Merry Christmas
VIETNAM
1967

May the Peace and Happiness of Christmas be yours today and throughout the New Year from The First Team
IN VIETNAM

1st Air Cavalry DIVISION

Christmas 1967

Commander's Message

Throughout the Christian world, the Christmas season is a time of joy and spiritual inspiration. Despite separation from our families and the hardships imposed by war, those of us in Vietnam will still share the traditional Christmas spirit this year. We can enjoy the spiritual satisfaction that comes from giving. As fighting representatives of the Free World, our gift is the help we give the Vietnamese people to secure their independence, their individual safety, and their future freedom. Each of you gives a part of this gift and deserves the satisfaction of having increased the happiness of others—the true Christmas spirit.

My best wishes to each of you and your families for the Christmas season. May you enjoy good fortune during the coming year.

W. C. WESTMORELAND

Christmas Day Dinner

Shrimp Cocktail

Crackers

Roast Turkey   Turkey Gravy

Cornbread Dressing   Cranberry Sauce

Mashed Potatoes

Glazed Sweet Potatoes

Buttered Mixed Vegetables

Assorted Crisp Relishes

Hot Rolls   Butter

Fruit Cake

Mincemeat Pie

Pumpkin Pie w/Whipped Topping

Assorted Fresh Fruits

Tea w/Lemon   Milk

Assorted Nuts and Candy

Prayer for Christmas

Our Father in Heaven, we give thee thanks for the gift of thy Son, Jesus Christ, our Savior, the Prince of Peace and Lord of Life. May thy gift of Bethlehem announced by the Angelic Chorus, be born again in our hearts this day. Help us to know and experience the meaning and blessedness of their message: "Peace on Earth, Good Will Toward Men." Remove from us fear and hate and help us to know by faith thy peace which passes all understanding. We pray that the spirit of Christmas will be shared by our loved ones. With them help us to ponder, like Mary, the deep mystery of Christmas. May the truth and love which the Holy Child of Bethlehem brought to earth abide in our lives. In His name receive our praise and thanks. AMEN

APPENDIX E

Faces of Vietnam

APPENDIX F

Reflections on Leadership

In later years when I was a college administrator, I had the opportunity to address the employee leadership class and offer my views on the subject. They wanted me to share a story that exemplifies the best of workplace leadership. I sometimes used my initial combat experience in Vietnam as an example. A summary of the story I told follows:

- I can tell you about a young infantry second lieutenant who went to Vietnam to lead men in combat; most men were around his age.
- About 4:00 p.m. one evening in March 1967, a helicopter flew the lieutenant to a hill in the Central Highlands of Vietnam to join his company. He was introduced to a seasoned, veteran sergeant who had led the platoon since the last lieutenant was killed several weeks earlier. The sergeant had the trust and respect of the platoon. This was evident from the words of the captain and the men of the platoon.
- The veteran sergeant introduced the lieutenant to the men, defined their mission for that night, and asked the lieutenant if he wanted to lead the mission. The lieutenant responded, "Why don't you continue to lead so I can become acclimated to the method of operations of the company and the men of the platoon. We will know when it is time for me to assume the full role."

- The mission that night was to lay in ambush all night along a well-worn trail in the mountains. Future days and nights included search and destroy and combat air missions.
- Jointly the two shared responsibilities and decisions. They learned each other's strengths and shared observations on the strengths of the men in the platoon.
- They played to everyone's strengths and shared many successes.
- The actions and examples of the two leaders rubbed off on the men. The men began to show greater teamwork and learned that they had two leaders to support and lead them.
- As new men joined the platoon, the men took them under their wings and mentored them. They followed the examples of leadership demonstrated by their leaders, as they themselves were learning valuable leadership lessons.
- Nothing was ever said between the lieutenant and sergeant about it being time to change roles. The roles merged and leadership emerged. It was natural. The pre-defined roles and relationships of lieutenant and sergeant evolved without fanfare or discussion.
- Several months after the lieutenant arrived, the veteran sergeant rotated back to the U.S. The transition was seamless, and the platoon continued to achieve.
- The lieutenant now mentored the new sergeant, who had just arrived in Vietnam, and the team continued to be successful.
- Several months later, the lieutenant was promoted to a battalion headquarters job and many of his men asked to follow him there. About six were promoted and joined the lieutenant at battalion.

SUMMARY:

Leadership is:
- Knowing the team and how to make it work together effectively,
- Inspiring in unpretentious and non-authoritarian ways,
- Planning and leading the mission, but focusing on the strategic horizon,
- Providing clear roles and expectations,

- Mentoring with a focus on the individual and playing to their strengths,
- Doing the right thing and always considering the feelings of others and the consequences of your actions,
- Leading by example and,
- Making yourself dispensable, not indispensable

APPENDIX G

Glossary

First Cav: First Air Cavalry Division.

Second/Fifth: Second Battalion, Fifth Cavalry Regiment.

AIT: Advanced infantry training.

An Khe: Village near the home of the First Cav at Camp Radcliff.

ao dai: Traditional Vietnamese dress.

APC: Aspirin.

AR15: Similar to the M16 but has a collapsible stock.

ARA: Aerial rocket artillery.

army mules: Supply transport flatbed vehicle.

ARVN: Army of the Republic of Vietnam.

ASA: Army Security Agency.

beer: Um, um good.

Bong Son Plains: In the Central Highlands, Binh Dinh Province, Vietnam.

boom-boom: Vietnamese slang for sexual intercourse.

BOQ: Bachelor officers' quarters.

C Company: Charlie Company.

C rations: Army field ration—individual food items sealed in cans.

C130: Four-engine turboprop military transport aircraft.

Camp Evans: New home of the First Cav in early 1968—halfway between Quang Tri and Hue.

Camp Radcliff: Headquarters of the First Cav, near the village of An Khe.

Central Highlands: Plains, mountains, and valleys in central Vietnam, bordered by the South China Sea.

Charlie: Slang for the enemy—NVA and VC.

Chinook helicopter: Twin-engine, tandem rotor heavy-lift helicopter, used to transport troops and heavy equipment.

chopper: Huey helicopters transported infantry units into enemy territory as well as medevac and S4 resupply missions. Huey gunships, equipped with machine guns, rockets, and grenade launchers, often escorted the transports.

CIB: Combat infantry badge.

claymore: Anti-personnel mine that propels a fan-shaped pattern of steel balls in a 60-degree horizontal arc with a maximum height of 6.6 feet.

CO: Commanding officer.

COL: Colonel.

CP: Command post.

CPT: Captain.

di di mau: Vietnamese slang for *go, go quickly*.

DMZ: Demilitarized Zone.

GI: Government issue—slang for soldier.

hot LZ: Taking fire from the enemy.

HQ: Headquarters.

KP: Kitchen patrol.

LRP: Long range patrol food pack.

LT: Lieutenant.

LTC: Lieutenant colonel.

LZ: Landing zone.

M16: Automatic rifle.

M60: A belt-fed machine gun that fires 7.62 mm caliber cartridges at a rate of 550 rounds per minute.

mad moment: Ammo and weapons check by firing into the area surrounding a field camp.

medevac: Medical evacuation of casualties by helicopter.

Montagnards: Vietnamese hill tribesmen.

MOS: Military occupational specialty.

NCO: Non-commissioned officer.

NVA: North Vietnamese Army.

O club: Officers' club.

OCS: Officer Candidate School.

OD: Olive-drab.

P38: Can opener for opening C rations.

point: Leading the company during missions.

pop smoke: Smoke grenade used to direct helicopters or other aircraft.

pungi pit: Sticks or stakes made out of wood or bamboo, spiked, and placed upright in a hole; some are rubbed with toxic plants or feces to cause infections in the wounded.

PX: Post exchange.

Quan Hai: ARVN first lieutenant.

R & R: Rest and relaxation.

RTO: Radio telephone operator—the man who carries his unit's radio on his back in the field.

S2: Army Intelligence.

S4: Army Supply and Logistics.

SFC: Army sergeant first class.

six: Radio identifier for company commander.

scuttlebutt: Gossip or hearsay.

snakey licks: Used by Bill Cosby in his *Wonderfulness* album, referring to the imaginary snakes surrounding his bed as a child. My wife used snakey licks as an affectionate way of kissing and being silly at the same time.

stand down: Period of rest and refitting—no combat operations except for security needs.

tact officer: Tactical officer in charge of our platoon.

Tet: Vietnamese New Year.

two-six: Radio identifier for second platoon leader.

two-six-alpha: Radio identifier for second platoon RTO.

two-six-mike: Radio identifier for second platoon first sergeant.

USO: United Service Organizations.

VC: Slang for Viet Cong.

Viet Cong: National Front for the Liberation of South Vietnam (NLF)—a political organization and army in South Vietnam and Cambodia that fought the United States and South Vietnamese governments during the Vietnam War.

XO: Executive officer.